The Gestiana

by

Alltud Eifion

Based on the translation by
Jack Kidd

Edited by Richard Walwyn

ACKNOWLEDGEMENTS

I am indebted to Suzanne Millard of Pentrefelin for giving me the opportunity to render Jack Kidd's translation into computer-readable form, and also to the late Mr Kidd's daughter-in-law, Mrs Iona Kidd, for kindly allowing me to use it as the basis of this edition.

RICHARD WALWYN

ISBN: 978-0-9561469-7-7

Published in 2013 by Delfryn Publications, Delfryn, Borth-y-Gest, Porthmadog, Gwynedd LL49 9TW, UK. Telephone: +44(0)1766 512115

Cover design by Cathy Woodhead from an early tinted print of the Cob with Porthmadog and Moel-y-Gest.

CONTENTS

EDITOR'S INTRODUCTION

The Gestiana was first published in Welsh in 1892 and it gives a vivid picture of how the history of the area was understood by a cultured Welshman at the end of the nineteenth century. This original Welsh edition is rare, but there are copies in Bangor University Library and the National Library of Wales in Aberystwyth. A near-facsimile of the original was published by Gwasg Tŷ ar y Graig in 1975.

Alltud Eifion which means 'the Exile from Eifion' was the pseudonym used by the author, Robert Isaac Jones, pharmacist, printer and littérateur. Jones was born in 1813 at Tyddyn Iolyn Uchaf, a small now-derelict cottage north of Pentrefelin. Robert's father was Owen Jones, an Overseer of the Poor who, like his own father, John Jones, was tenant of Tyddyn Iolyn, which was owned by the Rhiwlas estate and later by WA Madocks.

From his mother, Gaynor Jones, Robert Isaac Jones claimed descent from the family of Roberts of Isallt in Eifionydd who were renowned as physicians; he also claimed special gifts as a physician and veterinary surgeon. He was educated in his home neighbourhood and in about 1831 was apprenticed to a pharmacist at Pwllheli, after which he worked in Caernarfon and London. In 1838 he opened a business as a pharmacist in Tremadog and became famous for his celebrated 'Tremadoc Pills' which claimed to cure all sorts of ailments. His slate notice still adorns the building which he called the 'Cambrian Pill Depot' on the northeast corner of Y Sgwâr in Tremadog.

Jones started a printing-press at Tremadog and printed various leaflets and a number of Welsh books. In November 1858 he began publishing *Y Brython*, initially a weekly newspaper which, at the beginning of 1859 became a monthly magazine. Because of lack of support, its publication ceased in 1863. He was a keen supporter of eisteddfodau and he wrote a good deal of verse. He published and edited *Gwaith Barddonol Siôn Wyn o Eifion* in 1861; *Cyff Beuno* in 1863; *Cell Meudwy* in 1877; *John Ystumllyn* in 1888; *Yr Emynydd Cristionogol* in 1889 and *Y Gestiana* (this book) in 1892. He also edited and published *Baner y Groes*, a monthly church magazine, and contributed articles to *Yr Haul*, *Y Llan* and *Cymru*. He was by nature an antiquarian and it seems that he was only interested in the more ancient history of the area. Also, like the gentry of old, he had an almost obsessive interest in genealogy. He appears to have been determinedly conservative (with a small 'c'). He hardly refers to the important shipping and ship building industries of Porthmadog and Borth-y-Gest and the associated vast increase in population. As a history the book contains a good deal of repetition and some suspect archaeology.

Little attempt has been made to correct the book's historical or scientific accuracy.

For much of his historical material Jones relied heavily on the work of Thomas Pennant (*Tours in Wales*) and Sir John Wynn (*The History of the Gwydir Family*), but he also called on his own extensive acquaintance and the memories of local people.

Unusually for his time he abandoned his original Methodism and returned to the Established Church, a conversion which colours much of the book. He was a staunch member of the Anglican church in Tremadog and started a Sunday school in the town hall. He died on 7th March 1905, and was buried at Ynyscynhaearn.

The Gestiana was translated into English in 1988 by Jack Kidd of Pentrefelin. He was born of an English father and a Welsh mother. After Jack's father was invalided through gas poisoning in the First World War the family lived in poverty and Jack was self-educated. He worked first as a quarryman, and later for the GPO Engineering Department.

Kidd's translation was never formally published, though the County Library Service holds bound photocopies of the typescript. Most of the text in this book is based on Kidd's translation and retains much of his rather idiosyncratic phraseology which perhaps aimed to capture the spirit of the original Welsh. In places I have referred back to the original Welsh edition, in particular with regards to dates and where Kidd's translation appeared suspect. His translation was quite 'free', he did not attempt a word-for-word translation, and at times altered the order of paragraphs.

The spelling and capitalisation of Welsh place and personal names is not simple and for consistency I have used the original edition as far as possible. Alltud Eifion himself regularly used what we would now consider to be Anglicisms such as 'Tremadoc' rather than 'Tremadog', or 'Carnarvon' rather than 'Caernarfon' – where he does so I have retained these for historical reasons. The spelling in the original is not at all consistent; so we have Crucaeth, Cricieth and Criccieth or even Krickieth. Some passages in the original edition were in English, particularly when historical documents or epitaphs were being transcribed; I have retained the original English spelling in those cases.

RICHARD WALWYN
Borth-y-Gest, 2013

TRANSLATOR'S PREFACE

Y Gestiana, first published in 1892, is essentially the work of one man, Robert Isaac Jones, a man blessed with an enquiring mind and the dedication to record all that he found of interest in his native parish.

It is a book where fact and folklore, scholarship and speculation all combine happily to form a unique testament which has delighted readers for nearly a hundred years. Alltud Eifion's expressed wish that the book would be read not only by his generation but also those who came after them has happily been fulfilled.

It also provides some justification for this attempt to translate the book into English, for Tre'r Gest has altered considerably since the time the book was first offered to the public.

There is now a new type of parishioner – residents who, though choosing to make this part of Wales their home, do not read Cymraeg. Their lack of knowledge of the language handicaps, but does not lessen the interest they show in their new surroundings and it is to bring this charming book to their notice that this translation has been undertaken.

Translation inevitably has its dangers and pitfalls but care has been taken to change the contents of the book as little as possible, so certain minor inaccuracies for which Alltud Eifion apologises in his foreword, still remain. There has been a little rearrangement of the text and the grouping of some of the items has been simplified,

In essence, though, this remains *Y Gestiana* as Alltud Eifion wrote it. He would, it is hoped, approve of making the book available to a wider readership and also the manner in which the translation has been carried out. It is a great pity that it was not attempted by someone with far more academic qualities than I possess. One point that I would like to bring to the notice of the reader is that the original was written nearly a hundred years ago, so any reference to this century in the text usually refers to the 19th century. I would also like the reader to consider and appreciate the genius and foresight of Mr Madocks, to plan and carry out all those enterprises, all by manual labour, building a town and large village, a grand harbour, a mile-long causeway, an 11-mile railway, and then to die before he saw the fruits of his creation. Lastly but not least, I should like to express my sincere and grateful thanks to Mr Meirion Parry, Headmaster of Eifion Wyn School, Portmadoc, for his advice at the outset; to Mr Ellis Gwyn Jones of Llanystumdwy, for his exceptional skill in translating the vast number of poems and englynion and, especially so, to Mr Walter Thomas of Bryn Tyddyn, Gaelic historian, ornithologist, botanist and many other 'ists' for his special knowledge and skill in composing the translations to a more presentable and neater form.

JACK KIDD
Pentrefelin, 1988

Alltud Eifion

THE

Gestiana

THAT IS TO SAY

THE HISTORY OF TRE'R GEST

CONTAINING HISTORICAL NOTES ON

THE PARISHES OF YNYSCYNHAIARN AND TREFLYS

ALSO

EPITAPHS OF BOTH CEMETERIES, HISTORY OF THE VALE OF MADOG, &C

BY ALLTUD EIFION

Editor of 'Y Brython', 'Baner y Groes', Author of 'Cofiant Ellis Owen', &c

'KEEP MEMORIES OF THE PAST, CONSIDER THE PRESENT, AND JUDGE THE FUTURE'

PUBLISHED BY ROBERT ISAAC JONES, TREMADOG

TO MY FELLOW COUNTRYMEN

My reason for compiling this small volume stems from the belief that all that is worthy of remembrance concerning our national heritage should not be allowed to be forgotten. I feel that a debt is owed to my own and future generations to set down all that I have learnt about the area in which I live: a knowledge acquired by my own research into local history, from the recollection of others and from many other sources. Thus, I hope, it will be possible to preserve the history of Tre'r Gest, its places, people, customs and traditions.

Lack of space necessarily means that much has to be omitted, so it is my intention, should this first volume be successfully received, to publish a further book along similar lines. [This never happened. – Ed]

Hopefully my efforts in gathering all this information relating to Tre'r Gest and two centuries of its history will arouse the interest of the reader, especially those chapters dealing with Dyffryn Madog (the Vale of Madog) and the great venture of the building of the Cob.

In this, my first attempt to record all the antiquities of the area, it is almost inevitable that inaccuracies will occur, so while apologising for these in advance, I also cherish the hope that the reader will consider that such errors are outweighed by what is, I trust, the book's more meritorious content.

I gratefully acknowledge the valuable assistance given to me by that great and diligent historian Mr Robert Evans, of Beddgelert (formerly of Pentrefelin) and conclude with the hope that the following pages will provide both pleasurable and interesting reading, not only for the present generation but also those who come after them.

ALLTUD EIFION
Tremadoc, 1892

Readers amend the defects,
And the faults that you find.
Pass by all false notes,
The slips and errors of print.

Howel of the Axe

THE GESTIANA

THE HISTORY OF TRE'R GEST, AND THE PARISH OF YNYSCYNHAIARN

Geographically the area lies in southeast Caernarfonshire; historically in the Hundred of Dunodig and in the commote of Eifionydd. The name hundred (or cantref) and commote are titles given to early units of administration which preceded by many centuries the implementation of shires by Edward I. The hundred, being the larger unit, was composed usually of two or three commotes, thus the Hundred of Dunodig comprised both Eifionydd and Ardudwy. Eifionydd, in turn, consisted of many townships among them being Tre Benyfed, Tre Dolbenmaen and Tre'r Gest.

MOEL-Y-GEST

The isolated position of this mountain, which rises to nearly 1,000 feet, dominates the area of Tre'r Gest, although there is also high land which runs from Caer Dunawd, near Crucaeth in the direction of Bryn hywel to the edge of the Tre'r Gest boundary.

Moel literally means 'bald hill' and Gest may possibly be derived from the word 'cist' – a chest, hollow or void – for the south side is certainly hollow and cup-like. Viewed from the north, however, it gives the appearance of a lady spreading her arms to encircle Trwyn Cae Iago, Porthmadog and Cefn cyfanedd; a different impression is obtained from Garth Pen y clogwyn and Garreg wen – from here the mountain looks like two separate and distinct peaks. Visitors at Crucaeth and Ystumllyn are afforded much amusement and interest for, from that angle, the profile of Moel y Gest assumes a definite likeness to the features of the Duke of Wellington.

Whatever its appearance, it is said to contain many metals and minerals and sulphur has been obtained from its southern slopes; granite sets and road surfacing materials are extracted above Nant Adda near Penamser, and the eastern end has provided paving slabs. There is a slate quarry on the west flank whose product roofed many houses in the area during the latter part of the 18th century.

Near the top is a place called Gwastad y Farchnad (Market Level or Place) where old foundations reveal that habitations were in use here in bygone days. A well on each side of the mountain can also be found and the house called Bronyfoel, on the westward slope, is the likely site of the Plas or mansion of the ancient princes of Gest.

Moel Tuhwnt-i'r-bwlch is the name given to the eastern side of the mountain being derived from a house of the same name which is situated just above St John's Church.

On a fine day the summit is an excellent viewpoint, not only of the local area but also much further afield. Given ideal conditions, the following places may be seen:– Cardigan Bay, Penychain and Gimlet Rock at Pwllheli, Penrhyn du, Llanbedrog, St Tudwald's Islands, Pembrokeshire, the Wicklow Hills in Ireland, parts of Cardiganshire, Trwyn Celynin, Mochras, Cnicht, Moelwyn Mawr and Moelwyn Bach, Manod and Diphwys, Moelfre, Cadair Idris, the hills of Trawsfynydd and Ganllwyd, Black Rock, the Rhinogau, Llethr, Carn Fadryn, Carn Bodfean, Foel Ddu, Moel Hebog, and other mountains of Snowdonia.

THE TOWNSHIP OF GEST

Although the precise meaning of the word 'tref' is town, it was an appellation frequently given to many smaller clusters of habitations, such as villages, hamlets or tithings – the law making little distinction between them. What was considered important, however before bestowing a name on a community was that early provision be made to build a place of worship where religious services could be held, the communion offered, and a place for the burial of the dead established.

Note: Pentref signifies as such from pen-tir-ef, it is the head of the possessions. Cwm seem to be a primitive of the same meaning with the combs of the bees: Vicus or vicum, living or dwelling together: Village is from vil-le-gi, place of living together. – ROWLAND JONES, *Origin of Languages.*

Over the course of time, the area of Gest became further subdivided into Borth y Gest, Lower Gest (Gwaelod y Gest) and Upper Gest (Pen tir y Gest near Bachysaint). The village of Pentrefelin lies in Lower Gest and the combined parishes of Treflys and Ynyscynhaiarn are known as Tre'r Gest. The Pentir y Gest (which lies on the western boundary) is that area of land which stretches from Llwynmafon to the borders of Ystumllyn.

TREFLYS – Early records reveal that among the old houses in Tre'r Gest was one known as 'Gwely Wyn ap Ednewin'. This was a llys or court and in the year 1356 it was owned by Gwgan ap Madog, Ieuan Llwyd ap Ririd and others. Another house recorded during the reign of Edward III was Gwely'r Prydyddion (Poet's Estate or house), the owners being Ieuan Llwyd, Ieuan Chwith and Ieuan ap Adda ap Eingan. Gwely means resting place or bed, but in this context means estate or home. 'Ap' means 'son of'. Even further back in time it is known that in the 9th century there lived in the area a head of a tribe called 'Blaidd Rhudd o'r Gest' (Ruddy Wolf). His was one of the five democratic tribes of Wales (the others being: Gwenwys, Heilyn Ysteilfforch of Glamorgan, and Adda Fras ac Alo). From the Blaidd Rhudd are descended many of the old families of Eifionydd.

THE BOUNDARIES OF THE PARISH OF YNYSCYNHAIARN

Until about 80 years ago [ie 1810 – Ed] the ancient custom of walking the boundaries or 'beating the bounds' took place annually. Then it was important, both for religious and secular reasons, to know exactly to which parish you belonged. This custom ensured that the exact limits of the parish were known to all parishioners.

In Tre'r Gest this event usually took place during Ascension Week. Preceded by a short homily at the church, the incumbent, wardens, parishioners and the children would set off on the circuitous route around the confines of the parish.

I can offer two reasons why the parish is such an irregular shape: firstly that the area that now comprises the parish was once held by a local prince as a complete unit of land ownership, or secondly that freeholders' cottages were brought together in order that a church could be built to serve their needs. (The actual construction of the church would probably have been carried out on the orders of the landowners and these, from their revenue, would contribute to their upkeep.)

Although the boundary walks no longer take place it may be of interest to record the route taken. It will be noticed that the parish of Ynyscynhaiarn shares a boundary with the township of Tre'r Gest with the exception of the parish of Treflys or Dryll which is at its centre. It is also divided into two between Cwt-y-defaid and Tan-y-bryn.

Starting from the bank of the river Glaslyn at Ynys carregaethnen (Farmyard), through the centre of Farmyard – there used to be large stones to denote the limits – then up past Tanymarian, through a ravine between the fields of Erw Suran and Cwmbach, yr Einiog, Cefncoch and Gesail, then over the brow of Craig Wen to Castell y Graig, and down to the boundary between Tŷ Cerrig and Llidiart yr Yspytty, through the garden of Pwllgloewlas, close to the borders of Broncynan or Bwlch-y-fedwen, on to Wern and through Coed-y-cefn to the old road that came out by Cwtydefaid. It then runs along the borders of Coedycefn and Cefncyfanedd, along the top of the Moel and borders of Bronyfoel, towards the fields of Llanerch, through parts of Tyddynadi, and the boundaries of Tyddyn einion, and down to the stream that runs through

Glanymorfa mawr to the sea at Morfa bychan.

The sea is now the boundary namely: the Gest Bar, past Ynyscyngar and Carreg goch to a point at Cae Iago and along the river bed that separates the two counties to Borth, over the Embankment to the spot beyond Farmyard where we started.

The Upper Parcel or 'Gest uwch y Llŷn' starts by the stream below Cwt-y-defaid and follows along the boundaries of Carreg felen, Bryntwr y Wern and Bontfaen; then up towards the boundaries of Gwernyddwyrig or Gwern moreddig to the front of Cefnmeusydd uchaf, along Glanbyl, along the stream that divides Cefnperfedd bach and Cefnperfedd mawr, to Pencaenewydd, to a place called Ffrwd goch near Golan Chapel, and down along the same stream to the extremities of Ty'nrhos and through part of Tyddyn madyn and Drwsdeugoed, up along the stream that divides the fields of Ymwlch bach and Llwnymafon ucha, through the marsh to the boundary of Ymwlch fawr and along the ditch that runs from the garden wall of Bachysaint, below the 'Tir y Gest' shippon, down past Ffynnon Dunawd to the boundary of Eisteddfa, through part of Mynydd du towards Ystumllyn and Genau Mygram, below the church of Saint Cynhaiarn, up to Porthyrhirfaen and Cae Shon, the boundaries of Garregfawr, Garthymorthin to Glogyrog, ending there in the fields of Bronyfoel, below Brynmelyn Chapel, down to the stream near to a place called 'Cloddfa Shon Prys' (John Price's Mine) where the Cambrian Railway line deviates from the road by Wern Bridge, back to Cwtydefaid.

That roughly is the limit of the parish of Ynyscynhaiarn; the likelihood is that the boundaries of Tre'r Gest followed the same lines. West of the parish lies the Manor of Criccieth; to the north and northwest the township of Dolbenmaen and the Manor of Clynhenwy (or Clenenney). At its northern extremity is the township of Gorllwyn whilst to the east and southeast the commote ends at the beach and Traeth Mawr.

THE MILLS OF TRE'R GEST

The first record of a mill in Tre'r Gest comes from *The Extent of North Wales* where an entry, in Latin, reads:

> Et omes isti villani istuis ville fac medietatem opis g n gitis ad molend d n e Princ de Abdowargh.

Of the many mills in Eifionydd named in the Extent, that of ABERDOWARCH is the most conspicuous in the care taken for its upkeep in good order. The river here indicated is that which runs through Pentrefelin into Ystumllyn Lake, the overflow of which would be a frequent cause of damage to the Mill, and necessitate the precautions taken; the Lake being formerly under direct tide influence, and the Mill was nearer that part of the road to the Parish Church, called 'Sarn yr Ynys'.

The old mill was superseded by one built at Carregyfelin and this in turn gave way to the New Mill which was built by Colonel William Price of Rhiwlas in the year 1680. This was located close to the road at Pentrefelin and its now ruined walls are still to be seen as is also one of the roof trusses bearing the Inscription *'WP 1680'*. The New Mill had a working life of about 180 years but the gable end collapsed and severely damaged the wheel and it was not repaired, the mill being allowed to fall into decay. In this condition it was a frequent subject for artists in the period 1864 to 1870.

During the year 1810 WA Madocks had erected a new mill near his mansion, Tan'rallt, Tremadog, and it was to here or the mills of Clenenney and Brynkir that following the collapse of the mill at Pentrefelin, local farmers took their grain.

Mills were important features in olden days and were at the centre of village life, although the rates for milling and roasting were fixed, it is interesting to note that corn and flour measures differed in each commote. Many mills were owned by the Crown in olden times and then leased out. Thus we find that during the reign of Edward VI the local inhabitants were ordered 'to carry timber to the King's mills' as a punishment for failing to comply with English laws. As well as this penalty, the law-breakers earned for themselves the sobriquet 'The Surly Tribe of Gest'.

This is a list of the millers at the New Mill from 1756 until the time of its collapse:

Hugh Jones...1766
John Owen. 1776
Owen Jones...1777
Griffith the Miller, brother of Siôn Evan Gruffydd..............1779
William Roberts of Anglesey...1807
Robert Williams, his son...1820

THE ISLANDS AND ANCIENT DWELLINGS IN THE PARISH OF YNYSCYNHAIARN

The majority of the islands in the parish lie in the Vale of Madog and were, until the building of the Embankment, entirely surrounded by water. I intend to deal more fully with these in a separate chapter called 'The Vale of Madoc', but their names are (Ynys means island) Ynys Pensyflog, Ynys y Gwartheg, Ynys Hir, Ynys Fadog, Ynys Galch, Ynys Cerryg duon, Ynys Towyn, Ynys Carreg aethnen and Ynys Penrhynheli. There are three more islands which lie outside the Vale of Madog. These are: Ynys Cynhaiarn, Ynys Cyngar (son of Carthog son of Cynedda) and Ynys y Gorswaun. Remains of Cytiau Gwyddelod (Celtic Huts) were to be found at Nhyrra, Garregfelin, Garregfelen, between Beudy mawr and Ty'nllech. There are two ancient burial grounds; one on the land of Llwynmafon isaf and the other close to Llidiart Ysbytty.

Other place names which have strong historical connections are: Cae Llidiart Dunawd (Field of Dunawd's Gate), Mûr Gwgan (Gwgan's Wall) which is close to Ffynon Dunawd (Dunawd's Well), Gallt Rhodri on Tyddyniolyn land, Cae Gwenllian, Bryn Howel, Llwynmafon (Llwyn Mabon ap Enllech), Cae Pant Adda near Penrhynllwyd, and Cae Hwfa on the land of Tyddynllwyn. The area has two hendrefs; Hendregadno and Hendre'r Clochydd, near Sarn yr Ynys.

EISYNGRUG – This house lies close to the New Mill and its name means 'Rye Winnows' being the place where those who brought corn to the mill prepared it ready for the kiln.

TY'NDWR – The most unusual thing about this thatched cottage was that a stream ran through the house about 2 feet above floor level. It also has a tradition from about 120 years ago – the woman of the house was terrified of lightning and during a storm one day she climbed into the butter churn, which she hoped would be a safe place. Unfortunately this proved to be a very unwise refuge for lightning struck the churn and she was burnt to a cinder.

TWLL Y CAE, PENTREFELIN – This was an old thatched cottage, very similar in appearance to what it is today. Way back in time it was the only public house in the parish and so became a central focus for village life. Church vestries were held here as it was the most convenient place before Tremadoc and the Embankment were built. Old parish registers record the fact that a pound or two was spent on ale at vestry meetings, but no doubt this sum also included the cost of the hire of the room as well.

GOAT VILLA – In the year 1852, during a thunderstorm, a bolt of lightning entered and travelled a few yards up the chimney. The occupier of the house, an old lady of the name of Shiân Roberts, was sitting by the fire with her small grand-daughter on her knee, and had a miraculous escape from death or serious injury when the lightning burnt a hole in the brim of her hat. Neither she nor her grand-daughter were harmed; the bolt emerging before reaching the roof leaving a scar that can be seen to this day.

Y FELIN (THE MILL) – This attracted all the farmers to the village, since it was here that all corn was brought for milling. Below the mill were several small cottages close to the river bank. They were called 'Coldai' or College, names which suggest that, possibly, a school existed here at some tine or other.

PENYBRYN – This is now in ruins but was once the home of Joseph Parry. He is reputed to have planted an apple pip which grew into a tree so fruitful that it paid his rent for 20 years. Unfortunately a grub destroyed the roots and it decayed.

TAI'R FELIN – On the northwestern side of the mill pond were two small thatched cottages bearing this name. They were sited where Tanygraig Cottages now stand.

TY'N LLECH – The only difference in these old cottages, which lie on the old road to Penmorfa, is that the thatched roofs have now been replaced with slate.

EFAIL BACH – This was close to the entrance at Hendregadredd; two small houses stood where the present mansion of Hendregadredd is now built.

CEFNYMEUSYDD ISAF – This is a long house with an out-house in the front. The old house at the rear has been repaired but the 'Pen uchaf' (Top End) remains unaltered. It was here that Ellis Owen held his society meetings where the young were taught. See their history in *Cell Meudwy* (Hermit's Cell), by the bard Cynhaiarn, one of Ellis Owen's adherents.

CEFNYMEUSYDD UCHAF – This was a very insignificant house before its purchase by Mr Barnes and Captain Jones; the last named rebuilt it completely. The old house still stands below the old road leading to the farmyard. (A later amendment by Alltud Eifion concerning this house reads: 'It should have been said that Richard Thomas came here from Coed y Llyn and bought the farm from the trustees of Mr Price of Rhiwlas in 1798, leaving it to his two daughters Mrs Jones and Mrs Barnes.')

THE TWO LLWYNMAFONS – There is nothing left of the two old houses and the present buildings were erected on the ancient sites.

TYDDYNIOLYN OR TYDDYN IORWERTH – The original building was at a place called 'hen erddi' (Old Gardens) at the top end of a field called Cae'rpant (Field of or in the Hollow). This was before the property was divided and shared between brother and sister, Iorwerth and Gwenllian. Higher up the hill stands a small cottage, most probably the original farmhouse. This is now called Tyddyniolyn uchaf. It was here that the author of this book was born. The present house was built about 150 years ago.

CAE GWENLLIAN – Following the division of Tyddyniolyn land, this house was erected in a secluded spot and is constructed to a similar design.

EISTEDDFA – This was originally a small house that stood on the south side of the present building. Another dwelling, 'Ty isaf' lay with its gable to the hill. It was here that the Rev Richard Griffith, the incumbent at Criccieth, resided in the year 1727. About 70 years ago Ty isaf lay vacant and the opportunity was taken to start a Non-conformist Sunday School there. From the name Eisteddfa 'Sitting place' it might be assumed that it was the scene of a court where Druids or the Prince's overseers sat in judgment. It is possible that the residence at Dunawd (a name still remembered in Cae'r Llidiart Dunawd and Ffynnon Dunawd, 'the field of Dunawd's Gate and Dunawd's Well') lay above this site on the boundary of Tre'r Gest.

An urn was discovered in the ground when the field was being ploughed about 60 years ago. On top of the hill, near the boundary of Cae'r Llidiart Dunawd and Gallt Rhodri, there are many remains of old buildings.

TYDDYN-YSGUBORIAU – This building may be regarded as a middle-class house and was once part of the Ystumllyn estate. Before its conversion it was a barn where, most probably, the villagers would gather to enjoy their meetings and the opportunity taken to acquaint the newly-emerging generation with traditional Welsh customs. Opposite here, on Eisteddfa land, is a field called Cae blysig (Hungry Field) where many remains of old buildings were to be found. The tenant of the field, who lived at Garreg-y-felin, spent many years clearing them, but even so many foundations are still discernible. Cae Blysig is not far from Dunawd's Gate and Well.

CARREG-Y-EELIN – This was a small old house situated below Tyddyn-iolyn and alongside the old road leading from Penmorfa towards Criccieth, Pwllheli and Llangybi. It is also near the site of the mill-pond of the second mill, which has previously been mentioned. A portion of Eisteddfa land was added to this place about 65 years ago and Cae blysig lies slightly to the south.

DRWS-DEU-GOED – An important place in olden times and nobility lived there until about a century ago. The present house has been constructed on much older foundations. Plas-yn-ogrwth, or Plas-yn-eog-ruthr (Mansion of the Wild or rushing Salmon), so named because the river below was noted for its salmon. Ffrwd goch and Ty'nrhos were other dwellings on Drws-deu-goed land, which being near Dolbenmaen, is at the furthest extent of the parish.

CEFNPERFEDD BACH – An old insignificant house, unworthy of the land attached, the property of Lord Harlech. The outbuildings are in a dilapidated state. An old lady living there was noted for her white bread and buns.

BRON-Y-GADAIR – 'Bron' means brow, breast, hillock or hill. 'Cadair' – notably among the bards – could indicate presidency. Many places of a similar name can be found in central areas, such as Cadair Elwa near Llangybi, Cefn-y-gadair near Mold, and Cadair Rhys Goch in Y Gymwynas [which translates as The Favour; it is the local Welsh name for the Aberglaslyn Pass – Ed]. Bron-y-gadair was one of the old mansions of bygone days. The outbuildings stand close to where the old house once stood, with the gable end to the hill and a kitchen, or old house, in front of the door. A distance of about 8 feet separated the front of the house and the old kitchen which were both built on the same line. This remains the same as does also the old stable with the stone steps outside. The present house was built in the year 1839. Generally attached to old mansions were 'cots' or smaller houses, and ruins of two – Beudy Corn and Hendre Clochydd – can be seen along the present road to Ynyscynhaiarn. In the latter of the two houses, according to tradition, dwelt the parish sexton, and this was most probably church property – possessions which were slowly whittled away due to slackness and carelessness on the part of the wardens. Also Coldai lay on the river bank below the Penysingrug Mill, plus the two Penbryns, one on each side of the river. One is now in ruins and the other has been renamed Plas Llwyd.

A conch or seashell was sounded at 8 o'clock in the evening at Bron-y-gadair during the winter months about 100 years ago, before the animals were bedded down for the night. When they heard the sound they rose briskly to their feet ready for their suppers.

HENDRE-GAD-REDD – This name can be written in various ways: Hendre-gad-no, Hendre-gad-rodd and Hendre-gad-redd. The late Ellis Owen believed it was a place where militia were once trained: 'cadcno' means a sword or to repel an enemy (explanation of Dafydd ap Gwilym). 'Gad' means Army. This house was once two cottages, both with thatched roofs. One was a low building, whilst the other was tall and rambling. There was a little land attached. The present house, now a beautiful mansion, was built in 1829 by Mr John Williams of Tuhwnt-i'r-bwlch. He sold it to a Major Walker whose daughter, Mrs Ignatius Williams, is the present owner.

Y GARREG-FELEN – This old mansion, built in the Elizabethan style, is situated in a secluded situation, the style of the building, both exterior and interior, indicating that noteworthy persons lived here. It could be that descendants of the Prince of Gest made their home here and it is interesting to note that remains of a brass dial fixed to a wall in front of the house and orchard are still to be seen.

As at Bron-y-gadair, the estate included a number of smaller dwellings. Those remaining include: Ty'nllech which stands on the old road between Pentrefelin and Penmorfa; Beudy mawr, a house which is alongside the present road leading from Pentrefelin to Portmadoc and Tremadoc; it is said that the Rev John Wesley preached at Penyclogwyn when on his way to Criccieth and Lleyn. The tenants of Tanyclogwyn and also those of Ty Coch lived rent free but were required to give of their labour when it was required on the land; standing on the roadside at Pentrefelin, the fairly modern house called Cross Keys was previously known as y Dafarn Lôyw (the shining or crystal clear Inn). The Rev Y Evans who was incumbent at Crucaeth and Ynys had it constructed in a roadside recess in the year 1816 for the purpose of placing a tithe on the two parcels of land, as was the custom at the time.

One Jones of Mathafarn and also one David Hughes of Penmorfa accompanied John Wesley when he came over and preached at Penyclogwyn, Pentrefelin. This occasion was the likely commencement of the 'cause' started at the Wern.

Sycamore and beech trees used to be planted near older places and mansions, it being considered by the old people that they were non-conductors of lightning because of their smooth bark.

CEFN-CYFANEDD – This ancient residence, just below the Foel, lies in the parish of Treflys. An old 'mounting stone' and other traces of antiquity can be found in the area which indicates that the Prince or his descendants once lived here. Nearby is a small cottage called Brynmelyn which was used by the Calvinistic Methodists as a chapel around 1800. It was rebuilt at a later date but retained the same name. Under old Welsh laws specific dwellings in each cantref were given the duty of maintaining a constant fire, thus enabling any householder whose fire had gone out to rekindle it easily. Cefncyfanedd was such a house as was Gorllwyn in the Manor of Clenenney, and Cefn collwyn in the Ffriwlyd area.

COED-Y-CEFN or COED-Y-CEFNCYFANEDD – This isolated cottage stood on the main road and to the east of Cefncyfanedd land. Now a ruin, it was probably built in bygone days to watch over the forests in that area.

BRON-Y-FOEL or LYS BRON-Y-FOEL – Most probably this is the oldest mansion or dwelling house in Tre'r Gest and occupies a position on the westward slope of Moel-y-Gest. Little remains of the old mansion except the old stone staircase and the window through which Hywel ab Rhys fired the arrow which killed Gruffydd ab John ab Gorono from Gwynfryn when the latter and his armed band once attacked the mansion. This followed a dispute over fishing rights in Ystumllyn lake about the year 1390 (see *Y Brython* 1860, page 290). There was a hall in the old dwelling and morning devotions were held there each day. I have explained the meaning of the word 'Moel' before, meaning bald, baldpated, or barren, thus it is literally a treeless and heatherless point in a prepared or built up place. Interestingly there was a family in Cornwall bearing the name Moyle whose crest on their coat of arms was a hornless ox. Below the dwelling on the side nearest Ty Mawr are many traces of old habitations.

TY MAWR – Standing on a prominent point in the area, the present house of modern construction has replaced an excellent old house. This was the home of 'Bardd Treflys' (The Treflys Bard).

TYDDYN-EINION or ENGAN – Another old dwelling house in which once lived Einion ab Gwgan ab Iorwerth and other members of the family of the Prince.

TYDDYN-ADI – it is not known why this house is so-called, but perhaps after the an old inhabitant of Y Dryll, or part of Treflys. The present house, built at the turn of the century, replaced a small and insignificant structure. There is a large stone close to the back door which bears the Inscription '*RJ 1750*'. It is said that he (Adi) carried it on his back and placed it there.

GARTH-Y-MORTHIN – 'Garth', plural Geirth, means rocky, barren, poor or a collection of litter; Morthin is Welsh for Martin. Its association with cock fighting provides the main point of interest about this house for it was the venue of quite large gatherings at the 'cockpits' located there. Folk memory recalls a man who rejoiced in the name of 'The Little Cockerel of Garth-morthin' and some of the old steel cockspurs worn by the fighting cockerels have been found from time to time. Shôn Edward of yr Einiog composed an appropriate ballad in the year 1780. The present house is modern and stands beside the road leading to Bettws Treflys Church (or the Church of the Prince) and St Dyfynog's Bay and Morfa bychan.

Y GARREG FAWR – Lying under the lee of Garth-y-morthin Rocks, this small farmhouse is also on the bank of Ystumllyn lake in the parish of Ynyscynhaiarn. In a hollow below the house a gorse chopping machine was set up and it was used by farmers of both parishes to chop fodder for their animals.

CAE SHON – This was a small old dwelling house and small-holding in the parish of Treflys, lying in a southerly direction opposite Garreg fawr. Part of it was Cefn Cae Shon, this being built by one William Owen. In 1733 it was the home of William Efan of Leyn and Elin Jones, his wife; the latter is said to be the daughter of Cae Shon. There is a cupboard or dresser in the house on which is carved the inscription WE, EJ, 1733. A giant of a prize-fighter lived there at one time named Owen Cae Shon.

COED-Y-LLYN – The church of Treflys is built on Coed-yllyn land, which was once a single farm. Its division into two properties resulted in two houses with a few trees beyond them. Their boundaries extended to the centre of Llyn Ystumllyn and the borders of Ynys, where St Cynhaiarn's church is built. Close to the sea and near Lyn Morys (Morris's Lake) is a field called 'Clwt-ymryson' (field of Strife or Rivalry). This is aptly named as its ownership is a matter of dispute between Coed-y-llyn and Ystumllyn. A son of Coedyllyn called Richard Thomas lived at Garreg wen at some time or other. Not only is he reputed to be the first person to have a cart at Treflys but he was also the owner of the first clock in the parish.

PORTH-YR-HIRFAEN – This is a small north-facing dwelling house. Close by are two bays or anchorages: Porth St Dyfynog (called The Mount) on the eastern side of Penrhyn y Greig-ddu or Penrhyn-y-Pryfaid (Black Rock headland) and Porth-yr-hirfaen on the western side of the same headland. Black Rock is a name given to the headland by English visitors. Porth means anchorage or harbour and a location below the house looks as if it had been used for this purpose. 'Hirfaen' (long stone) takes its title from a large stone pillar that may have stood nearby, erected as a symbol of some certain heroism or deed of prowess.

PENRHYN – (meaning Peninsula) is of fairly recent construction, being built around the year 1839. In old documents the headland was called 'Penrhyn y Pryfaid' (Worm or Insect Headland) but I can give no explanation of this curious name. Hereabouts are large quantities of loose stone or scree making it an ideal haunt of foxes and hares.

Y TRIP – This is a small dwelling on Black Rock near where the path makes a steep descent to the Morfa bychan caves. Standing close to the cliff, it makes an excellent viewpoint of both sea and mountains.

NANT-Y-GWRAGEDD and BRYN-HOYW-LAS – Only the names remain of these two small cottages which once lay in a hollow below Treflys Church. Nothing of importance is known about them and only traces of the first named can be found.

GLAN-Y-MORFA MAWR – The fairly old farmhouse is situated on a slope to the southeast of Treflys Church but did not, to the best of my knowledge form part of the Bron-y-foel heritage. Evan Parry of Coldy, Pentrefelin was the builder of the first 'Ty Unos' (One-night house) in Morfa Bychan. It was an old Welsh custom that if you could build a house and have smoke through the chimney in a night you could claim it as your own.

GLAN-Y-MORFA BACH – This is the name of a smallholding which borders with Llanerch y Gest. It nestles in the protection of a sheltering rock and faces the beach; at one time the sea came very close to it.

PENRHYD-FECHAN – A small dwelling house built quite close to Glan-y-morfa Bach. It is apparent that in the past they had to ford the river that ran to the sea at Ynyscyngar. The river Glaslyn found its outlet between Ynyscyngar and Morfa bychan 200 years ago and traces of the old river bed can still be seen in some places.

YNYSCYNGAR – This was surrounded by water and before the construction of the Cob and harbour at Traeth mawr was an anchorage for ships. It was from here towards the end of the last century that shipments of slate from the Bronyfoel Quarry were made to Ireland and other places. Vast areas of Morfa Bychan land on which houses are now built were once under the sea.

LLANERCH Y GEST – In ancient times this was a mansion of note – possibly another home of the prince, who is believed to have had residences on both sides of the Moel, Llanerch being adjacent to the harbour at Borth-y-gest. The old mansion stood lower down than the present building, at a place called 'Cae yr Hen Dy' (the Field of the Old House). There is a belief, supported by names given to neighbouring places such as Ty'ndre etc, that it was the residence of the Blaidd Rhudd or Ririd Flaidd.

Y GARREG WEN – This was the birthplace of the harpist and noted musician Dafydd Owen (David of the White Rock), a composer also of many well-known hymns. There is nothing noteworthy about the small dwelling, which lies on the side of a hill overlooking a small lake.

TYDDYNLLWYN – A small farmhouse that lies on the eastern side of the Foel and close to the old road that led from Penamser via 'bwlch y Gest' (the Gest Gap) to Borth. It is close to a quarry where, 50 years ago, stone flags could be obtained.

TY'NDRE – These were old cottages, quite small, that were built in a nook near Llyn y Garreg Wen; unremarkable except for the name and an event associated with them which is said to have occurred at the beginning of the century. An old lady by the name of Shiân Owen lived in one of them and it was she who was sent to Barmouth by the other wives in the district on a special errand. Her task was to buy some 'dail dieithr' (strange or unknown leaves). These, of course, were tea-leaves but upon her return it is recalled that no-one knew how to prepare the beverage! Shiân Owen also trained her dog to assist her in her occupation of wool shredding but not, one supposes, in her other trade – that of making blue dye for her neighbours. Ty'ndre was also the home of a family of dwarfs about 60 years ago.

Y LLETTY – Situated on the old road to the Borth, this low rural cottage provided accommodation for travellers awaiting transport if the hotel was full.

Y BORTH – This house is on the harbour side and, although repaired, remains unchanged from its original design – it being like two houses previously. Borth had only one other house at the time, this being called Plas y Borth, of which nothing is left except some old foundations upon which the Pilots' Houses now stand. The owner of Plas y Borth in 1740 was a gentleman named Williams who traded in smuggled goods which came in over the 'Bar' from Cardigan Bay. 'Noson Lawen' or 'Merry Evenings' were often held here, the noted harpist Dafydd y Garreg wen entertaining the company. It was whilst he was on his way home from one of these gatherings, just as dawn was breaking, that Dafydd paused by a lonely rock enchanted by larks singing as they greeted the new day. This proved to be the inspiration for him to compose the well known tune The Rising of the Lark. The stone can still be seen on the footpath that leads to Garreg Wen, his home. [The stone now bears a plaque. – JK] Borth-y-Gest and Ynyscyngar were the chief ports an this coastline before the course of the river was diverted past Ynystowyn to create the harbour on the Traeth mawr, now Porthmadog.

PEN-Y-CLOGWYN – Now uninhabitable, the ancient farmhouse was, for many centuries, the home of a number of old families at the Gest. The attached land extended over the Garth to Trwyn Cae Iago (this now being the upper part of Portmadoc), to the mansion of Bronygarth and to the quay known as Cei Solly or the Welsh Slate Wharf. In past times there were other houses near here which were surrounded by gardens and there was also a road that led from Tywyn to Borth-y-Gest.

TUHWNT-I'R BWLCH – An older house stood more to the west than the present dwelling, which is on the northern slope of the Foel. The present mansion was built by Mr WA Madocks, being further enlarged by his agent Mr John Williams, and was the home of gentry for many years. Not far from 'Ffynnon Beudy'r Ychain' (the Ox Shippon Well) is 'the Gap' on the road which leads from Garregfelen and Bontfaen, through Coed y cefn and past Penamser bach above Pant Adda (where the Moel y Gest cemetery now stands). Below the Gap on the northern side could be found a variety of sea shells, and wild boar tusks were found when cultivation of the land was being carried out about 120 years ago. One further comment about the Gap may be of interest to the reader; it was at the beginning of the present century, during a period of little employment, that an old man went to the Gap with the intention of lowering it. He sought reward for his labours by holding out his hat for offerings from the travellers who had benefited from the enterprise. The task was never fully completed, however, as work commenced on the Embankment which, it is said, broke the old man's heart. The cut in the Gap is still visible in its unfinished state. Before the days of the Embankment it was only possible to cultivate the drier slopes and cattle were driven to graze on the Morfa when the tide allowed.

MORFA LODGE – An earlier name for this was Clog-y-berth, being part of Penyclogwyn. In 1809 Dr Robert Morris, MD built a small mansion on the site of the old house. This was on the road that led from Borth-y-gest past Penyclogwyn to the Traeth, but permission was given to move it to its present position. A low house called Clog-y-berth stood close to what is now called Dora Street, Portmadoc. This was enclosed common land in the ownership of Owen Dafydd, one of the Gest's older inhabitants. Later this was purloined by Mr Madocks for some small recompense during the time of the Embankment undertaking.

PENAMSER – The old mansion stands on a rocky outcrop with its front to the Moel. A crosswise section in the manner of these old mansions was built later. Although it excels that of ordinary houses built in the period, the architecture is not outstanding but it was the residence of the top gentry of Tre'r Gest during the 16th Century. The name Penamser possibly derives from the tidal flow which affected the road to the Traeth, since it was not possible to cross without using fords at low water or by using boats at other stages of the tide. Fifty years ago the sun never shone on this house until the first week in summer but it shines weeks earlier now.

BRON-Y-GADAIR BACH – This house is now called Tanycoed, and I feel it is a pity that the present generation in this and other cases have changed names that were in use for centuries. The dwelling, with a smallholding attached, occupies the site where the old smithy once stood. Evan Ellis, an accomplished blacksmith and a skilful veterinary surgeon, resided there about 70 years ago. On the opposite side of the road, a few yards nearer Criccieth, are two workmen's cottages: Pencraig, Evan Ellis Griffith's house and a later addition named Ty Mawr y Lon.

NHYRA OR NANT HYRA – On Nhyra land, close to the road that leads to Cefnymeusydd uchaf, are the remains of a number of old dwellings – the possible site of a former house and smallholding which were established there. Until recently there were also two cottages here, being called 'Nhyra uchaf' and 'Nhyra isa'. It is said that the latter was built for John Ystumllyn (Jack Black) whose life and history are contained in a small booklet, *Hanes John Ystumllyn,* which has been published by the Madoc Estate Office. Ellis Owen suggested that the name should be 'Nant Harri Ddu' (Black Harry's Valley) for which he gave his reasons. (Note: Sir Harri Ddu, a native of Llangathen, was the composer of the well known hymn of the same name. He was a churchman and, like all unmarried priests, was accorded the title 'Sir', this being the custom at the time. It is also recorded that one Abel Isaac and his wife Alice Jones lived at the old farmhouse in 1712. Their daughter was baptised at Ynyscynhaiarn on January 6th 1712 when the name 'NANHURAN' was entered on the register.

LLIDIART YSPYTTY – An ordinary old farmhouse standing at the foot of Graig wen near Tremadog. Being located on the banks of the Traeth in former times it was very close to the sea and from here one could wade across to the other side when the tide was favourable. The eastern end of an older house still stands and it is believed that a hospice existed here during the time of the wars of the Cross or Crusades. An old cemetery lies nearby and this, together with an account of its excavation, is more fully explained elsewhere in this book.

CASTELL Y GRAIG – Two fields higher up than Llidiart Yspytty were two small cottages, the home of many families from time to time. These were demolished about 35 years ago and evidence of earlier habitations could once be found.

TAN'RALLT – An older house stood to the east of the present mansion, which was built for Mr WA Madocks in 1808. In Eifionydd the house and its attached lands, which included all the Morfa as far back as Ynys carregaethnen (Farmyard) formed an important estate, and before its transfer to Mr Madocks the lease was held by Richard Humphries. The English poet Shelley stayed here during 1812 and 1813. Below the mansion stood a smaller dwelling called Tan'rallt isaf which was demolished about 40 years ago, enabling a start to be made on the construction of a residence for Miss Madocks (Mrs Roche). Parts of the wall are still to be seen.

Lack of space means that I can only deal but briefly with the cottages built on the islands in the Vale of Madog, whose situation underwent a great change when the Embankment was built at the beginning of the century as a result of the enterprise of Mr Madocks. YNYS PENRHYNHELI – This was a sheltered anchorage in which are two small cottages; only foundations of these remain. YNYS FADOG – Major Pilkington demolished the old houses on this island about 70 years ago. Gruffydd Ellis of 'The Union' Tremadog discovered a chest in one of the foundations and this was found to contain a number of spade-head guineas and some mint coins of the reign of William III; some of these I have seen. YNYS PENSYFLOG – A large farmhouse has now replaced a single chimneyed old cottage which stood where the barn is now. YNYS PENRHYNLLWYD – The house still stands in its original state. YNYS CERRIG-DUON – On this island was a cottage which possessed a deep cellar. Legend recalls that during its excavation a terrible thunderstorm blew up. YNYS HIR – In the lee of a rock in what is now the garden of Bodawen stood a dwelling house. About 60 years ago this was converted into a shippon for use on the farm. Later the Rev W Ambrose built a residence which he called Bodawen and further extensions were carried out by Mr FS Percival. There was a small house called 'Llidiart y Cil' close to the site of The Madocs Arms Hotel and Town Hall. This was demolished in 1805 when the hall was built,

CWM MAWR – Situated in an exposed and barren position above Craig wen, by Tanrallt and Tremadog, the large dwelling house has been occupied by members of the same family for hundreds of years. It formed part of the Tan'rallt estate, originally the property of Mr RW Price of Rhiwlas, Bala but a few years ago it was sold to Mr GA Huddart of Brynkir who, in turn, later relinquished ownership. The old farm has been split up and there are one or two more houses on the land today. In the year 1797 the Tanrallt Estate included half the parish of Llanfrothen. Up till that time estates were increased in size as a result of marriage settlements but, in more modern days, more by the acquisition by purchase.

CWM BACH – The site of this little house (which has now been converted to a shippon of Erw Suran) was called Pen Y Golwg (Sight or Vista Head). The present house at the foot of the hill was built in 1860. An earlier resident was Edward Jones, one of the sons of Ymwlch fawr, who is known to have lived there in about 1773.

This concludes the rather extensive list of details of the main houses and farms in the parishes of Ynyscynhaiarn and Treflys. Most of the two parishes were at one time or another owned either by the families of Rhiwlas, Brogyntyn or Clenenney. It used to be said that the Squire of Rhiwlas could make the journey on horseback from Bala to Llangybi without leaving his estate (except for a few miles) during the past century. It is rather strange to think that now the heir of Rhiwlas is without land in Eifionydd – an inheritance that descended to the family from Ririd Flaidd about 1150 and remaining in their ownership until 1890. Richard Tavistock Price Esq of Rhiwlas made his will on the 13th of November 1793, appointing Sir Robert Vaughan, Simon Yorke Esq, Richard Richards Esq of Caerynwch, David Ellis Esq of Gwynfryn and O Owen of Llwyndedwydd trustees to his will. He died on 6th August 1794. — *Gentlemen's Magazine*.

TRACES OF ANCIENT HISTORY IN TRE'R GEST

I intend to make only short references to the many ancient traces of history in which the area abounds, as these have been fully covered by other books or by tradition. The diligent historian can, by his own researches, greatly amplify the facts contained in these brief notes.

DRUIDICAL CIRCLE IN CWM MAWR – In a field called 'Maen Arch' (the Arch Stone) there used to be an elliptical circle comprised of 37 upright stones with one larger stone in the centre. This was anciently called Y Maen Arch or Arch Druid. This was in fairly good condition at the time of the historian Pennant (see Pennant's *Tour in Wales*) but, alas, it is only possible to indicate where they once were. In the company of the late JW Greaves and Sir Love Jones-Parry the writer visited the site in 1851. Mr William Owen (grandfather of the present Mr Owen) gave us the history of the stones and said that it was he who had blasted them when preparing the field for cultivation. He was able to show us several pieces of the Maen Arch which had been incorporated into parts of the wall!

BWLCH YR ESGOB – This is off Tan'rallt woods in an out-of-the-way spot on the side nearest Tremadog. One finds a wide large wall and, after crossing a small stream, there is an entrance of fairly straight stone door posts. From here a pathway leads to 'Pant Evan Esgob' (Bishop Evans' Hollow) which is nearby. At the top end of Cae'r Duntur old foundations can be found. Little is known about these although a lot of ashes and seashells found there indicates their use as a habitation in past ages. A stone coffin was found in this field but its present whereabouts is not known. In the nearby woods more old foundations can be found, possibly the site of an old farmhouse. Close by is a place called Ffynnon Corlan y Geifr (Well of the Goats' Fold) whose water is said to posses healing properties.

THE ROMAN ALTAR – Below the gatehouse of Tanrallt on the southern side of the hill is a place of this name, although it may well have been a Druidical altar. It consists of a large rock supported by two upright stones with doorways for entrance and exit. It is of sufficient height to allow an average sized man to stand upright without lowering his head. The stone steps leading through it to the top of the bank were in good condition a few years ago, it now being possible to ascend them right to the top. Mr Madocks laid a convenient pathway to the old altar under the sheer rock near the Gatehouse.

THE ROCKING STONE AT YNYS-CARREGAETHNEN (FARMYARD) –This stone which was on the island near Farmyard and lay across two other stones was blasted to pieces when the house and outbuildings were being built in 1810. It is possible the site was part of a Druidical circle as, from here, one can see the Circle at Cwm Mawr which, in turn, is in sight of a similar one at Yr Einiog.

THE OLD BURIAL PLACE AT LIDIART YSPYTTY NEAR TREMADOG – This was located in the banks of the junction of the two roads that lead to Pentrefelin and Penmorfa. Before excavation split it into two, it comprised a circular burial ground with traces of surrounding walls. Around the year 1820 a quantity of human bones were disinterred, these being carried by Evan Roberts, tenant of the Madocks Arms, for reburial at Penmorfa Churchyard. In 1868 a more thorough excavation was carried out on a section above the road and this revealed many graves and pieces of slate and thin pottery. Archaeologists differed in their opinion as to whether the tiles were Roman or of the Crusader period. *The Cambrian Journal* printed the following extract by a society called 'The Archaeological Association' (Vol XIV, 1868, page 470). — 'At Llidiart Yspytty explorations were made on the site of an old burial ground. Many Roman tiles, foundation of a building, traces of burnt limestone (not Early Roman), human bones and other traces were found'. The word 'Ysbytty' (hospital or hospitum) may indicate that the site was occupied by the Templars or Hospitalers, although there are no records to substantiate this view. That the tiles were Roman cannot be denied (some of them were painted) and one is hopeful that a more detailed survey will shed light on the question. About 1800 part of a bell was found on the bank above the burial ground. The local tradition is that in the early days of Christianity, work started on the building of a church on this site but the materials were moved during the night to where Penmorfa Church now stands! Some historians hold the view that the 'hospice' was used by the Romans, because it stood at the junction of a road between Segontium and Tomen y Mur, Trawsfynydd and near the crossing of the Traeth, which was fordable at ebb tides. A section of Roman road is discernible on the hillside above Penmorfa; this is paved and is called locally 'Pen-y-Palmant' (Head or end of the Pavement). Roman badges have been found at Penrhyndeudraeth and at Llysdin or Llys Dinas (Llystyn) beyond Dolbenmaen. The noted antiquarian, the late Rev John Jones MA, Vicar of Llanllyfni mentions this place in a letter to the historian Ellis Owen of Cefnymeusydd, which was published in *Y Brython* (see Vol 1861, page 347).

CASTELL Y GRAIG – This place is in a secluded grove about two fields' distance above Llidiart Yspytty, between the old road and Craig Wen. Very little remains of the old foundations and the rocky columns although a rough patch on one of the columns is called 'Crair Neidr' (the eye of the snake's needle). As well as the ruins of the old castle in the teeth of the rocks, there is a level place called 'Castell Uchaf' (Upper Castle) where other old foundations may be seen. Up till about 35 years ago, two occupied cottages stood on the castle site and those living in them had the word 'castle' tied to their name. A mineral outcrop, known as ironstone, lies below this spot and an old quarry existed about 100 years ago close to the road that went over the hill by 'Beudy y Llidiart' (Shippon Gate). No one knows when early work was carried out there but a Mr Cooper restarted operations in 1840. Many shipments of iron are were sent to Cardiff but the cost of transport made it unprofitable. To remedy this a smelting furnace was built but even this failed to reduce costs to an economic level.

THE OLD HOUSE OF YNYS FADOG – This was a meeting place and shelter for those wishing to cross the Traeth in the days before the Cob was built. Inclement weather and shifting fords often caused delays (which could last for several days) and many unfortunate travellers were drowned whilst attempting the hazardous crossing. Ynys Fadog was the point of departure of Madog ab Owen Gwynedd, who went to sea from this part of Eifionydd to seek land to the westward. This fact is confirmed by a reference to it in Madog's farewell speech. His father, Owain Gwynedd, Prince of Wales lived at Cefn y fan (see details of his speech in *Cylchgrawn Cymreig* and also *Madog* by Southey).

THE WATCH TOWER AT YNYSHIR – Foundations of a fort or tower and remains of a man-made wall and trench stood in an advantageous site to guard the beaches of Tre'r Gest against attack. Similar defences can be found at Wern and Penrhyndeudraeth, the latter called Castell Coed (Wooden or Timber Castle). This was built by Dafydd ab Owen Gwynedd close to the spot where the present castle is situated.

CELLAR AT YNYS CERRIG-DUON – A large cellar on the island was possibly used in later years as a hide-away for smuggled goods but its purpose in ancient times is not known. At the beginning of the last century a stone coffin containing large bones is reputed to have been found on the island.

PLAS Y BORTH – There is now no visible trace of this place apart from its cellars. Tradition recalls that these were fitted with doors which could be lowered at ebb tide, thus safeguarding the goods that were stored there.

CLOGWYN RUNER, TREFLYS – By the lake near Cae Shon is a section of rock called Clogwyn Runer and salt and spirits (smuggled goods) were known to have been hidden nearby. About 20 years ago one of these hiding places was found below Porth-yr-hirfaen.

PENRHYN-Y-PRYFAID – Someone called Stanley prospected in search of lead in the Trip rocks at Black Rock in the year 1770. Yellow Ochre has been found near Porth-yr-hirfaen.

Y GARREG WEN BACH or LETTY'R CENAW (CUBS LODGE OR LAIR) – Between this place and the sea is a cromlech which is partially buried in the sand [this seems to refer to Samson's Rock, a natural glacial erratic boulder – Ed].

YNYSCYNGAR – This is where Cyngar ab Gerinius or Geraint, grandson of Constantine, Duke of Cornwall, landed about the year 600 AD

CEFN-Y-GADAIR – This is a place at Morfa Bychan behind the site where the course officials sat on the winning-post platform when horse racing took place on Morfa Bychan circa 1810. At that time it was part of the Bronyfoel estate, but the present owner is Mr John Jones of Ynysfor.

The following note appeared in the *North Wales Gazette*:

> Tremadoc races came off in the year 1810. The following gentlemen were acting on the committee viz:- Sir WW Wynn Bart; Sir Robert Williams Bart; Sir EP Lloyd Bart, Thomas Boycott Esq, HW Wynne Esq, WA Madocks Esq, Bell Lloyd Esq, Sir Thos Mostyn Bart., John Wheatley Esq and John Madocks Esq. Five events were advertised to come off in addition to a match of 200 guineas between two horses owned by Mr Boycott and Mr Nanney. The entry to be made at The Madoc Arms Hotel, Tremadoc. Ordinary Ball, plays as usual. The racecourse was at Morfa Bychan. The stewards for the year were Love Jones-Parry, Esq, and Edward Lloyd, Esq.

MORFA BYCHAN (SMALL OR LTTLE MARSH) – It is called this to differentiate between Morfa or Traeth Mawr, now called the Vale of Madog. About 150 years ago the river flowed through the centre of Morfa Bychan.

Y TAN DIETHR (THE STRANGE FIRE) – According to legend a strange fire was seen in the neighbourhood in the year 1693; later it also affected parts of Meirionydd. It appeared around Christmas time and set alight haystacks belonging to Richard Davies of Erw wen, Richard Griffith of Llechwedd dû and Humphrey Owen of Garreg wen y Gest. These occurred on December 27th and three days later a stack belonging to John Phillips of Ynys Llanfihangel, two stacks belonging to John Griffith Owen of Cefn Trefor bach, two stacks belonging to Catherine Williams of Cefn Trefor mawr, and one belonging to Francis Evans of Glasfryn, were set ablaze. Later a shippon containing a large quantity of hay owned by Richard Davies of Erw wen was further affected. This strange phenomenon which aroused feelings both of wonder and fear, was a type of volatile marsh gas which rose from the wet and sandy marshes of Morfa Bychan and crossed both river and marsh to reach Ynys, Llanfihangel, Morfa Harlech and the banks of Traeth Bach. It differed from another type of fire which was known to destroy at night, and it left in the ground poisonous substances that caused the death of many cattle, horses, pigs and goats; this lasting for a long time. The after-effects of the fire were so harmful at Tyddyn Sion Wyn that, for a period of three years, they caused the death of all stock that grazed there; birds, too, were not immune. First appearing as a small blue flame, it seemed an easy matter to extinguish it, especially as it proved harmless to those trying to prevent the hay igniting. It was later found that noise diverted it, so horns were blown, shots fired and drums were beaten – actions which caused the flame to rise in the air. Following the discovery of this deterrent, little further damage was suffered although the flame was observed for a long while afterwards, especially on Saturday and Sunday nights.

The historian Pennant believed that its origin lay in a horde of locusts blown in from the sea by a westerly gale; these were drowned and drifted ashore at Morfa Bychan. Local people at the time believed that a cottager at Tyddyn Sion Wyn, who had been evicted from his home, had put a curse upon the place!! He was apprehended by the constable, Rowland Pritchard of Ynys Ddû, with the intention of bringing him to justice. It was found that there was no Justice of the Peace nearer than Penarth or Wern Fawr in Caernarfonshire so the prisoner was kept in custody at Llanystumdwy. During the night however, he managed to escape through a window and was never seen again.

Note: The learned historian Edward Llwyd wrote about the strange event in the *Philosophical Transactions* soon after the fires had occurred. The Rev Morris Jones, the Rector of Dolgelley, corresponded with many learned men at the time, describing 'the strange fire' in the year 1693. Mouffett, a French writer, mentions a plague in Normandy in 591 AD which caused 80,000 men and animals to perish – this, too, being caused by a plague of locusts which had poisoned the air to a high degree.

LLANERCH-Y-GEST – On the land of Llanerch many traces of olden times have been found, such as Muriau Gwyddelod (Celtic Huts), but there is not sufficient space to record them singly.

TY MAWR, TREFLYS – On the land between Ty Mawr and Bronyfoel in a field called 'Cae y Gist gerrig' (Field of the stone coffin or chest), a stone chest was discovered but there is no particular tradition attached to it in the area. The coffin or chest consists of six large stones, two at each side and one at each end; the two stones at the top end are the biggest by far, measuring about three yards in length. All of them are very wide and very plain. Around the chest were many circular or oval building foundations, these being known locally as Irish or Celtic huts. (See *Y Brython* 1860, pages 237 & 251. The writer of this publication makes detailed reference to the chest and puts forward the theory that the mountain of Moel y Gest might correctly be called Moel y Gist.) Some are of the opinion that a Prince or Princes of Gest were buried here, as the place is close to Bronyfoel, the home of Sir Howell of the Battle-axe. I do not share this view, but give all the information known to me so that the reader may decide whether or not satisfactory light has been shed on the subject.

It is well known that our forefathers marked the graves of old ancestors either by raising a mound of earth or by the erection of a large cairn or cromlech. Many of these graves have been opened and urns containing ashes have been found in unjointed stone coffins. Another method used to mark graves was the placing of large stones, sometimes singly, other times two, at the ends of graves. Such an example I have seen on one of the Merionethshire mountains which, when opened, was found to contain a few human bones that had not quite disintegrated. When more than one was buried additional upright stones would be erected as can be seen at Beddau Gwyr Ardudwy (Graves of the men of Ardudwy) at Hafod-yr-Ysbytty, Festiniog and also on Mynydd-y-Glyn on the Berwyn range close to Allt-y-Badi, Llangollen. At the latter site stones have been set up in regular rows with about a fathom distance between them. Some believe that cromlechs and circles which are to be seen in many places, are memorials, but no-one has yet discovered any traces of burial to confirm this view. It may well be that the various methods used relate either to different periods of time, to the customs of different families, or means of indicating the difference of rank of the people buried there. It is known that all are very ancient for they ceased to be used after the 6th century.

A stone chest was examined some time ago and was found to differ considerably from other burial traces examined previously. In this particular case the remains comprised stones set upright with a long cairn of smaller stones and pebbles. The chest stood close to the cairn and consisted of six stones – four large ones on the eastern end and two more making up the sides. One of the stones appears to have been placed there at a later date or, perhaps, to have been moved from its original position. More careful scrutiny indicated that the chest was once inside a circle and was most probably discovered by someone searching the site for treasure. I have no doubt that it was not a burial chest as it was usually the custom to place large stones at the head of graves, as related in the following poem from Englynion Beddau Milwyr Ynys Prydain (stanza of the Graves of Britain's Soldiers).

> Whose the four-sided grave
> With four stones about its head?
> The grave of Madog, the faithful knight.

Perhaps it may be asked whose grave it is and this is a question to which it is impossible to give a definite answer. The belief that the Princes of Gest were buried here I believe to be untrue. There is no record of the Bronyfoel family before the 14th century and it is certain that burial under cairns was a practice of much earlier times. During the Middle Ages burial usually took place in consecrated ground and nobility were usually buried inside the church. That was the Welsh custom in the 12th century and we can take, for example, Owen Gwynedd who was interred in the walls of Bangor Cathedral, and the wife of Llewellyn ab Gruffydd at Penmon, on Anglesey. (See also memorial stones in churches and cemeteries pertaining to that period, such as the column at Llanfihangel-y-traethau.)

Therefore we have to look to a period prior to the Middle Ages for the occupants of cairn graves and, amongst Englynion y Beddau (Stanzas of the Grave) the following verse may be found.

> The graves in Morfa Bychan....
> There is Sanant, gracious maiden,
> There Rhun, most ready for war,
> There Carwen, daughter of Henwy,
> There Lledin and Llywy.

Could it possibly be that it is the grave of these that lay under the cairn? If the reader can find time to visit the chest he will find its position off Morfa Bychan not far from the Morfa.

TYDDYN-ADI – 'Y MAEN LLWYD' – On a bank below the house, that is between the house and the Morfa, there is a noted stone known as y Maen Llwyd (The Grey Stone). It measures about three yards in length, is nearly as wide, and is slightly narrower in depth. One end of this stone rests on a smaller one (about 4 feet long) and a third stone is nearby resting on its side; the whole giving the appearance of a collapsed cromlech. The largest stone differs in quality from the others and also from the surrounding rocks. Many tales were told about the Maen Llwyd by the older inhabitants, including hearing strange and unearthly voices and noises and of other mystifying things that were seen around the rocks! [Actually this is a glacial erratic. – Ed]

OGOFEYDD Y GREIG-DDU (THE BLACK ROCK CAVES) – These can hardly be classed as 'antiquities' but many strange tales are associated with them. Some say that they extend many miles inland and, though they have been explored for a considerable distance, no-one has yet succeeded in reaching the far end. The story favoured by local tradition is that the caves were made by a wizard and that they reach as far as Braich-y-Bib in Cwmstradllyn, the point reached by one explorer who blew his shepherd's whistle ('Bib' means whistle) to indicate how far he had progressed. It is reported that he never returned to the cave entrance so the reader can attach as much credence to this story as he feels it merits! No doubt the caves do reach far inland and, although some believe them to be mine adits, it is more likely that they were created by erosion caused by waves, as at Porth St Dyfynog on the western side of Black Rock. They are still there for the curious to investigate.

LLYN MORUS AND YNYS Y CAPEL (MORRIS' LAKE AND THE CHAPEL ISLAND) – On a small hillock, not far from Ynyscynhaiarn, there are traces of old foundations which may be of a former chapel or church. The stretch of water nearest Criccieth from Lyn Ystumllyn is called Llyn or Llynau Morus (Llyn means lake), to which two legends are attached. The first concerns a man called Morus who lived at Mynydd-du at a time not known to us. It is said that he undertook the risky task of 'raising the old demons' but, having done so, he was overcome by them. He was lifted up into the air, carried over Ystumllyn woods and dropped into the lake. Later the body was recovered and buried by the side of the lake which now bears his name. Until about 25 years ago there was large cairn of small stones on the grave but this has disappeared under the Cambrian Railway track. The second story about the cairn by Llyn Morus was given by the late Ellis Owen. He stated that Morus hanged himself in one of the outbuildings of Mynydd-du and that he was buried by the lake because Welsh custom would not allow the bodies of suicides to be buried in consecrated ground. From early times it was the habit of everyone who passed the spot to add a stone or two to the grave, a custom which continued until the Cambrian Railway destroyed the cairn.

LLYS BRONYFOEL – There are two interpretations of the words 'palas' or 'plas' and 'llys'. The meaning of the first is a 'place to stay' and the other 'that which sticks or stands out'. The first was a dwelling place of the 15 tribes, possibly a fort or castle; the latter word 'llys' indicates that it was the residence of the ruling nobility or princes of the Royal blood or lineage. 'Cwrt' conveys the meaning of a sitting place of law and justice. When the hall and main entrance were being demolished about 60 years ago, cavities extending deeply into the walls were found on both sides of the doorposts, where bars could be fitted to strengthen the entrance against enemy attack. The window and stone staircase from where Gruffydd ap John ap Gorono of Gwynfryn was killed by an arrow fired by Evan ap Meredydd also remains. The attack on the mansion took place around 1490-1500 and arose from a dispute over fishing rights on Llyn Ystumllyn. The following is the complete story of this event as it was recorded in their family records called *The Pedigree of the Family of Ystumllyn*, a précis of which was translated and appeared in *Y Brython.*

THE STORY OF THE ONSLAUGHT AND BURNING OF BRONYFOEL

Gruffydd ab John ab Gorono, of Gwynfryn (a cousin of the sons of John ab Meredydd), who had served in the army in France for a long while, returning to his old country, as he was fishing with his manservant in Ystumllyn lake, the fish were stolen from the manservant and he was beaten up on the orders of Hywel ab Rhys of Bronyfoel. Gruffydd ab John ab Gorono took exception to this and challenged Hywel ab Rhys to meet him in the field, but he refused. After gathering the sons of John ab Meredydd and their friends together, they went to attack Hywel in his own house, Bronyfoel using the same methods as in the battles in France. He set the barns and outhouses on fire and then decided to set fire to the Hall in which Hywel ab Rhys was sheltering; this being a very strong building. Hywel shot at Gruffydd through an aperture in the wall; the arrow entered his head through his hat (he wore armour and this was the only place unprotected) thus killing him, but although he died the onslaught continued fiercely. Large bales of straw were placed against the entrance to the Hall and set alight.

The smoke from the burning outhouses prevented the men from repelling the attack, as they had to go under the benches to avoid the smoke which choked them. The exception was the old Hywel ab Rhys, who stood unshaken in the centre of the floor with a spear in his hand. He chided his men 'for shame' and ordered them to stand up saying that 'he had seen more smoke in the hall at Christmas time when roasting geese'. At last, when they found that they were surrounded and the smoke was becoming unbearable; Hywel ab Rhys agreed to surrender as a prisoner to Morus ab John ab Meredydd of Clenenney (the eldest son of John ab Meredydd of Cefnyfan) if he swore to him that he would escort him safely to the castle at Caernarfon to stand trial for the murder of Gruffydd ab John ab Gorono (who was second cousin of Hywel ab Rhys of Bronyfoel and of the same family). Morus undertook the task and placed a guard of his truest friends to keep Hywel from the revengeful family, especially from Owen ab John ab Meredydd, his brother, who was fiercely against him.

They travelled as an army arriving at Caernarfon safely, where practically the whole county had assembled. Hywel's friends sent a messenger an horseback to Bronyfoel to advise them that he had arrived safely, as they greatly feared that he would be murdered on the journey and that Morus ap John would not be able to defend him: neither would anyone of Hywel's family defend him because of fear of revenge. After reaching Caernarfon he was placed in the custody of the Keeper of the Castle, where he was kept in safety until the Assizes. It turned out that according to law, attacking Hywel in his own home and burning it was a more heinous crime by Morus ab John ab Meredydd and others than the killing of Gruffydd ab John ab Gorono by Hywel. Because of this, Morus ap John and thirty of his henchmen were charged with the massacre and pillage, as is learnt from a paper that Sir John Wynn found in the records. When Hywel left the Castle he would not risk going to his own home in Eifionydd, so he went to Penmachno to a relative of his mother and a son of Rhys Gethin.

It is interesting to note that the house has disintegrated from time to time and also that none of his descendants, of which there were four, have been buried in the family burial ground at Penmorfa. More comments on the brave men of Bronyfoel will be found amongst the details of Tre'r Gest.

The following (English) quotation from *Records of Carnarvon* deserves recording in conjunction with the saga of Bronyfoel.

> Meredith ap Howel, of Bronyfoel, held in farm from the Crown the Lordship of Gest 6. Richard II [this is the 6th year of the reign of Richard II. – Ed]. His son was Ifan ap Robert, died of plague in Gesail Gyfarch, in the year 1468, aged 31. He was the father of Meredydd ap Efan of Gesail, Creigiau (the Crug now) Dolwyddelen Castle and lately Gwydir. Howel y Fwyall was Raglot of Aberglaslyn (Aber y Porth); he held a lease on the villa of Bodewyn (Gwely

Wyn ap Ednewyn, or Treflys) and the fishing of Ystumllyn; Howel died between AD 1379 and 1383, between Michaelmas, 2. Richard II and the same 6. Richard II.

William Morris, Knight, fishing for the township of Gest £10.

William Morris, mil. pro villa de Gest £10 (son of the above).

William Bold, Esq, had the fishery of Ystumllyn and Aberglaslyn.

Jane, daughter of Rees Bold, Esq was the second wife of Morris Jones, Esq, of Wern, who died in 1624.

Y CAE BLYSIG (THE GREEDY OR HUNGRY FIELD) – This is located below the road leading to the field of Llidiart Dunawd and Bach-y-saint. The field contained many foundations of dwelling houses with a paved road below and a footbridge over the river to Nant flysig (nant means stream). Many mill-stones or querns were found here many years ago and were in the safekeeping of Ellis Owen of Cefnmeusydd.

BRONYGADAIR AND THE STONES OF THE OLD MILL – Bronygadair is a conspicuous landmark in this part of Gest. There were three accessible footpaths leading to Ynyscynhaiarn. One, near the hill called ffordd Gorph (Body road), started from Efail bach and Llidiart Bronygadair, through the woods on the westward side of the mansion, through Cae Calch (Lime field), Cae bysedd cochion (Red fingers or Foxglove field); bysedd cochion being the Welsh name for foxgloves in this part of the area, to Cae'r Sarn (Ford field), and Hendre'r clochydd (Sexton's old house). The last named has been demolished down to its foundations. Another path is Llwybr llan (Church path) starting from the boundary of Ystumllyn by the main road and along the southwestern slopes of the Moelygadair to Sarn yr Ynys (Island ford) to Hendre Clochydd. There was also an important footpath from Treflys towards Ynyscynhaiarn through the lake which the parishioners were unheeding enough to allow the tenant of Bronygadair to destroy. We may find space to comment further on the paths of Tre'rgest in conjunction with information about the roads.

MEINI MELIN ABERDOWARCH (THE MILL STONES OF ABERDOWARCH) – There was doubt about the site of the old mill until the stones were found in 1884, now in safekeeping at Bronygadair. The discovery confirmed that the mill was near Beudy'r Ychain (Oxen shippons), about 120 yards higher than Sarn yr Ynys, close to the banks of the river (now a stream). It must be remembered that before the year 1764 the river Aberdowarch ran through Gors Nadroedd (Snake's marsh) on the westward side of Ynyscynhaiarn to 'Lynau Morus'. It can be seen, therefore, that there was a need for a ford to enable worshippers to reach the church. Sarn yr Ynys was built by Owen Efan of Tyddyniolyn and Owen Ellis of Cefnymeusydd.

Sir J Owen

Y MAEN HIR, PENTREFELIN (THE LONG STONE) – This occupies a prominent position by the roadside in the village, on the bank of the mill-pond. It measures 9 feet above ground in height and 24 by 18 inches in girth; the date 1721 is inscribed on it. It is said that four brothers: Morris, Harry, Griffith and John Parry lived at Cefnymeusydd isa and that two of them tried to carry it from Y Geirth (where it was found) but failed to bring it any further than Tanlan, below The Geirth, to a spot called 'Llam llithrig' (Slippery leap). However the other two brothers managed to carry it the remaining distance and erect it in position on the bank. It was thought to be their mother's wish that they erect it by the roadside so that they would remember her when passing the stone on their way to church on Sundays. There is a similar stone close to the old house of Geirth from where this stone was brought; Ellis Owen called it 'the sister of the long stone'. The initials of the four brothers were inscribed on a stone that could be seen at the rear of the barn but when rebuilding the outhouses in 1824 the stonemasons placed the stone with the initials facing inwards; the stone is still visible.

CAE'R DUNAWD OR CAE LLIDIART DUNAWD (THE FIELD OF DUNAWD'S GATE) – This is on the southern side of Bachysaint hill on the boundary of Tre'rgest. From its position and traces of foundations found in the area, it is believed that it was a site of some importance. It is plain to see from the architecture, name and position of the well that it was a place of distinction and usefulness. It stands by the roadside close to the entrance called Llidiart Dunawd. The well has steps to it and is fed from a spring of crystal clear water. Higher up in a field called Cae Llidiart Dunawd are signs that many dwellings once stood there. When the son of Bach y Saint, the late Mr John Jones (who spent the last years of his life at Garth, Porthmadog) was ploughing the field about 45 years ago the plough struck a stone flagstone and when it was lifted an urn was found underneath which contained ashes. A piece of copper was also discovered but this was too badly corroded to see if there was any inscription on it. The urn was taken home but unfortunately on exposure to the air it shattered into pieces. It was seen later by the historian Ellis Owen of Cefnymeusydd. A relic similar to a stone coffin was found later in another part of the same field.

THE MINES OF GEST

In dealing with this subject it is not proposed to discuss either the principles of metallurgy or to comment on the merits of the veins or the mineral resources of the area. However, as much prospecting has taken place in Tre'r Gest for many years, an attempt will be made to record all the mines and quarries in the two parishes and to give the reader that knowledge that is known to me. Copper and lead were the metals most commonly found, although iron, sulphur, paving stones, ochre, slate and stone sets were other materials which were either mined or quarried. Professor Davies of Llanbadarn read a paper to the Geological Society in London about 45 years ago in which he speculated that coal deposits existed in the Vale of Madog, between Penamser and Llidiart Yspytty (extracts of his address appeared in the local papers at the time). Lewis Morris, in his survey of Cardigan Bay, also comments on the various minerals to be found but does not supply any information of their location.

If an analogy can be made, one can liken Moel-y-Gest to a hen sheltering her chicks, for the possibility is that under that mountain lie vast untapped riches still undiscovered and merely waiting development by some future industrialist. I feel that there is an ebb and flow in all things and that what has been once will come again. This is particularly true when one notes that old workings that have been abandoned for centuries are suddenly reopened and zealously explored for metals or slates – the need for them arising suddenly only to recede at a later date. There is nothing new under the sun.

THE COPPER MINE AT BRONYGADAIR – There is a tradition that this mine was first worked by the Romans; a tradition which probably stems from linking the early evidence of mining to the method used by them. Unlike other places, however, none of their old tools such as copper chisels and stone hammers have ever been found. The mine was worked by various small companies over a period of time and between the years 1824 and 1830 the mine owner was Mr Holland, father of Mr Samuel Holland of Cae'rdeon (formerly of Plas y Penrhyn). In 1836 a competent concern called the Cambrian Mining Company took it in hand and operated the mine successfully for many years, raising many tons of copper ore. They installed a 12 HP steam engine to drive a 48 feet diameter wheel in an endeavour to pump out water from the workings but the two pumps were unable cope with the rising water levels and work was unable to proceed. A lake or millpond was built close to Garregfelin from which water was taken, firstly by a ditch on the surface and then by a wooden trough which was raised in some places to a height of 66 feet until it reached the water-wheel. The pond the troughs and the installation of the wheel all were completed in 1838; the cost of the timber alone amounting to £700. Before the water was released into the troughs for the first time, Griffith Owen and Lewis Jones raced along the troughs in front of the water (the first of these two is still alive) and the completion of the work was marked by a celebration dinner and a firework display on top of the Foel. Note: Lewis Owen of Llanfair, Merioneth, was the planner and worker of the water-wheel and troughs. The troughs were 2 feet wide with 6 inch sides. His son is Mr Griffith Owen of Glaslyn Villa, Portmadoc.

The new generation may think it was the old mill-pond of Garregfelin Mill that was used, but this is not the case; the new work to enable water to be carried to the mine was carried out, as stated, in 1838. Before the pond was opened, a start was made at Cefnymogran bach to excavate a tunnel to the lowest level of the mine and also the shaft by the main road. It was hoped that this project would alleviate the serious flooding that was hampering mining operations – the two shafts on top of the hill being waterlogged. The loose nature of the rock was also thought to be helpful in solving the problem which, if successfully overcome, would allow extraction of the ore from the very rich veins as yet untapped; ore which had particularly good smelting qualities. Ultimately, however, the flooding could not be contained and mining operations ceased. There were two shafts close to the main road: one at the boundary between Bronygadair bach and Cefnymogran, which was said to produce the best copper, and one on the eastern side at a depth of 89 yards. There is a huge space between the shafts with a large cavern at the bottom. Some little excavation was carried out at Cefnymogran at some time or other – possibly when the old shaft which lies on Ystumllyn land was dug out, for here the Bronygadair land terminates.

I knew an old man named Harri Roberts of Garregfawr (he died in 1836), who sank the old shaft about 100 years ago; this shaft is now covered by a stone flagstone. The Cambrian Copper Mine also had a takenote on a copper mine near Migneint, Festiniog during the same period, both being on land owned by Mr RW Price of Rhiwlas, who received £700 in royalties annually from both places. The whole works – machines, steam and water – were in constant use day and night, weekdays, Sundays and holidays, making it a non-stop operation which continued for many years until 1843. Ellis Owen of Cefnmeusydd sang of the Bronygadair mine when Mr Holland of Plas Penrhyn worked it in 1826.

A cave portal to intricate depths,
Old and dreadful den of demons;
We stand beyond this bleak mouth,
The entrance to Eifion's Vesuvius.

The stench of sulphur, of cold dark water
Is raised from the hollow of hell;
The vapours of the black cauldron
Would overcome a multitude.

Let me be saved from its soils,
Its earth and the dark pits;
Never may I set eyes on the cave
Or its hideous creatures.

Old inhabitants recall hearing their fathers tell the story of a strange blue flame which moved around the hill and across Cefnymogran at night-time. This was believed to indicate the location of an abundance of copper! Evan Ellis of Bronygadair bach used to say that the hooves of the horses and cattle which grazed on the field would turn a coppery colour. Some people were afraid to pass the mine at night, claiming to hear sounds of working when no work was being carried out. Wmffre Dafydd said that he was once working at the bottom on a Sunday night shift when 'a lady in white with a haughty look about her' suddenly appeared. Such was his fright that he said that 'he was took short' and vowed never to work on a Sunday night shift again. Such was the superstition of the people in the area at that time, and their belief in ghosts!

Since information of the early history of this mine is scant, no one knows just how much copper was raised but the most likely prolific era was during the time of the Cambrian Mining Company, the last to work the mine. Because of flooding it has been unworked since 1844, although it was an accepted fact that the deeper the mine was driven the more plentiful the copper ore, which promised a continuity of production for many years.

THE COPPER MINE AT GLANYMORFA BACH – Considerable exploration and work was carried out on this level in the search for copper; there were workings here before the memory of men who were alive at the start of this century. It is believed by same that the level or cave extends as far as Penrhyd-fechan. A Mr Hughes of Amnodd sold the lease of Glanymorfa Bach Copper Mine for £800 about 40 years ago. He had worked it himself for a while but said that due to the vein being so deep, the flooding became too strong. If this problem could be overcome there still remains sufficient copper to make it a viable proposition.

THE COPPER MINE AT CWM MAWR – About 30 years ago some work was carried out on a site on the side of Allt Wen, above Pwll-gloewlas (Penmorfa). It showed great promise but, being on the edge of an estate, there was no place to dispose of the spoil, so the work was abandoned.

THE SULPHUR MINE AT MOELYGEST ABOVE PENAMSER – There was a fairly large sulphur works on the northern side of Moel y Gest, the owner of which was a Mr Parry, a solicitor. At the time he lived at Plas isa in Penmorfa and also owned Penamser. This was about 100 years ago. A long level was opened out, it being discovered that the quality of the mineral improved as the work extended. The story is told that the workers persuaded Hwmffra William of Llanerch that the vein extended right under his hearth, and this remained the unshakeable belief of this simple old soul.

BRONYFOEL QUARRY – There is not much evidence of slate in Tre'r Gest and this quarry is the only place that was worked with any zeal. It was about the year 1793 that the quarry was first opened by a local man. It flourished for a time. The manager's name was Evan Jones. Sulphur and impurities ran through the slates which caused them to change colour and disintegrate when they had been on a roof for a while. Tremadog when first built was roofed with them and some of the old slates can still be seen on older houses even today. It is possible that the workings did not go deep enough to reach material of a better quality. About 70 years ago the quarry was worked by a tenant, Mr Humphrey Humphreys, grandfather of Mrs Roberts (Wife of the distinguished writer, Mr Edward Roberts), who is still there. A few small ships were loaded at Ynyscyngar with slates from this quarry which were carried in wicker hampers over Cerbi to the harbour.

THE LEAD WORKS AT TAN'RALLT – Lead was mined here at an early period because a level was found which entered into the side of Allt Wen (where the Factory, Tremadog, now stands) towards the end of the last century. Work recommenced about 70 years ago (if not earlier) and hundreds of tons lead of the purest quality were raised by a local company. It is said that differences of opinion between management and workers about the run of the vein caused it to be lost – the workers favouring one direction and the owners another. That was how things stood about the year 1825. Lone prospectors have made unsuccessful attempts to locate the vein and it is felt that it needs a rich speculator to exploit the rocks behind Tremadog which could contain rich minerals.

THE IRON ORE MINE AT LLIDIART YSPYTTY – This hill was called Bryn y Garreg Haiarn (the Hill of the Iron Stone) well before present day memory. There was an old road going past the level of the ironstone, which had a door on it to prevent animals entering. They seemed to be old workings when I passed them on my way to school about 70 years ago. In the year 1840 a Mr Cooper (who lived at Aberglaslyn at that time) took a lease on the hill and started to work it in earnest; he then sold it to a Mr Heyward. Much of the ore was shipped in small vessels from Porthmadog to Cardiff but the freight charges proved too high to make the work profitable. A smelting furnace was installed but even that did not succeed in reducing costs sufficiently, although the ore was of a high quality. It is judged that if operations could be carried out methodically, it would be a paying concern as the whole hill extending to Allt Wen is full of ore. There is also a vein of iron ore in a small hill near Pensyflog. A person called Trefor raised some ore from this spot, but the work was not strongly pursued.

THE FLAG QUARRY AT TYDDYN LLWYN – Excellent flagstones were raised from this quarry during the years 1830 to 1844. Dafydd Jones of Carmarthen, who worked it about 1840, also built the old Commercial Hotel in Porthmadog. From this quarry came the flagstones which were used to floor Ynyscynhaiarn Church. About half a century ago, and even later, flags to floor houses, their frontages, and the streets of Tremadog and Porthmadog were obtained from this source.

THE QUARRY AT TU-HWNT-I'R-BWLCH – Later a quarry for flooring slabs and buildings was opened up in a field between Tu-hwnt-i'r-bwlch and Penrhynllwyd; the stones in this quarry were easier to work and split better than those at Tyddynllwyn.

GLODDFA SHON PRYS (JOHN PRICE'S MINE) – This was a flag quarry that was worked by an old man who was well known to most of the middle-aged of the district. It stood close to a spot on the main Cambrian Railway Line on a bend near Wern Bridge. Fine stones were quarried by the Railway Company from a spot lower down, the site of which was expected to be a station for the convenience of the parishioners of Penmorfa, Treflys, Pentrefelin and Morfa bychan.

THE SETTS OR PAVING STONES QUARRY – This was opened a few years ago on the northern side of Moel y Gest, above Penamser. The stones are of an excellent quality (feldspar trap) and an incline was built to bring the stones down to the road, where they were loaded into trams and then taken to the Cambrian Railway Station. Although there is an ample supply it is proving costly to produce. There was a noted brewery at Penamser until 1842, when it was demolished and the present house was built. Evan Hughes brewed here in 1793.

THE LAKES OF TRE'R GEST

There are only three lakes of any note in Tre'r Gest. These are Llyn y Garregwen, Llyn y Garregaethnen (Farmyard), and Llyn Ystumllyn, the latter being the chief one. There is a reservoir at Tanrallt which is called Llyn Cwmbach, but originally this was only a collection of ditches from the gully above Bwlch Efan Esgob (the Gap of Evan the Bishop). A strong dam was built here to hold water to work the factories and mills of Mr WA Madocks at the start of the century. A few trout were introduced into the lake some years ago and the numbers have increased a great deal over the years. During periods of prolonged drought the water level drops considerably as it is dependent on rainwater from a small catchment area.

LLYN GARREGAETHNEN – This small but very deep lake by the buildings of Farmyard, was created when the Embankment was breached in 1812. It has a continuous outflow although the lake is only replenished by rain water.

LLYN Y GARREGWEN – This is in the Gest, below the house of Garregwen (the home of Dafydd Owen the noted harpist). I know of nothing to interest the reader about this lake apart from the fact that many years ago there were many medical leeches which declined in number when farmers started to lime their land. Some local women used to go into the water to catch them, these then being sold to those in need of them. It must be remembered that leeches were used far more extensively for medical purposes than they are today.

LLYN YSTUMLLYN – This is the 'king' of the Gest lakes and it is often asked why is it called Llyn Ystumllyn rather than Llyn Treflys, it being much closer nowadays to that side of Ynys. Perhaps the following explanation will throw light an the subject. The river Aberdowarch (or Aber-dwy-erchwyn Aber means estuary, dwy means two, erchwyn means sides or bank) is probably named from the two banks below the mill, which was between Ynys and Moel Bron-y-gadair; therefore the main part of the lake was closer to Ystumllyn as far as Llynau Morus. The lake extends from the banks of Nantyglyndwy up to Porthyrhirfaen, to the beach at Black Rock, encircling Ynys y Capel and Ynyscynhaiarn, up to Gors-nadrodd (Snake's marsh or bog), and Llynau Morus. During dry seasons in the summer it practically dries up, apart from a small section near Coed-y-llyn.

About the year 1763, John Parry of Garregyfelen, Goruchwyliwr (agent) for WR Price Esq, of Rhiwlas, moved the bed of the river Aberdowarch from the northern end of Gors-nadrodd to its present position along the boundaries of Garregfelen, Garregfawr, Cae-shon, Coedyllyn, Porthyrhirfaen and Penrhyn, then along the southwestern boundary of Bronygadair. It is still possible to follow the bed of the river before it was diverted. From Gors-las, at the western end of Bronygadair meadows, below the field of Beudy'r ychain (where the mill stones were found) to Sarn yr Ynys, through Ystumllyn meadows to the centre of Gorswaen, then crossing over Ystumllyn land until one arrives at Lyn Morus and lower down to Nheraig; thence in wooden troughs (with a sluice at each end) to the sea. Before John Parry made an opening through Black Rock (as it is at present) it was necessary to keep careful watch on the sluices. In 1879 the covers collapsed and the troughs were broken, thereby obstructing the flow of water. This caused the level of the water to rise to a height never seen before, and it was some time before the cause was detected. It was found that the canal had given way and that the damage to the sluice made it impossible to fit it as before.

There used to be a rock below Gae'rdyni called 'Craig Gofer y Llyn' (rock of the Lake's Overflow) but this is now covered in sand from the beach. In olden times, however, it was in the estuary of the river Aberdowarch from Lyn Ystumllyn as it entered the sea.

Reference has already been made to Ystumllyn lake when Sir Howel y Fwyall (Howel of the Battle-axe) was Raglot (governor) of the lake or fishery at Aberglaslyn and it is interesting to note that in the year 1620 the fishing rights for Llyn Ystumllyn and Aberglaslyn were held by William Bold, of Tre'rddol and Caernarfon. It must be realised that in these earlier times the grant of such rights came from the King, whose sole prerogative they were. (Morris Jones of Wern married one of the daughters of Rees Bold, who was High Sheriff of Merionethshire in 1622. Richard Phillips, the bard, composed an elegy for him. William Maurice married Jane, another daughter of Mr Bold.)

It is probable that small boats came up the creek to Porthyrhirfaen, as iron mooring rings were to be seen in the rocks as far as Clogwyn Runer, below Cae-shon. Visitors, some of whom had travelled quite a distance would gather at Porthyrhirfaen to collect scarce herbs, osiers for the weavers and also medical leeches. Wild ducks, geese and swans were also attracted to the lake, especially when there was migration from Northern Europe to escape the freezing conditions – these were hunted and shot by many people.

That part of the lake that fronts Garregfelen was called Llyn Gloyw (Clear Lake). This was the deepest section and also the spot where many osiers grew. Some of the lower sections between Ynyscynhaiarn and Treflys were called Y Gwyllt (The Rough or Wild) and here too were many groves of willows and osiers. Llyn Ystumllyn once contained ample quantities of leeches, salmon and eels, but supplies of these dwindled following the re-opening of the Bronygadair Copper mine by the Cambrian Mining Company. There was footpath called Llwybr y Llan (Church path) from the cemetery at Ynyscynhaiarn which crossed the river below Coed y Llyn and then went to Treflys Church. The stone footbridge was removed about 15 years ago. Another path went through Ystumllyn meadows towards Porthyrhirfaen, but this was only passable during the summer months.

Speculative thought often starts with the words 'if only', and this is recalled by an old saying which is known to many local people:

If Snowdon's hill were made of cheese,
A better hope of cheer,
And Moelygest all whitened bread,
And the Llyn of yellow beer.

A SCHEME TO DRAIN YSTUMLLYN LAKE

Mr James Spooner (father of the late Charles E Spooner, CE, of Bronygarth, Porthmadog) submitted plans for draining the lake and for the reclamation of the land and also gave an estimate of the costs about the year 1840. He devoted a lot of time to the project, walking the lakes in the summer and around the land surrounding it in the winter. This enabled him to estimate the area, test the varying depths and also the composition of the bed of the lake. His studies resulted in the preparation of many plans and references, in which attention was drawn to the various types of soil that were hidden under the water. He said that the eastern section, called the Gwyllt, was composed of excellent soil and that, if drained, was capable of bearing wheat of a comparable quality to that found in the Vale of Clwyd.

The method he advocated was to cut one large ditch or canal about 4 yards wide at the bottom and with sloping sides; these to be paved with stone and the surplus soil carried along the top of the walls to act as flood banks. The bed of the canal was to be of uniform width throughout, incorporating the necessary fall towards Black Rock (this to be about a foot lower than the present outlet to the sea). Strong tidal gates would be fitted at Black Rock, being similar in operation to those at the Cob, Porthmadog.

Mr Spooner said that the canal would be capable of carrying all the flood waters in the lake when it was high tide and would ensure its quick dispersal when the tide began to ebb. He gave a warning that the land which would be reclaimed would require some time to elapse before it could be got into good condition as it had been submerged over a long period. He gave the opinion, however, that in time it would bear an abundance of crops and that the valley would be 'one of the prettiest'. It is understood that the survey cost the owners of the adjoining land about £400. The lands of Garregfelen and Bronygadair are those mostly under water (the Rhiwlas estate until recently).

The agents for Mr Price (of Rhiwlas) in Eifionydd were; Mr Griffith Parry (1728), John Parry of Garregfelen (1765), John Jones of Bronygadair; Owen Owens of Llwyndedwydd (1798), then Hugh Owen, John Roberts, John Evans, Mr Parmeter, Mr Owen Evans, etc.

THE NOTABLES OF GEST AND THE OLD CHARACTERS OF THE TWO PARISHES

Although many of these that I will record under this heading have previously had much written about them, also included are those whose history has passed from father to son over many generations. References to the latter, therefore, are from my own recollections of stories told to me over a period of many years. It is possible that my forgetfulness will lead to the omission of some persons whom otherwise I should have liked to include.

SAINT CYNHAIARN

An old proverb says 'Good is the Rock of the Gospels' and so it is fitting that the name of the bringer of Christianity to Tre'rgest should receive priority over all others.

St Cynhaiarn lived in the 6th century, being the son of Hygarfael ab Cyndrwyn of Llystynwerian, Caereinion in Powys. He was Bishop of Llanbadarn fawr during the 6th century – a period when Wales was served by seven bishoprics.

Note: From old registers – St Kynhaiarn of Eifionydd ap Cyndrwyn from Llys Tedwynan in Kered (Ceredigion).

Kynhaiarn in Eifionydd and Hungaroal ap Cyndrwyn, from Llys Tedwynan in Caereinion.

Cynhaiarn in Ynys in Eifionydd, son of Garanvael ap Cyndrwyn, from Lys Tedwynan in Ceredigion in the 6th century.

Elhaiarn ymmaes Regitum in Powys and Llwch-haiarn in Cetewyn and Chynhaiarn in Eifionydd – sons of Hygarfoel ap Cyndrwyn from Llys Tenwynau, Caereinion.

Slight differences will be noted in these four references.

GWION AB CYNDRWYN

He was Prince of Powys and a cousin of St Cynhaiarn. Gwion ab Cyndrwyn, Gwgan Cleddyf Rhudd and Madawg ab Rhudd were a trinity of three guards at the battle of Bangor-is-y-coed AD 602–7. Llanbadarn Fawr near Aberystwyth was a cathedral in ancient times and St Cynhaiarn was its bishop, he also had two brothers, Llwchaiarn and Aelhaiarn whose names are given to two churches, one in Montgomeryshire and Llanaelhaiarn in Caernarfonshire.

It is most likely that those named lived in Eifionydd at some time or other for reference to these can be found in many places throughout the commote; Gwion's grave is at Beddgelert, Mur Gwgan at Bach y Saint and Castell Gwgan near Dolbenmaen. NOTE: There is a stream running down to the sea at the eastern end of Criccieth, near Tanrhiwiau Cochion, called Abergeraint.

SAINT DYFNOG

It is believed that the dwelling place of this man was somewhere in Treflys, perhaps Porth-yr-Hirfaen. The bay to the east of Black Rock is called 'Porth St Dyfynog'. He was the son of Mardredd ap Cawrda ap Caradoc of Freichfras. Some maintain that he established Treflys Church and that there was a church or chapel before the Princes of Gest used it as their family church.

COUNSELS OF CATAWG THE WISE TO ASUR, SON OF ST CYNHAIARN

Know thyself to know others.
To serve others is to serve thyself.
Censure thyself, censure not another.
To see thyself more foolish than another
Will make thee wiser than the other.
Be not like a wolf to thy kinsmen.
Be not like a sow in thy bed.
Be not like a cat in thy falsity.
Be not like a dog in thy confessions.
Be not like a he-goat in the herd.
Be not like a frog in thy lair.
Be not like a sea in thy breast.
Be not like a woman in thy report.
Be not like a woman in thy embrace.
Accuse thyself and no other.
Teach thyself before teaching others.
Lower thyself and not another. – RHIRID FLAIDD

It appears that he took the name 'Blaidd' (Wolf) from the elders on his mother's side. Rhudd means rosy or red, so his name translates to 'Bloody (Red) Wolf of Gest'. He was the son of Gwrgenau ab Collwyn from the daughter of Bleddyn, Prince of Powys. Rhirid was lord of Penllyn in Meirionnydd and Gest but lived near Bala at a place called Rhiwaedog. Woodward says that Henry III, in 1241, built a castle on a steep rock by Dyserth. The castle was granted to Prince Edward in 1254, along with Rhuddlan and others. In 1263 Prince Llewellyn carried it by assault and immediately levelled it with the ground. During the siege, Einion, son of 'Ririd Flaidd', was slain and a cross was erected in his memory on the spot, the shaft of which, ornamented with rude sculpture, was subsequently made to form part of a stile into the churchyard.

CYNGAR

Little is known about this brave knight other than that a residence and an island were named after him. Ynyscyngar is in a corner of Gest by the sea and once boasted a harbour. His ancestry is given in one of the trinity as follows: Cyngar ap Iestyn and Chetaw and Selyf, sons of Geraint, ap Erbin, ap Cystenin Cornen, ap Cynbron, ap Tudwal ap Eurmur, or Morfawr, ap Cudan, ap Cynan, ap Endaf, ap Caradol, ap Bran, ap Llediaith.

CILLYN AP Y BLAIDD RHUDD

Cillyn ap y Blaidd Rhudd had a daughter named Maer who was noted for her beauty. She married Bleddyn ap Cynfryn, Prince of Powys, who was killed at Ystrad Tywi in the year 1073. Her second husband was Cynfyn Hirdref (so named because he was heir to an estate of Hirdref in Lleyn), by whom he had a daughter, Enerys. This daughter was later to marry Gwrgenau ap Collwyn ap Moreddig from Pennant Melangell in Powys. Their son was Ririd Flaidd, who lived around the year 1150, and from whom most of the older families of North Wales can trace their ancestry.

Because the men of Gest were noted for their skill in making back-chains (used on the stirrups of carthorses) it gave rise to the following old proverb

> Praise the chains of the men of Gest,
> As tough as the chains of the men of Gest.

BLAIDD RUDD

The nobilities of Gwynedd and North Wales were divided amongst the fifteen tribes from which various families are descended. Blaidd Rhudd yn Gyff was not really part of this tree; his descendants being called 'the unruly or surly tribe of Gest' – their militancy was recorded when they refused obeisance to King Edward I. As punishment for this they were ordered to carry timber for the King's mills in Gest. There is little factual history about Blaidd Rhudd apart from the fact that he lived in his 'plas' somewhere in Gest and that he had many descendants, some of whom may be living up to the present.

EINION AB ITHEL

He was the fifth descendant of Ririd Flaidd and was squire to John of Ghent, Duke of Caerwerydd, Sheriff of Meirion for the year in which he died. Margaret, his daughter, became heiress of Rhiwaedog and estates in Eifionydd. She married Meredydd ap Jefan from Ystumcegid and bore a son who became the famous John ab Meredydd, Constable of Crugaeth Castle who, as captain, supported Henry, Earl of Richmond at the battle of Bosworth in 1485 (see *The History of the Gwydir Family*). From his descent from Rhirid Flaidd and John ap Meredydd, Lord Harlech owns most of his estates in Eifionydd. So, also, do the well known family of Price of Rhiwlas, near Bala, who have held almost the whole of the parish of Ynyscynhaiarn for centuries, together with half the parish of Llanfrothen. The estate of Plas du and Pentyrch did not descend to this family from their forefathers, but was bought by John Price Esq in 1610, from Owen Owens, heir of Plas Du. He was a brother of John Owen, the accomplished Latin poet.

RHYS FAWR OF YSBYTTY

Rhys Fawr was standard bearer to Henry, Earl of Richmond, at the battle of Bosworth and from whom descend the Prices of Giler, Foelas and Rhiwlas near Bala. This honourable family was fairly numerous and kinfolk spread to England, many to become knighted and become landed gentry and also to hold important Government posts.

LANDOWNERS OF GEST AND THE PARISH

Practically the whole of the Tre'rgest belonged to the Rhiwlas Estate, apart from a few places owned by Mr Ormsby Gore of Brogyntyn (now Lord Harlech). The family of Rhiwlas were sheriffs of Merioneth as follows:

John Wyn ab Cadwaladr of Rhiwlas	1576 – 7
Cadwaladr Price of Rhiwlas	1592
John Price, eldest son and heir to the above	1608 – 9
Roger Price	1709
William Price	1730 – 1
Richard Tavistock Price	1778 – 9

FIRST COUNSEL OF CATAWG THE WISE, TO ASUR, SON OF ST CYNHAIARN

Be not like a dog in thy confessions.
Be not like a cow in thy herd.
Be not like a frog in thy shelter.
Be not like a wolf to thy kinsman.
Be not like a cat in thy caress.
Be not like a saw in thy bed.
Be not like the sea in thy bosom.
Be not like a woman in thy gossip.

SECOND COUNSEL OF CATAWG THE WISE

Accuse thyself and not others.
Demean thyself but not others.
Teach thyself 'ere teaching others.
Chastise thyself 'ere chastising others.
Better thyself by aiding others.
See thyself more foolish than others.
'Tis impossible to be wiser than others.

THIRD COUNSEL OF CATAWG THE WISE

Be not sluggish or idle slothful.
Take not to drink in the way of a fool.
Take not to women of wanton ways.

Beware of oaths and all rough words.
Be generous where there is need.
Do no ill or bear excess of it.
Strive always to behave without vanity.
Devote thyself to God in thy whole life.
In every turn of fate, consider how it shall be in the end.

HYWEL AP MEREDYDD OR SIR HOWEL OF THE BATTLE AXE

Meredydd, the father, was the son of Einion ap Iorwerth ap Gwgan etc whose main residence was his mansion at Bronyfoel. Howel ap Meredith was Raglot of Aberglaslyn and also held lands in the district of Bodewyn (that is to say Treflys in the Gest), the estate being Gwely Wynn ap Ednewyn. He also held the fishing rights of Ystumllyn Lake.

An old essay in the *Records of Carnarvon* states that John ap Efan ap Robert ap Meredydd (one of the Bronyfoel and Gesail family, on his mother's side) bequeathed Garthmorthin in Tre'rgest to Efan ab Robert on June 30th 1538 in the reign of Henry VIII. In his will Evan ap Robert passed it to Evan ap John in 1697; the executor to the will was Gruffydd ap John.

He achieved fame at the battle of Poitiers in 1346 when serving as a captain in the army of Edward the Black Prince when they were opposed by French forces with King John at their head. During the battle it is said that Howel chopped off the head of the horse on which King John was riding, thus taking the French monarch prisoner. For his bravery and for his prowess on the field Howel was created a knight by the Black Prince, who also ordered that a banquet be held annually in London to commemorate the event. This custom continued for many years but was discontinued during the reign of Queen Elizabeth I. Eight Yeomen (who were given the title Yeomen of the Crown) were paid eight pence a day and were always in attendance at the feast, afterwards distributing the food to the poor. Howel was also created Constable of Criccieth Castle and from the King received many other gifts including the taxes on Aberdowarch mill and other King's mills on the river Dee. It is not possible from his pedigree to discover whether or not he was married and there is also doubt as to where he was buried. Some maintain that his grave is in St Michael's Churchyard at Treflys (the Bronyfoel family chapel), whilst others hold the view that his ashes lie in St Catherine's cemetery at Criccieth, for it is as Constable of Criccieth Castle that we last hear of him. His valour in battle forms the subject of a poem by Hugh ap Rheinallt.

Och am Howel heb gelu
Ai fwyall ddichall y bu
Yn erchyll y fwyall i Ffraingc
Troi chwalfa trwy uchelfainge
Dal en brenin heb flino
Dal ei fab a'i deulu fo
A wnaeth Howel Ryfelwr
Reneiliwr y gamp pwyn ail i'r gŵr
Er ei farw o'i urdd fawredd
I ach yw fawl uwch ei fedd

Wynn's *The History of the Gwydir Family*

His brother, Einion, had a large family by his wife Nest, who was the daughter of Gruffydd ap Gruffydd ap Madog ap Gadifor. Nest bore a son, Ieuan, who married Gwenhwyfer or Gaynor (Genevieve), who was the daughter of Ynyr Fychan of Nannau, in Merionydd, ap Ynyr ap Meurig, ap Cadwgan, ap Bleddyn, Prince of Gwynedd and Powys, who died in 1073. From the lineage of Madog, their son, we get the families of Peniarth, Bodfel, Madryn, Bodfean, Glynllifon, Bodwrdda, Pontddu, Talhenbont, Wern, etc.

Hywel Fychan of Bronyfoel and Ystumllyn, another son of the above Einion married Angharad, daughter of Llewelyn ap Hywel from Manaw (the Isle of Man), to whom a son, Rhys of Bronyfoel, was born. Rhys later married Gwerfyl (daughter of Gethin of Nant Conwy) and their daughter Catherine married Ieuan ap Robert of Cesail Gyfarch (ancestors of Sir John Wynn of Gwydir).

HYWEL AP RHYS

A son born to Ieuan and Catherine was Hywel ap Rhys of Bronyfoel and Ystumllyn, who married a sister of Ieuan ap Robert (of Gesail), but she died soon after the marriage. A dispute is said to have arisen between the two families and details of the feud are contained in the family history of Sir John of Gwydir. The culmination of their differences was an affray which ultimately led to the destruction of both the old princely families of Bronyfoel and Gesail Gyfarch (see *The History of the Gwydir Family*, *Y Brython* 1860, pages 290 to 294).

Hywel ap Rhys of Bronyfoel was a fierce fighter during the struggles for ascendancy between the Houses of York and Lancaster and was said to have possessed great physical strength. So strong was he that he was able to straighten horseshoes with his bare hands thus earning himself the name 'Hywel y Pedolau' (Howel of the Horseshoes) which helps to distinguish him from his forebear, Howel of the Battle-axe.

The pedigree of Wynn contained in *The History of the Gwydir Family* show that from him, in direct lineage, sprang the family of Bronyfoel right down to the Wynns and Ellises of Ystumllyn (to which 'plas' the family had moved at the time of the affray over the fishing in Ystumllyn lake, which has been mentioned previously).

MARGARET OF BRONYFOEL

According to some manuscripts, Margaret of Bronyfoel, mother of Howel y Pedolau was the nurse of Edward II, the first English Prince of Wales, at Penllyn near Bala. She sprang from the stock of Hwfa ap Cynddelw, one of the fifteen tribes of Gwynedd. She was the daughter of Einion ap Ithel of Rhiwaedog in the township of Penllyn near Bala, from the lineage of Ririd Flaidd of Gest and Hywel ap Ifan ap Meredydd ap Ifan of Bronyfoel. This Einion was squire to John of Gaunt, Duke of Lancaster, and from this tree sprang most of the nation's nobility in North Wales.

Sir John Wynn had in his possession the will, bearing the date 1416, belonging to Morfydd (daughter-in-law of Hywel y Pedolau). This had been proved in the Probate Court at Cricciaeth by one Robert Saethon, for the Archdeacon of Merioneth. Hywel y Pedolau's second wife was the daughter of Tudur ap Gruffydd ap Einion of Ardudwy. It is said that this woman was the cause of the murder of the Vicar at Llanfrothen, because he was guardian of the heir of Plasnewydd yn Rhôs, Penrhyndeudraeth.

SIR JOHN OWEN OF CLENNENEY

Although this loyal and brave man was not resident in Tre'r Gest, his lineage from his mother's side can be traced through the marriage of the sister of Hywel ap Rhys of Bronyfoel to Ifan ap Robert ap Meredydd of the Gesail family. Sir John, who was born in the year 1600, was the son of John Owen Esq, son of Robert Owen of Bodsilin, from Elin Morys of Clenenau and Brogyntyn. His grandfather, Robert Owen of Bodsilin was secretary to the famous Walsingham and while in his service accumulated the sum of £10,000 which was an enormous fortune in those days. Very little has been recorded about the early days of Sir John and the first important mention we have of him is when he was appointed a Colonel and a Vice-Admiral in the Army. He was steadfastly loyal to King Charles I and served under Prince Rupert at the siege of Bristol, where he was sorely wounded during the action.

His qualities were recognised by the King who appointed him to take charge of the defence of Conwy Castle and to relieve Archbishop Williams of that responsibility. This led to bad feelings between the two men and it was the treachery of the Archbishop and his friends that led to the Castle being overcome by Cromwell's forces. Following this Sir John retired to the peace of his home in Eifionydd. He was created a knight in 1629 and also in that year he was appointed High Sheriff, a position he was to hold again in 1664.

In the year 1648 he raised an army to carry out what was to be the last effort in support of the King, maybe in council with Ambassadors from Kent and Essex. This proved unsuccessful, for the Royalist forces were overcome by those of William Lloyd (Sheriff of Caernarfon) and Sir John was wounded and taken prisoner.

The following is a copy of an old manuscript letter from Prince Rupert to Colonel Owen confirming the authority to take charge of the defence and control of Harlech Castle.

Shrewsbury 16th May 1644

To Colonel Owen. I noticed the interest and attention taken by you in the keeping and control of Harlech Castle in the County of Meirionydd and the services of Captain John Morgan of Gelli Iorwerth, Trawsfynydd in his governing under you. I am prepared to confirm your authority required and to advise my acceptance of Captain Morgan to increase the Guards, so long as the costs will not be any higher than will be the advantage to the country.

Thus I rest,

Your friend

RUPERT

This to Colonel Owen, Keeper and Constable of Harlech Castle.

Then Sir John went to attack Caernarfon, but on hearing that Parliamentary forces under Colonels Carter and Twisleton were on their way to oppose him he made haste to meet them. A fierce battle was fought near Llandegai with the advantage, initially, going to Colonel Owen. Later, however, troops under the command of Captain Taylor succeeded in dismounting and capturing the Royalist commander whose men became disheartened and fled the field of battle. The Sheriff also died the same day. Captain Taylor was despatched to Parliament to acquaint them with the news of victory – news that gave them so much pleasure that they awarded the captain with the sum of £200, all of which was to be paid from the estate of Sir John.

Our hero was taken to Windsor Castle to join four peers who were already in custody for the same reason and, with the Duke of Hamilton, Earl Holland, Lord Goring and Lord Capel, he later stood trial. He was not overawed by the court and with great bravery and Welsh spirit told the Judge 'that he was only an ordinary Welsh gentleman from Wales who had tried to obey the King on all occasions and that he had carried out his obligations faithfully throughout the war'. He said that he had seen many true and loyal men trying to assemble an army so that they could get their King released from prison and that he had done likewise. He apologised to them as a man and said 'That he did not care much what they did with him'.

The court found him guilty and pronounced sentence of death by beheading whereupon Sir John bowed with great dignity and expressed his thanks for such a verdict. When asked to explain his attitude he said in a loud voice 'It is a great honour for an ordinary gentleman from Wales to lose his head in the midst of so many peers; for I thought I might have been hanged'. He was later pardoned, serving only few months imprisonment before his release. He neither sought a pardon nor was a petition forwarded to Parliament on his behalf. He returned to his own country to live out the rest of his life quietly. He died in his sleep in the year 1666 at his mansion, Clenneney in Eifionydd and his body was laid to rest in the cemetery of St Beuno, Penmorfa. A type of tower was erected to his memory at the eastern end of the church and a tablet with the following epitaph was installed inside the church.

MS
JOHANNES OWEN de
Clenneney, in Co. Carnarvon. Militis
Viri
in patriam amoris ardentissimi:
in regem (Beatissmum Martyrem CAROLUM I)
indubitatæ fidelitatis clari
quiad sancrosanctam majestatem a perdnellionum
rabie eripiendam, summa pericula, lubentissimé oblivit,
Hostium copias non semel fudit, ac fregit;
religonem vindicavit:
donec, infelici sorte in perditissimorum hominum manus
Regali jam sanguine imbutas,
inciderit Dux præstantissimus
unde supplex sese obsessum redimerat,
nisi quod Heroi consummatissimo
famæ plus, quam vitæ sollicito, tale displicuit,
collo igitur imperterrite oblato,
securis aciem retudit divina vis.
volucrisque fati tardavit alas, donec senex lætissimus
CAROLUM 2um & sibi & suis restitutum viderat.
Ao. Doni. 1666, & Ætatis suae 66, placide expiravit.
Atque hic cum charissimâ conjuge IONETTA filia
GRIFFINI VAUGHAN de Gorsygedol arni
In pace reguiescit
ELENA OWEN
gratitudinis & pietatis ergo
Avo Aviæelbmpos

[This is taken from the actual tablet and is more accurate than the original version. – Ed]

The following is an English translation of the above Latin epitaph by Professor J Rhys MA:

> Sacred to the memory of John Owen, a soldier and man, the most fervent in his love for his country and most illustrious for his undoubted loyalty to his King (the Most Blessed Martyr Charles I) who in order to snatch his sacrosanct Majesty from the rage of public enemies, faced the greatest perils, and more than once routed the forces of the enemy, and crushed them, and avenged the cause of religion, when, by a most unfortunate accident, he fell into the hands of the most desperate of men, which had already been stained with royal blood their foremost leader (duke, prince) entreating (on his behalf) would have redeemed him for 6 [there is something wrong or omitted here – Ed] from his confinement, had not such a ransom displeased (this our) most consummate hero, who was more concerned for his good name than for his life. When, therefore, he fearlessly offered his neck, a force divine blunted the edge of the axe, and retarded the wings of the bird of fate, until he lived a most happy old man to see Charles II restored to him and to his AD 1666 and his 66th of his own age he peacefully died, and here, with his most illustrious wife, Jeanetti, daughter of Griffith Vaughan, Gors y Gedol, Knight, he rests in peace. Ellin Owen, from gratitude and dutifulness – (there is something wrong here) – towards her grandfather and grandmother put (up this monument) to their blessed memory.

SIR JOHN OWEN, CLENENAU AND OLIVER CROMWELL

The following letter was copied from *Letters and Speeches of Cromwell by Carlyle*, second edition, page 96. This is given in the language in which it was written (English) so this must be borne in mind out of loyalty to our hero, Sir John Owen.

Knottingley, near Pontefract
20th November, 1648

> Gentlemen:—I received an order from the Governor of Nottingham directed to him from you, to bring up COLONEL OWEN, to take bail for his coming up to make his composition, he having made a Humble petition to the Parliament for the same.
>
> OLIVER CROMWELL

From the same book, Vol I, page 369, Cromwell makes another reference (in English) to Sir John:

> Colonel Owen is a Welsh Delinquent. I find he is a Sir John Owen—The same Sir John Owen who seized my Lord Archbishop's Castle of Conway in that Violent manner long since. A violent man now got into trouble enough; of whom there arises a *life* and *death* question bye and bye.

NOTE: Close by the old mansion (Clenenney) is a 'gadle' (army place, parade ground) where Sir John and maybe Col Owen after him trained his soldiers. There is also part of a garrison chapel still not completely destroyed, though used as an outbuilding for the farm. It is a pity that a more detailed history of Sir John Owen is not available for he stood so bravely for his King and country.

He fought so bravely and unyieldingly. He stood firmly for his principles even when his life was endangered. Our ardour as a nation is far too low, if half the brave deeds carried out in Wales by our patriot had occurred in other countries then there would be volumes of their biography containing dates and times and their deeds of heroism would survive in family tales and folklore.

THE REV EDWARD SAMUEL

The Rev Edward Samuel, Vicar of Llangar near Corwen was born at Cwt-y-defaid in Tre'r Gest in the year 1673. He was the father of the Rev William Samuel, Vicar of Nantglyn, and the Rev Edward Samuel, Rector of Llanddulas. His grandson was Dr David Samwell MD who was born at Nantglyn and was with Captain Cook as surgeon's mate when Cook was murdered by the natives of one of the South Sea Islands. He wrote the narrative of the massacre.

The Rev Edward translated several important books, among them being the work of Bishop Beveridge, Bishop of St Asaph – Chief Duties of a Christian; the necessity and Advantages of Common Prayer and frequent Commune which was published in Shrewsbury in 1728. An eminent scholar and possessing an extensive knowledge of the English language, he died on April 8th 1748, at the age of 75 and is buried at Llangar.

His entry into the ministry came about in a most unusual way and has since become a legend in the district. With his friend John Jones, he was playing at Ty'nlôn, Penmorfa, one day when they attracted the attention of Bishop Humphries, the pious Bishop of Bangor who at that time was living at nearby Gesail Gyfarch. Intrigued by the fact that they were wearing their shirts over all their other clothing, he asked them the nature of the game they were playing. When told they were pretending to be 'little priests' the Godly Father asked them if that was what they wished to be. When they replied that it was, the Bishop arranged for them to be educated at Rhuthyn School. In the course of time both became learned men; John Jones was appointed Vicar of Northop, and Edward Samuel Vicar of Llangar.

William Owen (or Gwilym Ddu) of Glan Hafren was a descendant on his mother's side. In addition to running schools in various places in Eifionydd, he was a bard of the highest repute and also the author of a book on music entitled The Religious Singer. Also from this family came the Rev Samuel Williams, Baptist Minister of Clynnog.

DR DAVID SAMUEL MD

Son of the Rev William Samuel, Vicar of Nantglyn, and grandson of the above Rev Edward Samuel, he too was a bard of distinction. He received medical training and was appointed ship's doctor of the *Discovery*, in which vessel Captain Cook sailed for the Northern Seas in 1776. He was with Cook also when efforts were made to discover the Southern Continent. An eyewitness of the murder of Cook at the hands of the natives of the Sandwich Islands, he wrote about the tragic event in the *Biographia Britannica* and was also the author of a separate booklet called *Narratives* which was published in 1786. Most of the doctor's written work was done in English and his collection of curios and relics from his voyage were entrusted to Trinity College, Cambridge. His portrait was exhibited in Paris and some of his writings were published in the Cambrian Register. His death occurred in 1799, and he is buried at St Andrews, Holborn, London, which is close to the Welsh School

SAMUEL LLWYD OF PENAMSER

Penamser is an old mansion where many families of landed gentry of Tre'r Gest have lived from time to time, although nothing of note has been recorded about the house. Samuel Lloyd, who lived there in 1580, had a daughter, Jane Lloyd (died 1740), who was married to Henry Griffiths Esq (died 1725 and is buried at Ynyscynhaiarn Church). Their daughter, Catherine (died 1750) was married to John Vaughan of Penmaen (Dyfi) who died in 1740.

A later heir was Mr Henry Parry, a solicitor, known locally as 'Parry Bach y Twrna' (Little Harry the Solicitor), who lived at Plas Isa, Penmorfa. He sold the Penamser estate to Mr WA Madocks and, following the death of the latter, some members placed the matter into Chancery. His wife is buried at Penmorfa Church, having died in 1833, at the age of 89. He is buried at Dolgelley. Family graves can be found at Ynyscynhaiarn Church, some of whom were buried under the altar of the old building, a memorial stone being fixed to the wall with a transcription above the fireplace. The following are details taken from gravestones which are now by the door of the church (previously they were inside the chancel rails of the old church):

Here lye the remains of Henry Griffith, who married Jane, daughter and heiress to Samuel Lloyd, Penamser. He dyed May 4th 1725, aged 85. She

dyed May 24th 1734, aged 74.

Here lye the remains of John Vaughan, of Penmaen (Dyfi), and Catherine, his wife. He dyed 4th June 1740, aged 60, and she dyed 1750, aged 67.

One of the two stones is of black marble.

RICHARD THOMAS OF TUHWNT-I'R-BWLCH

Richard Thomas was born at Tuhwnt-i'r-bwlch in Gest on December 15 1753, and was educated at Jesus College, Oxford, where he gained a BA degree. He was the son of Thomas Rowlands and Jane Jones and brother of the Rev John Thomas, AC who was Headmaster of Beaumaris County School. A learned historian and genealogist, he compiled a collection of his heritages that can be found at the 'Herald's College' and at Rhug and Peniarth. Before leaving to become Curate at Ruthyn, he stayed for a long while at Peniarth with his old neighbour, Mr Wynn (late of Wern, Penmorfa). Following his death at Ruthin (where he is buried) on April 23rd 1780, at the age of 27, his books were sent to Lundain (London), Dinbych, Caernarfon, Meirionydd etc. Mrs Ann Thomas (mother of Ellis Owen Esq, Cefnymeusyd) was a sister of the two Thomas's of Tuhwnt-i'r-bwlch. Thomas Rowlands and his wife Jane Jones (a daughter of John Griffith and Ann Humphrey of Tuhwnt-i'r-bwlch), lived for a while at Tyddynysguboriau soon after their marriage, and it was here that their first son was born on October 22nd 1736. He was the Rev John Thomas, MA who was to become famous as a scholar and historian. A brass plaque on the wall of Llandegfan Church, Anglesey, marks his death in the year 1769.

DAFYDD OWEN OR DAVID OF THE WHITE ROCK

This renowned harpist and composer was born at Garreg Wen, a small cottage near the sea at Tre'r Gest, lying between Morfa bychan and Traethmawr (Porthmadog). He was the son of Owen Humphrey and Gwen Roberts, daughter of Isallt Fawr in Eifionydd, son of Humphrey, son of Humphrey Owen, who lived at Garreg Wen in 1693 at the time of the strange fires in Morfa Bychan that have been previously mentioned. There has been nothing written about his early childhood or his days as a young musician, yet it is apparent that he had an inherent talent for music. His mother was from that well known and talented family of Isallt, Cwm Pennant, a sister (it is believed) of Robert Roberts the eminent physician. At y Borth (that is Borth y Gest) there lived a gentleman called Captain Williams (the Smuggler). His house, called 'Plas y Borth', was the venue for many a 'Noswaith Lawen' (Merry evenings) and it was here that David would entertain the company with his harp. By doing so it is said that he was able to extend his musical activity and that in his early days he received some instruction on the harp from Captain Williams. Local legend says that it was when he was returning from a late night session at Plas y Borth that he rested beside a large rock (which can be seen to this day) that lies beside the path that leads from y Borth to Garreg Wen. The dawn was breaking and larks were rising and it was from this incident that he drew the inspiration to compose the famous air 'The Rising of the Lark'. His mother, Gwen Roberts, was also an accomplished harpist and was well versed in singing to harp accompaniment. She is said to have visited Maesyneuoedd and other places to entertain on feast days and holidays. She was a beautiful woman and an excellent singer and had the ability to compose a poem at will. Soon after her marriage she was feeling rather homesick for her birthplace. Looking around the area of her new home with its bare sandy soil full of gorse, she composed the following:

> Time was when I would gaily tread
> Moel Hebog's slopes in haste,
> But now you see me driving past
> The gorse-clad foot of Gest.

David Owen was born in the year 1720, baptized at Ynyscynhaiarn Church, died in 1749 and was buried in the churchyard of St Cynhaiarn – thus the sun set on this talented musician from Garreg Wen, though his genius remains alive embodied in his popular airs.

It is a complete fallacy to believe that Dafydd was born, brought up, died and was buried other than in the Gest; reports that he was born at Llanberis on Anglesey or in Glamorgan or that he is buried in any of these places are quite untrue. He did, of course, often visit the mansions of the gentry at the places mentioned to entertain them. He was the composer of three popular airs – 'The Conceit of Dafydd y Garreg Wen', 'The Rising of the Lark' and 'The Pleasures of the Men of Criccieth'. The last named is thought to be a Scottish tune called Roslyn Castle but this mistake has been explained by Lewis Roberts of Maentwrog. He states that 'The Pleasures of the Men of Criccieth' was sent by Dafydd to his cousin, who was a gardener at Roslyn Castle; the Scottish musicians liked the tune so much that it was dedicated to the family who lived in the Castle and thus received its Scottish name. The late Ieuan Glan Geirionydd composed words to suit the air 'Fenyw fwyn, gwrando gwyn' (Pretty Maiden hear my song) on the occasion of one of the annual fairs.

Dafydd was well-known to Sir Walter Scott, the composer of the sad verses to 'The Dying Bard'. He wrote, 'The Welsh tradition bears that a Bard on his death bed demanded his Harp, and played the Air, to which these Verses are adapted, and requested that it might be performed at his funeral'.

This is true. Owen Owens, nephew of the bard (his brother's son) told Ellis Owen of Cefnymeusydd that Dafydd had indeed asked for his harp before he died and had attempted to play his 'Conceit' on it and asked that that air should be played on a harp before the start of his funeral. When the mourners had gathered, however, it was found that there was no-one available to play so, after bringing the coffin to the door, the vast crowd sang the air and the harp was carried in front of the cortège to the burial ground.

For a time he was harpist at Nant Eos and also kept 'Nosweithiau llawen' in his own home area, where he played more for his own satisfaction rather than for the encouragement of any immoderation. Ellis Owen has stated that he himself had heard a woman called Betti Robert of Cwr Clwt recall that as a girl she had danced when Dafydd had sang and played the harp and that he was a large and handsome man. There was an old lady living at Prenteg about 50 years ago who was well known to me. She could sing 'Conceit of Dafydd y Garreg Wen' and 'The Rising of the Lark' having picked up the tunes by ear from her father, a harpist and pupil of Dafydd Owen; the late Mr William Owen, a merchant of Porthmadog, copied the metre of both airs from their lips. Dafydd died a bachelor at the early age of 29 and tradition maintains that it was as a result of a chill caught when returning from Roslyn Castle in Scotland following a visit to his cousin. It is traditionally believed that two white doves followed his cortège and only flew away when the words 'dust to dust' were intoned, but it is not possible to verify this. Prior to the year 1840 there was only a scrap of slate on his grave. This was found partly hidden amongst the Garreg Wen plots and in addition to a small harp carved in one corner it had the following inscription:

DO, 1749
A, 29.

In 1840 a more fitting memorial stone was erected, the cost being met by donations, but before going any further I would like to say something about his burial place. Before 1840 the grave was marked only by a small ordinary headstone with the initials on it (as above). The late Ellis Owen took the matter in hand and designed a new headstone for the bard; it measured four feet in height by two and a half feet square on which was carved a harp, his name, his age, the year of his death and an englyn composed by Ellis Owen. The old stone was placed at the end of the northern side of the column but in time, due to the opening of adjacent graves and insufficient care being taken with the foundations, the whole lot collapsed in ruins in 1864. The grave was rebuilt in a similar style to the other graves and the present slate was placed upon it, as seen today.

The old stone was incorporated into the western end but this is now out of sight below ground (it was visible in 1875). A large harp was carved on the new stone underneath which is the following epitaph and verse.

BEDD DAFYDD OWEN	*THE GRAVE OF DAVID OWEN*
Neu Dafydd y Garreg Wen.	*or David of the White Rock.*
Y telynor rhagorol,	*The splendid harpist,*
A gladdwyd 1749	*Who was buried in 1749*
Yn 29 mlwydd oed.	*Aged 29 years old.*

He charmed the breast, gave joy to all,
His song was the glory of Cymru;
Here he lies buried,
With no equal, a Jubal was he.

Ellis Owen collected £2 15s 6d towards the cost of rebuilding and repairing the grave, limiting the subscribers to 29 (the bard's age); the list can be seen in *Y Brython* for September 1858.

The following are notes on the tune 'The Rising of the Lark' compiled by the late Ceiriog Hughes.

CODIAD YR EHEDYDD (THE RISING OF THE LARK)

As regards age the tune is only 150 years old and was said to have been composed by David Owen, composer of the air Dafydd y Garreg Wen. One is saddened when it is realised that he died at the early age of 29 years for, had he lived and enjoyed good health, one wonders how many more airs would have been credited to his name today. It can be said of him as a musician what my co-bard Talhaiarn said of Ieuan Glan Geirionydd as a bard. David composed the most melancholy and the most light hearted airs that we have in Wales. It is true that in every nation the most lively tunes have been written by men noted for their melancholy. For example, there is John Gilpin by Cowper, a man who was 'down in the dumps', and also Ieuan Glan Geirionydd the composer of Cyflafan Morfa Rhuddlan and the light-hearted words of Old Morgan and his Wife. It is said that David Owen had gone to a 'Merry Evening' at Plas y Borth, Porthmadog and, according to the privileges and customs of the old times at these parties (there is no need to mention that these customs still prevail), the bard stayed late at the minstrel festivities until 2 or 3 am on the clock. The lateness of the hour was definitely due to the clocks (the 'Newport clock' had not then been invented for reference as a measure of time). However, the dawn broke on David's heels as, with his harp, he made his way home. The youth sat down by a rock that is still to be seen, 'Y Clogwyn Llwyd' (the Grey Crag) and he noticed a lark above his head striking a chord in his heart at the break of day. This was the time and place where he composed 'The Rising of the Lark'.

J CEIRIOG HUGHES

The poem of the Bardic Priest Glasynys is very apt:

My harp! O mother, bring me my harp,
The angel slowly appears,
The sound of eternity holds me in thrall
My elegy I sing in tears,

My harp! my soul fills its chords.
Hope whispers that a saint I'll be then;
I go! I go to the courts of heaven
With the sweet air of old Garreg Wen.

I see the dove, Oh! I see the pair,
To the churchyard bearing my pall,
I long for a harp in the city of peace
And a harp on my grave so small.

Farewell! the angel is calling me still,
The harps are his to bestow,
I depart in peace to the courts of heaven,
Singing old Garreg Wen as I go.

THE ANCESTRY OF THE HARPIST

The son of Humphrey Owen of Garreg Wen (1693) was Owen, who married Gwen Roberts of Isallt to whom was born a son, David Owen (the subject of our biography), who died a bachelor. Humphrey Owen's daughter, Anne Humphreys, married Owen Dafydd and they had two sons, Dafydd and Owen. Dafydd first married Elizabeth Roberts of Ty mawr in Treflys and among their children was a daughter, Jane, who married Owen Roberts of Glanymorfa and later Gwernddwyryd. (From this lineage is descended the chaired bard, Gwilym Eryri of Porthmadog.)

Owen Owens, son of Owen Dafydd, married Elizabeth Jones first and they had two sons and two daughters, one of whom, Catherine, married Hugh Owen of Trwyn-tywyn, whose son was the late Owen Owen Esq of Llwyn yr Hudol. Owen Owens, son of Dafydd, later married Mari Evans by whom he had a son, Robert Owen, who became a ship's carpenter, and also a daughter, Ellen, who became the wife of Griffith Jones, a shopkeeper at Garn. Anne Humphreys, daughter of Humphrey Owen (1693) was married to John Griffiths of Tuhwnt i'r bwlch. They had one daughter, Jane Jones, who married Thomas Rowland and their children were John, Rowland, Richard, Ann and Gaynor. Ann married Owen Ellis of Cefnymeusydd, father of the late Ellis Owen. Lack of space prevents any further details being given of various branches of this family. Note: David Morris of Dyffryn Ardudwy (a native of Pennant in Eifionydd) carved the harp and the inscription on the gravestone of Dafydd y Garreg Wen.

JOHN YSTUMLLYN OR 'JACK BLACK'

He was a native of some part of Africa and, according to tradition, was captured in a very wild state in a forest of that country by one of the Squires of Ystumllyn (probably Ellis Wynne) in around 1742. The tradition is as follows: 'One of the Wynnes of Ystumllyn owned a yacht and whilst sailing up river in Africa, captured a little black boy in a forest. He brought him back home to his house at Ystumllyn and that he was later baptised in either Ynyscynhaiarn Church or Criccieth Church and was given the name 'John Ystumllyn'. When he first arrived he could not speak any known language – only screaming – and was frightened of all strangers. He was thought to be about eight years old at that time and when his portrait was painted in about 1754 his age was reckoned to be about 16. The ladies of Ystumllyn went to considerable trouble to tame and train him and due to their patience he learnt both languages and was able to relate that at the time of his capture he was catching fish in a river close to nearby woods where his mother screamed her head off when he was taken away. He was taught gardening and quickly became proficient as he was a smart and lively youth. It is said that the fair sex were very enamoured by him although his skin was black and that they used to contend for his favours. It is strange, therefore, that one of the little maidservants at Ystumllyn was frightened by his appearance but it was she who, a few years later, was to marry him. Her name was Margaret Griffith, daughter of Hendre Mur, Trawsfynydd.

They were married at Dolgellau Church about the year 1768 and seven children were born to them; one of them became gamekeeper to the Hon Lord Newborough until he died in the year 1862, aged 92 years. John Ystumllyn served at MaesyNeuoedd near Talsarnau with another branch of the family, but returned to Ystumllyn towards the end of his days where he was given a house (Nhyra), a garden and small field sufficient to keep a cow, and here he lived until the end of his life. It was an old thatched cottage that lay close to Nhyra Stream and when his health gave way he was attended by Dr R Isaac Roberts (grandfather of the writer). He died in 1786 (according to the register) although the year 1790 is shown on his gravestone. This discrepancy is most probably due to the delay in the provision of a memorial stone by one of the Wynne family, who were also unsure of the date of his death. He was buried at Ynyscynhaiarn churchyard.

JOHN YSTUMLLYN OR 'JACK BLACK'
This engraving is from a portrait painted in 1754

The following epitaph appears on the gravestone, the work of Dafydd Shon James of Penrhyndeudraeth.

Erstwhile in India I was born, and brought
To Wales to be christened;
Here, beneath the grey stone
In the cold dark earth I lie.

His wife lived until 1828 aged 81 years and there are many descendants in Eifionydd, Llandwrog and other places.

THE REV ROWLAND JONES

The above prelate lived at Drwsdeugoed in the Upper Gest and was Curate of Llanfihangel. In 1755 he moved to Edeyrn, being incumbent of that parish. He died in the year 1760 and was buried at Edeyrn Church. His wife, who died in 1762, was buried at Ynyscynhaiarn and the following epitaph may be seen on her grave: 'Margaret Jones, widow of the late prelate of Edeyrn, the Rev Rowland Jones, who died May 5th 1762, aged 75 years'. Their son was John Jones, Gent. who came to live at Bronygadair, and was agent for the estate of RT Price Esq of Rhiwlas. He also had a son, the Rev Owen Jones of Llangadwaladr on Anglesey, who died on September 10th 1815, aged 50 years. He is buried in the churchyard at Llangadwaladr.

His sister was Mrs Williams of Bronygadair, second wife of William Williams Esq of Bryngoleu. She held a lease on Bronygadair farm but this ended with her death. Another sister of the Rev Owen Jones was Margaret, mother of the Rev John Jones MA of Mynydd Ednyfed near Criccieth who was incumbent at Ynyscynhaiarn, Criccieth, Llanfihangel and Treflys. He died on February 8th 1863, and was buried at St Catherine's Churchyard in Criccieth. Mrs Williams had three daughters – the eldest, Mary, married Mr Elizeus Griffith of Afon Wen Farm and their sons were John Griffith of the George Inn in Criccieth who died in 1856, William who died in 1827, Griffith who was drowned aboard the 'The Eagles' of Porthmadog while sailing off Bardsey, and Owen Lloyd Griffith who died in 1864, aged 40 years; Their father died in 1840 and their mother in 1863 (aged 75 years). Their only daughter, Mary, became wife of Mr GJ Hughes of Harlech and is still alive. Their only daughter is Mary Winifred (Gwenllian Meirion). Mr Hughes was the son of the late Rev J Hughes who was incumbent at Llanystumdwy.

COLONEL WILLIAM PRICE OF RHIWLAS

Colonel Price lived during the years 1630 to 1690 and although he was not born nor resided permanently in the Gest, he would sometimes stay at Garregfelen near Pentrefelin. The Price's main residence was at Rhiwlas and Tre Rhiwaedog, near Bala. The family descended in direct lineage from Blaidd Rhudd (Red or Ruddy Wolf), prince of Gest, through Rhirid Flaidd of Penllyn, Bala and of the descendants of Blaidd Rhudd, intermingled with the gentry of Tre'r Gest. Practically the whole of the lands in Tre'r Gest were owned by this family, including 6,000 acres of Ynyscynhaiarn, plus half of Llanfrothen at one time. Their properties in Gest descended wholly in line from Rhirid Flaidd. We find that Colonel Price presented a bell and also communion vessels to Ynyscynhaiarn Church in the year 1683.

Colonel William Price was the son of John Price (1709), son of John Price (1689), son of Cadwaladr Price (1608), son of John Wynne ap Cadwaladr, etc, and they were High Sheriffs of Meirionydd for many years. The daughter and heiress of John Llwyd of Faenol in Flintshire, was the mother of the second John Price who also became High Sheriff of Meirionydd in 1612 and 1613. Colonel William Price had a brother, Robert, who was appointed Bishop of Bangor but who died before taking up his appointment. The wife of Colonel W Price was Mary, whose father was David Holland of Gimmel. A daughter of Colonel Price married James Bryncir, to whom the bard Owen Griffith of Llanystumdwy composed a hymn in 1687. Roger Price (heir to Colonel W Price) was High Sheriff of Caernarfonshire in the year 1711–12. William Price (son of Roger Price, married Mary daughter of J Price, Earl of Hereford. Richard Tavistock Price, their son, was the grandfather of RLl Price Esq, the present owner. The estate of Plasdû was purchased by one of the Price's about the year 1612. The previous owner was Owen Owens, the brother of John Owen the exceptionally talented Latin poet, and brother of Hugh Owen who was also well known in his day and served the Earl of Arundel for many years. It is understood that the Price family today do not own a square inch of land in Eifionydd although extensive estates in the area had been in their possession for over 600 years!

WILLIAM ALEXANDER MADOCKS ESQ, MP

The above gentleman sprang from the gentry of Yale, a district of Denbighshire. He was the third son of John Madocks, Esq KC of Fron Yw, Denbighshire. John Madocks was MP for the Borough of Presbury and was also a leading King's Counsellor; he lived at a place called Mount Market which is near Llundain. WA Madocks was born in the year 1774 and after receiving a good home education was sent to one of the Oxford Colleges, where he gained an MA degree in 1802. In that same year he was elected Member of Parliament for Boston, whom he represented until 1820, when he became MP for Chippenham in Wiltshire. In 1809 he raised a charge in Parliament against Lord Castlereagh and Mr Percival whom he accused of bribery and corruption in an election campaign. His father died about the year 1798 and from the estate he received a considerable amount of money. He chose to visit his old home Fron Yw and Glanywern, where his brother, John Madocks, now lived.

Later bought a small place at Llanelltyd near Dolgelley called Dolymelynllyn. About the same time he became interested in the possibility of enclosing Traethmawr, having read the correspondence an the subject between Sir John Wynn of Gwydir and Sir Hugh Middleton which is contained in Pennant's *History of Wales.* In 1798 the farms around Traethmawr were offered for sale by the trustees of R Tavistock Price of Rhiwlas; these being Tan'rallt, Llidiart Ysbytty and Tuhwnt i'r bwlch etc. Madocks was able to buy these quite cheaply (as there was a lease on them) together with the right to enter a vast area of common land which now forms the Vale of Madog and, having built a mansion on the old building at Tan'rallt, soon came to live there. His most remarkable achievement was the building of the Embankment across the straits of Gest, from Ynystowyn to Trwynypenrhyn, which linked the two counties and which will be dealt with more fully under the heading 'History of the Vale of Madog'. In the year 1818 he married a widow named Mrs Gwynn of Treguntur near Talgarth in Brycheiniog (Brecknockshire). They had one daughter who was born about the year 1820. Later the enterprises he had started ran into difficulties and he also failed to gain re-election to Parliament. Leaving everything in the hands of his brother John and his faithful agent, John Williams of Tuhwnt i'r bwlch, he departed for the Continent and died in France or Italy in 1829. In the coming pages details will be given of the immense changes made by his works to the Vale of Madog and the surrounding area and this will include a summary of a winning essay entered for one of the Eisteddfodau held in Tre'rgest.

JOHN WILLIAMS, TUHWNT I'R BWLCH

He was the son of William Williams, a responsible farmer, who lived at Ty'nllan in Llanfihangel Ysgeifiog on Anglesey. He was employed as a gardener at Plas newydd (the home of the Marquis) but, after hearing of the marvellous undertaking at Traeth mawr (which had caught the imagination of all Welshmen at the time) he made up his mind to visit the place. His skill and ability soon attracted the attention of Mr Madocks who saw that he possessed the qualifications to become his foreman and he was put in charge of the tree planting and the preparations of the gardens. Later he was appointed agent over all the works, where his talents and his conscientious attention to his duties soon earned him the trust of his adventurous employer. He supervised all the many projects that were going on at the time and through his hands all wages were paid.

He showed great resourcefulness and bravery when the Embankment was breached following a storm in 1812. Thus sang Dewi Wyn of him:

> To halt the water's vengeance
> A neighbourhood brought its might,
> And the overseer's heart
> Is now the heart of man.

For a time he lived at Ynystowyn, which was built as an office and dwelling house and he married Anne, daughter of D Williams of Saethon in Lleyn, sister of the late David Williams of Castell Deudraeth. They later moved to Tuhwnt i'r bwlch, which mansion he rebuilt. He was in charge of the estate until the day he died, overcoming many difficulties following the death of Mr Madocks when the estate was placed in the trusteeship of the Court of Chancery. He was an ardent member of the church and would allow nothing to prevent his attendance at services held in Tremadog Church. He died in 1850 at the age of 72 and was buried in a vault below the church (on the northern side). Here, too, are buried his wife and their only son, WT Massey Williams. A plaque of white marble on the church wall reads as follows:

Sacred to the memory of

JOHN WILLIAMS, ESQUIRE

Of Tuhwnt i'r bwlch, in this parish, for a long series of years he was the faithful Agent and attached friend of the late Wm Alexander Madocks Esq, MP, the great founder of this place, after whose death, he zealously and energetically carried out those plans which had previously been so ably projected for the development of the natural capabilities of this part of the country, endowed with a strong mind and equally strong affections, he secured the good opinion of the public, the deep regards of his friends and the constant devotedness of his family and dependents; he died as he had lived, a sincere and devout christian. Born 9th May 1778, – died 26th November 1850. Also of their only son, WT Massey Williams, Esq who died the 19th day of October, 1856, aged 34. Also to the memory of Anne, Relict of the above John Williams, who died on 31st August 1865, aged 73, and was buried with her husband and son in the vault beneath this tablet.

THE REV JOHN JONES, TREMADOG

He was born at the Tymawr Inn in Penmorfa, in the year 1779, son of Evan Jones, Apothecary, and Ellen, his wife. He received a good education at the Church Schools of Llanystumdwy and Bottwnog and became a currier. He joined the Methodist movement in 1795 which had been established under the leadership of Hywel Harris and the Rev Daniel Rowlands. He himself started preaching in 1803. He married Jane, daughter of Ann Roberts of Shop, Penmorfa, and they moved to Tremadoc when it was built in 1806. Following a period of dedicated work as preacher, he was ordained in 1814 (that was three years after the Methodists left the church). He died on January 30th 1857 and was interred at the family burial ground at St Beuno's Churchyard Penmorfa. NOTE: He was a zealous Conservative and never prayed in public without a plea for the Crowned Heads, the Heads of State and members of the Government. Job Thomas composed an elegy for him, which is recorded in his Biography.

ELLIS OWEN, CEFNYMEUSYDD

Ellis Owen was born in the year 1789 at Cefnymeusydd in the parish of Ynyscynhaiarn, Tre'r Gest, which is in the commote of Eifionydd. Here he lived without a break until his death – that is for 79 years; he never married.

The following is his own transcription, dated 1862, recording the details of his birth:

> Ellis, son of Owen Ellis of Cefnymeusydd Isa by Ann his wife, was baptised April 3rd 1789.

The above is a true copy taken from the Register Book of Baptisms for the parish of Ynyscynhaiarn, year 1789.

> My father the above Owen Ellis wrote the following in the Cefnmeusydd family Bible: 'Ellis, son of Owen Ellis and Ann Thomas, his wife, was born March 3rd between 11 and 12 at night 1789, and the 5th day of the moon's age.
>
> It appears that I was born on Tuesday night between 11 and 12 o'clock, 31st March 1789 and baptised on the following Friday, 3rd April (Lenten service) by the Rev Robert Anwyl, BA of Bach y Saint, Vicar of Crugaeth (he died that year. After him came the Rev David Ellis, MA, a famous poet and historian). This was all written by me, Ellis Owen, on 25th March 1862 and I shall be 75 years of age if I live until Monday Next. - ELLIS OWEN

It seems that the subject of our memoirs wrote the history of his own life, as can be seen from the following summary which he wrote in the year 1858 and which has been copied from his own handwritten account.

> Ellis Owen was born at Cefnymeusydd in the parish of Ynyscynhaiarn, Caernarvonshire, on 31st March 1789. He was the son of Owen Ellis of the same place. His father's mother was Margaret Pritchard of Tymawr, Treflys, daughter of Richard Williams of Cae'rynwch, Meirionydd.

Ellis Owen, Cefnymeusydd

His mother was Ann Thomas, who was born at Tuhwnt i'r bwlch an October 3rd 1748. She died on Sunday the 19th of December, 1841, having lived 93 years two months and one day. Daughter of Thomas Rolant of Tuhwnt i'r bwlch, son of Richard, son of Thomas, son of Richard, son of Gwenric (or Kenrick) from Newtown, Montgomeryshire. His mother's brother was the Rev John Thomas, Headmaster of Beaumaris School, and also the Rev Richard Thomas, GC who died at Ruthin (see Williams' *Eminent Welshman*). His mother's mother was Jane, daughter of John Griffith of Tuhwnt i'r bwlch, near Portmadoc, son of Griffith Owen of Fronoleu, son of Richard, son of Hugh, son of Reinallt of Frongoch near Bala. Griffith Owen of Fronoleu was the son of Richard Humphreys, Esq of Hendre, Penrhyndeudraeth, the father of Bishop Humphreys of Bangor.

Ellis Owen wrote articles for various papers such as *Y Seren Gomer* (the Gomer Star), *Y Brython* (The Briton), *Y Drysorfa* (The Treasury), *Y Gwyliedydd* (The Watcher or Sentinel), Y *Gwladgarwr* (The Country Lover), *Y Traethodydd* (The Essayist) etc. He discussed antiquities with many of the foremost historians of the time, among them being Professor Wray. He wrote a hundred and twenty pages of poetry, in free and strict metre (this in his own handwriting) and also composed over thirty epitaphs which can be seen in many cemeteries, among others on Ieuan Llwyd, Ieuan Glan Geirionydd and Robert ap Gwilym Ddu. He was secretary to many and various organisations, such as The Eifionydd Association for the Punishment of Wrongdoers (for 40 years!), The Bible Society of Tremadog and District (for 26 years, being chairman also of this society until his death), and the Eifionydd Sunday Schools Association (for 34 years). He was Supervisor of Brynmelyn Sunday School for 45 years! He held a Literary Society at Cefnymeusydd which was in his charge for 11 years. The poems he composed were almost always the result of careful and thoughtful preparation and although occasionally a witty couplet might be quite spontaneous his work was always meticulous, exact and extremely precise.

After reaching the ripe old age of eighty minus one year, with 'only slight pain and tiredness' affecting his health, he passed away at 2 pm on Monday 27th January 1868. He had been hale and hearty until the last three years of his life and had been capable of carrying out all his duties to within six weeks of his death. In later years he had complained of headaches but he died from bronchitis which developed into inflammation of the brain. He was in sound mind and fully conscious of his impending release up to his last moments.

He was buried on Friday 31st January 1868 at Ynyscynhaiarn

Churchyard. His grave is on the left-hand side of the path and about two yards from the church door (a location which he had himself chosen). There is not, even now, a memorial stone erected to his memory.... when will the nation awaken to such things?

HIR A THODDAID – One of the strict metres composed by Mr John Williams (Ioan Madog) as an epitaph for the late Ellis Owen Esq, winner at Eisteddfod Madog 1872.

> And now has ended the long Joyful day
> Of Cefnymeusydd's Just and upright poet,
> A true protector of our noble tongue
> In the kind spirit of his poetry.
>
> He welcomed many, was governor and guide
> Of great enjoyment to Eifionydd's bards.
> The fruit of his fair gift will always live
> And the historians' fame forever stay.

SHON EVAN GRIFFITH, MUSICIAN OF THE NEW MILL, PENTRE'RFELIN

Shon Evan Griffith (John Evan Griffith) was a remarkable man of his age and blossomed about the year 1761. He became greatly involved in the arguments which arose when the calendar was adjusted and feast and saints days changed from the old dates to the new (change of Julian calendar – 3rd September 1751 was reckoned as 14th September and 29th February was omitted in the year 1800).

So ardent was he in his convictions that he made the long journey on foot to Glastonbury in Somerset where he asked for a sprig of a tree that blossomed on a certain feast day. The tree was called 'The Rod of Joseph' (Glastonbury Thorn). Poor old Shon could speak hardly any English except Stick of Joseph, but he was successful in his efforts to obtain a sprig, which he brought back to Pentre'rfelin. He was able to persuade the villagers that it was on the newer dates that the cattle knelt in the shippons and that the bees hummed as well, reasoning that because it was a mild year with little frost that the 'Rod of Joseph' flowered on the new date. John was a skilled craftsman as a mill carpenter and miller, and also excellent as a musician. He was often called to Maesyneuoedd in Meirion on feast days to sing for the Wynns. 'Griffith the Miller' of the same place was his brother and was said to be similar in character. They were descendants of the old saintly bard, Owen Gruffydd of Tymawr in Llanystumdwy (who died and was buried in that parish about 1730). Shon Evan Gruffydd died at Liverpool and was buried there in the year 1792, leaving a widow and children.

Ieuan Lleyn composed an elegy to his memory and it can be seen from the following poem that he was competent bard:

> What world, what sadness, what terror – what sorrow
> What grief to remember,
> What cold sigh and lament,
> What cold wrath and cruel world.
>
> Wild dread and savage blow – strange fear
> A chill blow each day,
> The dread and the wound remain,
> Great dread, O! when will it come.
>
> When will cease the long cold betrayal,
> A betrayal that entombed the aged poet,
> We attest the wound of violence and fright,
> The fright that is the Land's bruise.

Up to a few years ago the older inhabitants of the parish remained staunch in their conviction of the correctness of the old calendar and believed unwaveringly that it was according to the old date that the birthday of Our Redeemer fell. I record below some of their reasons for this belief:

1) The cattle on this morning would kneel when commencing to graze.
2) That on that day the bees would be humming in their hives.
3) Singing could often be heard in the air at old Christmas gatherings.
4) That it was always mild on that day, even during a frosty spell.
5) That the herb rosemary flowered on that day.
6) And, especially, 'The Rod of Joseph' at Glastonbury (the rod that Joseph of Arimathea held in his hand when he came to preach the Gospel, the same tree that he planted at Glastonbury) flowered on the old Christmas day.

The older parishioners of Ynyscynhaiarn were, therefore, extremely loath to adopt the new calendar with its modified dates and sent down Owen Griffith of the Old Mill, Pentrefelin (brother of Griffith the Miller) in the year 1759 to Glastonbury, to see whether 'The Rod of Joseph' bloomed on the same date as it had previously, regardless of the changes in dates that had been made. He found this was so – it bloomed on the old Christmas Day – and he was able to bring back to Pentrefelin a branch of this historical thorn.

The anxiety about the re-arrangements of the calendar was shared by other people as well as those from Ynyscynhaiarn as is evident from the following report which appeared in *The Gentleman's Magazine* regarding 'the curious thorn' which grew in the Abbestry Churchyard at Glastonbury.

> A vast concourse of people attended the noted Thorn on Christmas day new style but great was their disappointment. Those that watched closely on 5th January (the old Christmas day) saw that it flowered as usual.
>
> It seems that in the days of Queen Elizabeth, the original tree, planted on the south ridge of Warrel Hill, had a double branch. The largest of these was cut down by a Puritan but, according to Layston, he cut his leg and was blinded in one eye by a fragment which flew from it into his face, and so he left his proposed work uncompleted. The remaining branch was as large as a man's body; this also was cut down by a Puritan (Temp. Charles I) according to Mr Andrew Paschal, but many trees were procured by grafting from the original stock, having the extraordinary property of blossoming in the same way. The Bishop of Bath and Wells, Dr James Montague (Temp. James II), presented a branch of this Thorn to Queen Anne.

LIEUT COL ISAAC WALKER

Although not born in Tre'r Gest, the above gentleman bought Hendregadredd in 1836 and lived there until the end of his days. There was a son, Isaac J Walker, who was a barrister, and one daughter, who married Mr Ignatius Williams, a Stipendiary Magistrate. Lieut Walker was the son and heir of the Rev W Walker, of Wisbeach St Peter in Cambridgeshire and Greatfield Priory in the County of Suffolk. He was a descendant of Sir Edward Walker (Knight of the Garter), who fought under the Royal Standard at the Battle of Edgehill. He was born in 1613 and died in the year 1736 in the 123rd year of his life!

Lieut Col Walker joined the Army as a young man and was present at the unfortunate battle of Buenos Ayres in 1807. Faithful service followed during the Peninsula War, the defence of Cadiz in 1810 and in Canada during the American Wars.

The late Lieut Col Walker was a descendant of the families of the Earl of Cornwall, Clarke of Wisbeach, Clifford in Herefordshire and the Middletons of Denbighshire, of Welsh descent. He was High Sheriff of Caernarfonshire in the year 1850. A quiet gentleman, neighbourly and friendly, he died at the age of 80 in 1865 and was buried at Ynyscynhaiarn Churchyard.

Mrs Walker died many years later and she is buried in the family vault. The religious lady was noted for her benevolence and generosity in the neighbourhood. She was also a great credit to the church, to which she was a great benefactor, being a stalwart of St Cynhaiarn Church. Her death was a great loss to the area, nowhere more than to the village of Pentrefelin. Councillor Walker, their son, died in 1862 at the age of 45, and there is a memorial tablet to the family on the wall of Ynyscynhaiarn Church (above the seats of the Hendregadredd family).

DANIEL MORRIS

He was born in Llanystumdwy in 1789 but came to the district of Gest when very young. Later he was in service with Mr Bidwell at Tan'rallt, and Ffarm yard, Tremadog, when that gentleman rented the mill at Tremadog. He sold the flour and carted it to Pwllheli and other places in a cart on which he allowed the old and poor people to ride on his return Journey. In 1816 he married Mary, daughter of William Owen of Ynyscyngar (the first Bar-y-Gest Pilot) and came to live at Tywyn (later to become Porthmadog). When an Act of Parliament was passed concerning the port, Mr Madocks appointed Daniel Norris as its first harbour-master, a post which he conscientiously filled until the end of his days.

He was a very truthful man, both kindly and wise and gained the respect of the sailors and all who knew him. The problems arising from his post were known to be dealt with both efficiently and wisely. There were twelve children from the marriage, four sons and eight daughters, and their issue is probably the most prolific in the area. Daniel Morris died on December 29th 1840 and is buried at Ynyscynhaiarn Churchyard (see his biography in a later chapter).

Two of his sons are still alive; William Evans Morris of Lombard St and Mr Maurice E Morris the chemist. After his father's death, Mr William E Morris was appointed to carry out his duties as harbour-master and collector of dues, even though he was very young; he holds these offices at the present time. He has filled the post of Guardian for nearly 40 years and has been vice-chairman of the Union for 25 years. Mr WE Morris married Jane, the youngest daughter of Captain William Jones and Gwen Jones of Talsarnau. They had nine sons and one daughter (who died recently), and also another son who died in infancy. The rest of the sons are alive and occupy responsible posts in the parish and the neighbourhood viz: Dr Jones Morris, Daniel Morris (bank manager), Robert Jones Morris of Tycerrig, TE Morris (barrister), John Jones Morris (solicitor) the others being in positions of influence and responsibility.

THE REV WILLIAM AMBROSE (EMRYS) OF PORTHMADOG

This bard, preacher and noted literary genius was born at The Penrhyn Arms Hotel, Bangor, on August 1st 1813, the only son of John and Elizabeth Ambrose. He was educated at Friars School, Bangor and then by the Rev William Griffith of Holyhead (son of Mr J Griffith of Tyddyn y

Graig in Eifionydd. He was brought up to be a draper in Liverpool and later moved to London. On his return he started preaching and in 1836 became Minister with the Independents at Porthmadog, for which denomination he proved to be a hardworking and successful Minister for 30 years. He died in 1873 at the age of 60 and was buried at Capel Helyg Cemetery, Llangybi. He married Mrs Pierce, the widow of Captain Pierce; they had no issue. The late Gwilym Hiraethog wrote about him in a lengthy biography for he was known to be a fluent preacher, an erudite speaker and possessed of much literary ability; he was a Chaired Bard and a winner at many Eisteddfodau.

MR WILLIAM OWEN (MUSICIAN) OF PORTMADOC

This talented musician was born at Tremadog, the son of William Owen (timber merchant) and his wife Elizabeth Owen. He was born an May 3rd 1830, and died August 2nd 1865, being a descendant of one of the old families of Gest and Cwm Mawr. He showed a strong inclination towards music from a very early age, and his chief delight was said to be playing the harmonium constantly. For many years he was a choir member at Tremadog Church and it was about this time that he made the acquaintance of a visitor to the town (a niece of Lord Coventry). She encouraged his love for music and gave him every assistance and instruction, it being said that 'he drank from the river of knowledge in excellent style' – so successful and talented was he that other musicians and composers sought his advice and benefited from his knowledge. He was of a gentle disposition and completely unaffected; he was also an excellent florist.

For many years he was organist at Tremadog Church, and was the composer of a number of anthems (many of which were prize-winners at various Eisteddfodau), carols and community hymns. One person to benefit from William Owen's help and instruction was Ieuan Gwyllt. One of Ieuan Gwyllt's masterpieces is the anthem 'By the Rivers of Babylon' which, no doubt, is renowned even today. On September 12th 1855 William Owen married a Miss Catherine Jones at St Pancras Church in Llundain; for business reasons they returned to Portmadog, where he assisted his mother and brothers in running the timber merchants E Owen & Sons. There were two children from the marriage; Francis Goronwy (who died at an early age) and Mr William R Owen of Porthmadog (Assistant Overseer and Accountant), who is married and has issue. He is said to possess his father's talent in full, but his duties give him little time to develop them. Mr W Owen died a young man at 35 years of age and is buried at St Beuno's Churchyard in Penmorfa where a beautiful memorial stone has been erected to his memory. On it is carved the following verse, the work of loan Madog.

For gentle William now the nations mourn,
He who to kindness gave a human name,
With constant leadership to music's men
And whose sweet choir brought his people fame.
The mark of his great teaching will endure,
His place in literature ever sure.

Gwilym Gwent won a competition for funeral anthems in remembrance of him; this appeared in *Y Cerddor Cymraeg* (The Welsh Musician)

MR RICHARD ROBERTS (BARD OF TREFLYS)

The son of Thomas Roberts of Carth-y-morthin in Treflys, Gest. He was also a descendant of the talented family of Dafydd y Garreg Wen. He was born in 1818, and went to Tymawr, the adjoining farm, where his uncle lived. He was a bachelor, and at the age of 58 he died on June 19th 1876, and was buried at St Michael's Churchyard, Treflys. The Chaired Bard Gwilym Eryri of Portmadog composed an excellent elegy to his memory and the verse is on his gravestone. He was a member of the Literary Society at Cefnymeusydd since its inception, and supported it faithfully during the eleven years of its existence. He was a bard of great originality and, possessing a very strong imagination, he could have become one of the foremost novelists of his era. He was faithful to the Sunday School and was a Chapel Deacon with the Calvinistic Methodists at Chapel Brynmelyn.

JOHN OWEN OF PORTHMADOG

It is not known where this brave Meirioneth sailor was born. After leaving the sea, he lived the last years of his life in the High Street, Porthmadog. The reason for his inclusion among the notables of Gest is that be served aboard a man-of-war under Sir Charles Napier. He received £100 prize money from the Portuguese Government and also a pension (which was paid to him under the name 'John Bull' as he was wounded during an attack on the Mignelite Squadron off Cape St Vincent on July 5th 1832. He died on February 8th 1872, aged 76 years and was buried at the Moel y Gest Cemetery, Porthmadog.

ROBERT ISAAC ROBERTS, DOCTOR AND SURGEON

He was the son of Dr Robert Roberts of Isallt in Llanfihangel-y-pennant in Eifionydd and Jane Anwyl of Park, Llanfrothen. He was a descendant of Owen Gwynedd on his father's side. He was born at Isallt Fawr in the above parish in the year 1733, being one of five brothers who were all medical men, and many sisters. One of his brothers was Dr Roberts of Oakland. On 18th March 1865 [1765? – Ed], at Llanfihangel, he married

Dorothy Griffith, a daughter of John Griffith of Ymwlch (of the family of Sir John Morys of Ymwlch and William Morys of Clenenney). Seven sons and four daughters were born to them. Five of the sons became Doctors; their names were: Robert, John, Griffith, Edward, William, David and Henry; his daughters were Margaret, Jane, Dorothy and Gaynor. The youngest daughter, Gaynor, married Owen Jones of Tyddyniolyn (nephew of the Rev Robert Jones, formerly of Rhoslan). One of her sons is the author of this book. After his marriage he settled at Ymwlch and his sons and daughters were born there. There was a scarcity of doctors in those days, so his practice extended throughout Eifionydd, the Lleyn and parts of Arfon which meant that there were many demands on his professional services. It was while returning from attending a patient that he met with an accident, his horse taking fright and causing him to fall. He sustained a broken thigh, which kept him confined to bed for seven years, but even this incapacitation did not prevent him from resetting bones and healing the sores and cuts of patients who attended him at his bedside. After an arduous and dedicated professional life he lived out the last few years at Ystumllyn and Plymouth. After his sons and two of his daughters had settled down in life, he gave up Ystumllyn and Colonel Wynn erected a new house for him named Bronheulog (now called Plymouth) with as much land attached as he wished; here he spent the last four years before his death in 1809 aged 66. The funeral cortege extended from Plymouth to Bronygadair crossroads (where the turning is for Tyddyn Ysguboriau and this man of unusually large stature was laid to rest in his father's grave at St Michael's, Llanfihangel-y-pennant in Eifionydd. The following inscription can be seen on his tombstone:

> *Also here lyeth the remains of Robert Isaac Roberts, Surgeon (son of the above Robert Roberts) who departed this life on 15th April 1809, aged 66 years.*
>
> *A physician and author, willingly*
> *He cured many.*
> *Never through the whole of Wales*
> *was his like, or ever will be.*

The above englyn is said to be the work of Dafydd Shon James of Penrhyndeudraeth. A poem of praise to the doctor was also composed by Gutyn Peris, who was a patient for a while with a painful limb. There are many of his descendants to this day who are following the medical profession, known under the name used by the country as Teulu Isallt (The Isallt Family).

IOAN MADOG

John Williams or as he was better known for the last 40 years of his life Ioan Madog, was one of nine children born to Richard and Eleanor

Williams of Tremadog. Richard Williams was the son of William Thomas of Ysgubor goch in Penmorfa. Margaret Williams was an issue of Enwogion Eifionydd (Notables of Eifionydd). See *Y Brython* Vol III, page 66. Richard Williams, Ioan Madog's father, was a blacksmith, and he too was brought up in the same calling. His father worked for Mr WA Madocks in the years 1809 and 1810 at the time of the building of the Embankment. In 1811 the family moved to the Ruabon district (to Pont Newydd) and it was here, on 3rd May 1812, that Ioan Madog was born. Nine years later they returned to their old home at Porthmadog. The father was a good rhymester and composed a few englynion. He was also proficient in reciting from memory the works of old bards. To the delight of visitors to the smithy Ioan Madog and his father would compose poems, each quoting alternate lines.

Ioan received very little formal education before he came to Tremadog and here he attended the school of John Wynn which was held at the Town Hall where he showed an intelligence far higher than normal. A gentleman in the area offered to bring him up as a man of the Law or the Church; this offer he declined and regretted for ever afterwards. He composed the following englyn:

> A blacksmith I became, fie me eightfold, for not
> Entering the field of the perfect word,
> Or gaining worthy distinction through my work,
> On the registers of the multitude of the Law.

From his early days he had learnt the art of oral verse and proved to be a worthy muse, receiving the Order of Bard at Bala Eisteddfod in April 1836 (the same time as the famous Talhaiarn). He was also a winner at various eisteddfodau: Eisteddfod Rhuddlan, Eisteddfod Aberffraw and Eisteddfod Madog (in 1851).

He married Ann, daughter of Humphrey Evans of Llanfair near Harlech. They had nine children. Ioan established a smithy at Porthmadog which he kept until the day of his death. A skilful craftsman, he invented many improvements connected with shipping and mining, but his retiring nature prevented him from establishing his rights and no patents were taken out on these inventions.

Of a kindly, truthful and pure disposition all his work was natural and self-explanatory in its nature. He died on 5th May 1878 at the age of 66, being buried at Ynyscynhaiarn close to the grave of his famous mentor Ellis Owen, on the right of the path as you enter and close to the church door. At the time of writing only a green sod marks his grave.

Two-thirds of his talent has fallen on his nephew, Mr W Williams

(Gwilym Meirion) of Boston Lodge, Porthmadog. The bardic vein flows very strongly in his patriarchal brother 'Beuno' (Mr Richard Williams of Cornhill, Porthmadog). He was a refined bard but so self-effacing that his work has received very little attention or publicity up to now.

JAMES SPOONER

He was born in 1789, coming to the Maentwrog area from Birmingham at the start of this century. He once lived at Glanwilliam, Maentwrog (around 1818) but moved fairly soon to Tan'rallt, Tremadog. He had five sons and five daughters; three of the daughters are still alive.

He surveyed the route of the railway from Festiniog to Porthmadog in 1824 and was at Tan'rallt when the plans of the railway were amended in 1829. A barrister named Mr Henry Archer came to the area in the year 1830, and in 1831 Mr Spooner completed his survey and plans. These were included in a Bill which was submitted to Parliament and, although it was rejected the first time, it was passed in 1832. The first foundation stone of the tramway was laid on 26th February 1833. The whole enterprise is a wonderful monument to the skill and ability of Mr James Spooner. He moved to Morfa Lodge in 1829 and it was here that Mrs Spooner died (a memorial window was placed in St John's Church, Porthmadog). Mr Spooner died on August 18th 1856, aged 67 years and was buried in the family vault in Ynyscynhaiarn Churchyard, where there is a beautiful memorial stone. His sons and daughters were very talented and had a high intellectual ability. One daughter (Louisa Maud) wrote an excellent mystery novel under the nom-de-plume 'Gwladys Harlech'. She died on February 18th 1890, and was buried at the same churchyard. His son, Charles E Spooner, came to supervise the Narrow gauge Railway after his father's death and was the recipient of a Gold Medal from the Tsar of Russia when he came to inspect the railway.

The following paragraph appeared in *The English Mechanic* dated November 20th 1889, a fitting testimony to the talents of Mr Charles E Spooner and his family:

> The death is announced of Mr Charles Easton Spooner, whose name is closely associated with the designing and development of Narrow Gauge Railways. He was born at Glanwilliam, Maentwrog, in the year 1818. After leaving school he was engaged with his father from 1832 to 1836 in engineering & constructing the Festiniog railway which was designed by his father for the purpose of conveying the slate from the quarries in the hills to Portmadoc. The line, which is 13 miles in length, has a gauge of only 1 feet 11½ inches and was scooped out of the cliffs overhanging The Vale of Festiniog. On his father's death Mr CE Spooner became manager and engineer of the line, and did much to advance knowledge of the system by his addresses and writing.

The Festiniog Railway thus became the pioneer of narrow gauge railways throughout the world and Mr Spooner's 'Narrow Gauge Railways' which was published by Spon in 1871 is well known to all interested in the work of constructing small railways in difficult places.

Mr Charles E Spooner died an November 18th 1889, and was buried at St Mary's Churchyard, Beddgelert. Friends are placing a remembrance window in his memory at St John's Church, Porthmadog. He was a faithful member of the established Church.

NOTE: Mr Archer, to whom reference was made above, invented a machine for perforating postage stamps in 1846. The Government paid him £4,000 for the patent and I was allowed to see the machine as Mr Archer was lodging at The Royal Madocks Arms in Tremadog at the time.

CAPTAIN R PRITCHARD

He was born in the year 1783 at Ty gwyn y Gamlas on Ynys Llanfihangel-y-traethau, Meirioneth. He married Janet, daughter of Robert Jones of Plas ucha, Meirioneth and came to live at Porthmadog around the year 1828. He started voyages to America in his ship *Y Gomer* and crossed the Atlantic at least 10 times (journeys to the New World were uncommon in those days) but about 1835 he left the sea to start a business at Porthmadog. This operated from the first house in the Terrace now known as Lombard Street when the port consisted of only those few houses. He was of a lively disposition – a generous, friendly character, full of the spirit of adventure. In the year 1836, the National Provincial Bank at Pwllheli established a branch in Porthmadog in Captain Pritchard's house. He became the manager and the bank was held in a room at the rear, where iron bars fitted to the windows can be seen to this day. He traded in Porter, which his vessels brought back from Dublin, but in the year 1838 when the Temperance Movement throughout Eifionydd was gathering momentum he broke his connection with the trading of alcoholic drinks. He had become aware of the harm done by drunkenness in the area, especially in the vicinity of the port, and as a symbol of his convictions, allowed the last barrel of porter that he owned to drain into the street. It is said that this had a humorous sequel – a sow from 'The Ship' lapped it all up and got very drunk. He took an active part in the Temperance Movement and argued its merits very strongly in fiery speeches which he made in Penrhyn, Llanfrothen, Beddgelert and other parts of Eifionydd. He was among the founders in the provision of a chapel for the Calvinistic Methodists at Porthmadog and served as a deacon. Until the building of Garth Chapel, Portmadoc, this denomination worshipped at Peniel Chapel, Tremadog. It was to him and the Harbour-master (Daniel Morris) that all sailors came when seeking advice and instruction in their calling; the chief topics would all relate to seafaring matters. After being ashore for over 20 years, Captain Pritchard returned to the sea and his old trade but caught a fever when sailing from one of the Californian ports and, after a short illness, died in 1855, aged 72 years. His remains were committed to the deep sea on whose waves he had lived for many years. Besides being a matchless boatman and one of the most knowledgeable about every aspect of seafaring life, he possessed a medical knowledge far above the ordinary. It is said that the big toe on the foot of a black man (one of his ship's hands) was badly affected by frost-bite. The captain gave his opinion that there was no option other than amputation; this he undertook and the black fellow recovered straightaway.

When ashore, for a short while he managed the Britannia Foundry, but sold it afterwards. He had four daughters and one son (Mr RJ Pritchard of Tynewydd, Llangybi), but only one daughter is still alive, Miss Pritchard of The National Bank of Wales, Porthmadog. Grandsons who are still living are Daniel and Laura Williams of Ivy House, Richard G Pritchard of Llwynon (engineer), Mrs Lloyd Jones of Bronant, and Mr JR Pritchard, Manager of the National Bank of Wales, Porthmadog.

EDWARD BREESE, FSA

He was the second son of the Rev John Breese, formerly of Carmarthen and afterwards Minister of the Tabernacle Chapel, Lerpwl (Liverpool). His mother was Margaret, second daughter of David Williams of Saethon in Lleyn, Caernarfon. He was born at Carmarthen on 13th April 1835 and completed his education at The Independent College, Lewisham. Shortly after leaving this establishment he became a Law student, receiving instruction from his uncle, Mr David Williams of Castell Deudraeth. Successfully passing his examinations, he became a Barrister in 1857 and established a practice at Porthmadog. In 1863, he married Margaret Jane, second daughter of Mr Lewis Williams of Fronwnion in Dolgellau, and four sons and one daughter were born to them.

As a Solicitor, Mr Breese held an influential position in the Counties of Caernarfon and Meirionydd and when his uncle, Mr David Williams, retired as a Justice of the Peace, he was appointed as his successor. He also served as Secretary to the Lord Lieutenant of The County, the Porthmadog District magistrates in Caernarfonshire and to the magistrates of Penrhyndeudraeth district of Meirion. Following the death of his uncle, Mr David Williams, MP of Castell Deudraeth, the vast estate of the Vale of Madog came under his charge. Mr Breeze was well known in literary circles and was a painstaking and persistent historian. He enriched the

Archæologia Cambrensis with essays which he contributed from time to time, but his main work was the book *The Kalendars of Gwynedd* in which he co-operated with the late Mr RW Wynne of Peniarth. He was honoured as a Fellow of the Society of Archaeologists (FSA) and over the years was a generous donor to many similar societies. He wrote many articles for publication and he had an insatiable passion for old books, documents and manuscripts, and possessed an extensive collection of both rare and ancient manuscripts. A few years before he died his strength started to fail and he went to London to undergo a surgical operation from which, unfortunately, he never recovered. He died in 1881, aged 46 years and his mortal remains were laid to rest in the family grave at Penrhyndeudraeth Churchyard.

JOHN WHITEHEAD GREAVES ESQ

This gentleman came to Wales around the year 1833 when, in conjunction with Mr Shelton, he purchased the Llechwedd quarry. He lived at Tan'rallt isaf in Tremadog and was a native of Leamington, being the son of Richard Greaves, Banker, of that town. He married Miss Steadman of Ty Nanney, Tremadog and, after the death of Dr Carreg, they moved in to Tan'rallt uchaf. They later moved to a mansion he had built at Blaenau Festiniog which was more convenient for the quarry. He died in Brighton (where he had moved to improve his health) on February 12th 1880, aged 73; he was buried in Leamington Cemetery.

He was one of the leading men in the establishment of education in the Vale of Madog (this at a time when education relied on voluntary support), and was a generous contributor towards the salaries of schoolmasters. At one time he undertook the costs of Pontynysgalch school (where the Queen's Hotel now stands) and later zealously involved himself with the National school in Snowdon Street. The latter school also benefited from the arduous and painstaking work of his clerk, Mr John Thomas. Llechwedd Quarry (JW Greaves & Sons) is nowadays one of the most successful in Festiniog. His eldest son, Mr JE Greaves of Broneifion, is Lord Lieutenant of the county; ES Greaves now lives in London, and Richard A Greaves at The Wern, Penmorfa, where he has bought large tracts of land in Tre'r Gest. His daughters married as follows: Edith to the Rev Hansard, May to the Rev Clough Williams-Ellis, Evelyn to Mr Osmond Williams of Deudraeth Castle and Mary is unmarried.

JOHN PHILLIPS OF TEGIDION

He was born in the parish of Llanycil, Bala, in 1810. He was brought up to be a printer in the well known offices of Robert Saunderson. He became sub-editor of an old publication *Y Gwyliedydd* (The Watcher or

Sentinel) during the last few years of its existence. He moved to Caerlleon (Chester) where he was in charge of the offices of Mr Thomas of that city. He moved to Porthmadog around the year 1854, where he was secretary and later agent for The Welsh Slate Company. He married twice and had two daughters from the first marriage. He died in 1877, aged 67, and was buried at Llanycil Churchyard, Bala. He was a brilliant bard and the composer of many songs in free metre, among them the well known 'Hen Feibl mawr fy Mam' (My Mother's Large Old Bible). He was a peaceful neighbour, a quiet citizen, a good musician and was a deacon of the Calvinistic Methodist Chapel in Porthmadog.

MARY DAVIES (MAIR EIFION)

She was the eldest daughter of Captain Lewis Davies and Janet, his wife, of the Treguntur Arms in Porthmadog. A pleasant and kind young lady of brilliant talents and of a pure and unsullied character, she competed regularly in literary meetings at Porthmadog and the outlying district and won many prizes for poetic pieces and essays. A small neat volume of her bardic composition of free metre verses was published under the editorship of the Chaired Bard Gwilym Eryri. It contains many tender and pleasing pieces including 'Cryd gwag fy mlentyn yw' ('Tis my Baby's Empty Cradle). After a long and painful illness she died quietly on October 8th 1882, aged 35. Her mortal remains were buried at Talsarnau Cemetery. She was unmarried.

DR JOHN JONES OF DOLWYDDELEN

This popular doctor was born at Tyddyniolyn y Gest in 1819. He was the third son of Owen Jones and Gaynor Jones, son of John Jones and Sïan (Jane) Owen; son of John Edward Suntur, of the Gwynfryn family. Sïan Owen was the daughter of Owen Evan and Catherine Williams of Tyddyniolyn, who lived around 1685. There is a curious old will pertaining to the old lady, in which she bequeathed the family bible to one son and a 'Gwif' (a type of large crowbar) to another. The wîf can still be seen at Rhyd-ddu. Gaynor Jones, the doctor's mother, was the youngest daughter of Dr Isaac Roberts of Ystumllyn, whose biography has already been given.

Dr John Jones took an interest in medical techniques whilst still young, but was brought up to be a farmer, receiving an education no higher than was necessary for that occupation. In the year 1843 he took over Bryntirion Farm near Castell Dolwyddelen (at that time in an isolated and inaccessible place) and took an interest in medical matters and also carried out skilful work as a bonesetter. He later went to one of the medical colleges in Dublin and, on his return, answered the many calls on his services which came from all parts of the country. His success with his patients and his integrity soon gained him recognition, so much so that the sting of jealousy raised its head and efforts were made to discredit his name. This was a worry to him and led to a shortening of his life – it is said that there is 'a black mark' (Blottyn Dû) against his enemy, even today. After a fairly long illness he died in July 1878, aged 59, and was buried in the family plot at Ynyscynhaiarn Churchyard.

The proof of his popularity was shown when Dolwyddelen Choir and a multitude of others followed his remains from Dolwyddelen to Ynyscynhaiarn (a distance of over 20 miles) on a very hot day. It was printed on his memorial card: 'An approved doctor, a faithful deacon, a lovable neighbour and a true Christian'.

He was married to Jane, daughter of Griffith Roberts of Pen'rallt, Llanystumdwy and they had one child. He was a deacon with the Calvinistic Methodists at Dolwyddelen and was held in high esteem. The place of his burial, like those of Ellis Owen and Ioan Madog, is devoid of any stone to mark the place.

It would be possible to elaborate further on the notables already mentioned and to add many more to them but further references will be made when dealing with the epitaphs in the churchyards of both churches.

SOME OF THE RESIDENTS IN HOUSEHOLDS IN TRE'R GEST AT VARIOUS TIMES

This section deals with the size of holdings as shown on the Parish Map (which was prepared in 1838 when the parish was valued for the commutation of tithes). Also shown are the dates and names of the various holders. The list is complete as far as possible and if there are any omissions it is due to no details being forthcoming even after careful research.

What is recorded may throw light on the movement of families from one district to another. It may also assist many families to trace the pedigree of their ancestors. I believe it will be of particular interest to those who now live in the various farmhouses who will note the changes that have taken place during the past 150 to 200 years in this rural area. The record is given as it has been collated and notes are made at the bottom of the pages giving some details of the residences.

MEASUREMENTS OF THE FARMS WITH THE NAMES OF THOSE WHO LIVED IN THEM

Measures of area for those taught only in metric.
4 roods to 1 acre
40 poles or perches to 1 rood
30 sq yards to 1 pole J KIDD

Bronygadair	A	R	P
	271	3	38

John Owen 1680
John Jones, Gent 1778
Mrs Jones, his wife 1817
Mrs Mary Jane Williams daughter, married 1838
Eliseus Griffith 1822
Robert Jones, son of Abercin
Robert Roberts 1849
Mrs Sarah Roberts and Robert Roberts, their son 1890

Bronygadair bach	A	R	P
	12	3	39

John Roberts 1783
Ambrose Lewis Esq 1790
Evan Ellis 1791
William Roberts 1830
Capt Eliseus Jones
Mrs Jones, formerly of Eisteddfa
John Jones, their son
Ellis W Roberts 1890

Mynydd du	A	R	P
	36	2	24

Robert Jones 1784
Morris Owen 1797
Gaynor Evans, his wife
Robert Owen
Capt Morris Roberts
Robert Owen 1890

Cefnymeusydd uchaf	A	R	P
	58	3	12

Ellen Jones 1773
Owen Owens 1798
Richard Thomas 1800
Mrs Thomas, his wife 1822
Capt Thomas Jones 1843
Mrs Jones, his wife 1861
Owen Owens 1876
Richard Jones 1890

Cefnymeusydd isaf	A	R	P
	99	0	31

Morris Parry 1721
Robert Roberts
Ellis Owen & Margaret Pritchard, his wife 1734
Owen Ellis, their son1803
Ann Thomas, his 2nd wife 1841
Ellis Owen (the historian) 1846
Rev W Williams 1880

Twllycae	A	R	P
	32	3	13

Formed part of Cefnymeusydd Isaf.
Robert Roberts 1766
Janet Williams, his 2nd wife 1828
Owen Roberts 1847
Jane Roberts, his wife
Owen Jones 1890

Tyddynysyuboriau	A	R	P
	42	3	14

Thom Rowlands & Jane Jones, his wife 1736
John Williams 1773
Owen Griffith 1778
Henry Humphrey 1791
Henry Parry 1792
Owen Williams 1798
Janet Owen, his wife 1860
John Williams, their son 1890

Llidiart Yspytty	A	R	P
	34	2	2

Robert Parry 1773
William Williams 1784
Griffith Griffiths 1809
William Owen 1838
Henry Jones 1879
John Jones 1890

	A	R	P
Drwsdeugoed	66	3	18

Rev Rowland Jones, who became
Vicar of Edeyrn 1727
Mrs Jones, his wife 1760
Owen Hughes of Caerhengaer,
Llanllyfni (Ynysmaen family) 1789
Evan Williams 1824
William Roberts 1832
William Roberts, his son 1869

	A	R	P
Cwm mawr	376	4	28

Griffith Williams 1695
William Griffith 1708
Owen Williams 1734
Humphrey Owen
Wm Owen & D Hughes
William Owen 1796
William Owen (nephew) 1840
William Owen 1890

	A	R	P
Cwm bach	123	0	39

Edward Jones 1773
Hywel Parry 1786
John Richard 1790
Richard Jones 1796
Mary Jones, his wife 1810
Rbt Roberts, her 2nd husband
Griffith Roberts, the son 1834
Thomas Roberts 1840
William Thomas 1870
David Thomas 1890

	A	R	P
Tan'rallt uchaf	54	2	5

Eleanor Pritchard 1773
Richard Humphreys 1787
WA Madocks 1802
Dr Carreg 1830–1838
JW Greaves 1850
J Lee (Barrister)
Lady Nisbet 1886
Mr Ainger 1891

	A	R	P
Glanymorfa bach	123	2	5

Catherine Jones 1784
J and D Roberts 1795
William Humphreys 1885
Humphrey Humphreys 1890

	A	R	P
Garreg fawr	31	2	2

Humphrey Pritchard 1774
Dafydd & Eliza Davies 1776
Henry Thomas 1784
Rev M Anwyl 1785–1788
Henry Roberts 1820
Jane Hughes 1846
Griffith Evans 1850
Jane, his wife 1862
Robert Roberts (the bard Moelwyn)
her 2nd husband 1880
His daughter who married
Richard Jones 1890

	A	R	P
Llanerch	344	1	32

Richard Dafydd 1690
David Pritchard 1717
Richard Ellis 1722
Ellis Dafydd 1750
John Ellis
Ann Ellis, wife of
Humphrey Williams 1823
William Williams 1856
William Williams, his son 1890

	A	R	P
Eisteddfa	96	3	11

Rev R Griffith BA 1727
Daniel Williams 1773
Griffith Williams 1799
Cath. Griffith, his wife 1810
Richard Griffith, their son 1820
Humph. Griffith, his son,
Robert Jones
Mrs Jones, his wife
Rev Thomas Jones 1890

Garregfelen	A	R	P
	216	3	0

Susana George 1701
Rev R Griffith, Vicar of Penmorfa, later of Eisteddfa 1715
John Parry (Agent of the Rhiwlas Estate) 1765
Jane Parry or Griffiths, his wife 1781
Owen Evans 1782
Evan Owen 1824
Henry Llewelyn 1844
William Llewelyn 1890

Hendregadredd	A	R	P
	12	0	0

Ellis Owen and Margaret, his wife 1714
Henry Thomas
Robt. & Ann Williams 1781
Margaret Rowlands 1791
Robert Evans 1796
Robert Edwards 1806
Griffith & Richard Roberts
Griffith Lloyd (tanner)
Capt John Barnes 1832
Sir John Kingston James (ex Mayor of Dublin)
Mr George Lee
Major & Mrs Walker
Ignatius Williams Esq, who married Miss Walker 1890

Caegwenllian	A	R	P
	49	2	14

Robert Jones 1789
Hugh Evans 1799
Henry Hughes, his son 1830
Evan Owen 1890

Caegwenllian was held in the same way as Tyddyniolyn at this time.

Tyddyniolyn	A	R	P
	41	3	30

Owen Evan 1687
Ann William 1767
John Jones 1810
Owen Jones 1820
Gaynor Jones 1838
Owen Jones, their son 1846
Griffith Jones 1890

Llwynmafon isaf	A	R	P
	128	4	0

John Williams & Elizabeth Griffith, his wife 1695
Ellis Jones 1769
Martha Roberts 1773
David Parry 1825
Henry Parry 1834
Griffith Parry
Rev T Jones 1859
Owen Jones 1880
Mrs E Jones, his widow 1890

Llwynymafon uchaf	A	R	P
	235	1	18

Richard Williams 1762
William Pritchard 1778
Jane Hughes 1804
Griffith Jones 1815
Morris Llewelyn 1822
Morris Griffith 1838
Edward Llewelyn 1860
The Family 1890

Tan'rallt Isaf	A	R	P
	13	3	3

Humphrey Pierce 1773
William Davies 1778
Thomas Owen 1795
James Spooner 1827
JW Greaves 1838
House demolished in 1842

	A	R	P
Tuhwnt i'r bwlch	110	1	11

John Griffith 1720
Jane Jones 1740
Thomas Rowland 1750
Rowland Thomas 1805
William Roberts 1809
John Williams (Agent) 1830
Mrs Williams, his wife 1840
Dr R Roberts 1890–1891
Tuhwnt i'r bwlch at this time included all the area where the Cambrian Railway now stands and also lands around Pensyflog, Ynyscalch etc

	A	R	P
Penyclogwyn	69	2	15

Evan Thomas 1773
Elizabeth Evans 1784
John Roberts 1794 –1840
Elizabeth, his wife 1840
Evan Roberts, their son 1860
Cath. Roberts, their daughter 1875
Richard Jones 1890
His children 1892

	A	R	P
Borth y Gest	129	2	3

Dafydd Humphrey 1750
Robert Dafydd 1773
Dafydd Humphrey 1784
John Davies 1880
John Owen 1890
Lowry Owen 1892

	A	R	P
Tyddyn Adi	123	1	7

Robert Jones 1750
Lowry Pritchard 1773
Robert Dafydd 1784
William Pritchard 1790
Humphrey Pritchard 1801
Robert Dafydd 1811
Henry Owen 1825
John Prys 1830
Margaret Prys, his wife 1834
William Roberts 1840
John Morris 1850
William M Roberts 1890

	A	R	P
Tyddynllwyn	69	2	15

Richard Davies 1750
Robert Griffith 1773
Ann Jones for her brother,
Owen Jones 1812
John Griffith, their son 1880
Griffith Griffiths 1892

NOTES: Humphrey Williams was the son of John Williams, Dolwgan; he also owned Derwin Bach through his first wife. Humphrey Williams married Ann Ellis, daughter of Ellis Dafydd and Jane Owen, his wife, of Llanerch. Their sons were William Williams, who married firstly Mary, daughter of Hugh Parry of Tyddynygraig, Dolbenmaen (cattle dealer), who died in 1796, aged 55 years. His wife Mary died in Mary 1829, aged 44 years. They had three sons and three daughters. William Williams' second wife was Margaret, widow of John Prys of Tyddyn Adi (formerly Glyncywarch). She was the daughter of the Rev John Morris, Rector of Llanfihangel-y-traethau. She died in November 1874, aged 86 years.

Hugh Parry (Tyddynygraig) had another son and daughter. The son was Lieut Hugh Parry who was on board the 'Victory' at Trafalgar; he was one of the four who carried Lord Nelson down to his cabin after he received the wound that proved fatal.

Hugh Parry's widow married the Rev John Griffiths, independent Minister of Caernarfon; they had two sons: the Rev William Griffith, and the Rev John Griffith, one at Holyhead, the other at Buckley in Flintshire.

MEASURMENTS OF FARMS IN THE PARISH OF YNYSCYNHAIARN IN THE YEARS 1838 AND 1842, AS SHOWN IN THE SURVEY PREPARED AT THAT TIME

The surveyor was Mr Edwards of Gwynfryn, Pwllheli; he also looked after the main road from Capel Currig to Porthdinlleyn for a number of years. Cadwaladr Williams of Glanybyl and Griffith Roberts of Gelli Grîn, Llanarmon were the parish valuers at the time. There are many changes and divisions in the lands of the parish. Most of them have changed hands and the leaseholders in most cases have died, 'The mode of the world passes by' in this parish as in other parts of the earth.

	A	R	P
Llwynmafon uchaf	235	1	18
Llwynmafon isaf	128	4	0
Drwsdeugoed	66	3	18
Cwm mawr	376	0	38
Ty'nrhos	7	2	20
Bronygadair	271	3	38
Y Felin newydd	2	3	17
Twllycae (Goat Villa)	32	3	13
Garregfelen	216	3	0
Tyddyn Ysguboriau	42	3	14
Tyddynyniolyn	41	3	30
Cwm bach	123	0	39
Nhyrra uchaf & isaf	37	2	18
Mynydd-du (part)	36	2	24
Ffridd Newydd	16	0	21
Pencraig, Tymawr (Ty Evan Ellis)	0	1	39
Tanycoed, (Bronygadair bach)	12	3	29
Eisteddfa	96	3	11
Cefnymeusydd uchaf	58	3	12
Cefnymeusydd isaf	99	0	31
Caegwenllian	49	2	14
Carreg y Felin	15	3	17
Hendregadredd	13	0	0
Coed y Cefn	75	2	15
Gweirglodd y Cefn	6	2	16
Borth y Gest	129	2	3
Tyddyn Adi	123	1	7
Tyddyn Madyn (part)	32	2	18
Garreg fawr	31	2	2
Cefnperfedd bach	59	3	14
Pentir Gest (part of Bachysaint)	100	1	31
Pwllygloewlas	6	0	0
Ffriddoedd (Morfa Bychan)	29	2	8
Cefn y Gadair	12	1	13
Ffridd Glanmorfa Mawr	13	1	0
Fridd Trip	2	2	12
Penamser	137	2	30
Tan'rallt uchaf	54	2	5
Tan'rallt isaf	13	3	13
Llidiart Yspytty	34	2	2
Ty Nanney	23	1	7
Pensyflog	215	1	22
Tuhwnt i'r bwlch	110	1	11

	A	R	P
Morfa Lodge	21	0	10
Pen y Clogwyn	69	2	15
Tyddyn Llwyn	52	1	15
Llanerch y Gest	334	1	32
Y Lletty	8	2	5
Glanmorfa Bach	123	2	5
Tynymynydd	0	3	14
Garregwen	244	2	35
Garregwen bach	13	0	29
Ynys Cyngar	7	3	53
Penrhydfechan	23	0	10
Ynystowyn	31	1	36
Ynys Cerrig Duon	1	0	37
Ynys Calch	2	3	6
Ynys Hir	54	1	24
Ynys Fadog	9	2	18
Ynys Carregaethnen (Farmyard)	149	0	31
Penmount (part of above)			
The old sea wall	3	0	10
Morfa Traethmawr	618	0	25
Porthreuddyn, part of above	3	0	28
Penrhyn Llwyd	10	1	16
Penrhyn Heli	34	2	13
Weirglodd Penrhyn Heli	5	3	1
Land at Bwlchymoch	10	0	2
Ty Eiddew (Glan y Gamlas)	16	3	13
Bryn Ellis (Griffith)	7	1	8
Caemawr (William Owen)	12	2	0
Madock's Arms Hotel	37	2	35
Cae Brics	20	3	10
Brynarddol	5	1	10
Cae yr Ynys Fadog	10	3	6
Llaingyd	2	2	12
Market Sq Houses, Tremadoc	4	0	12
Chapel Land (Moiety)	6	3	2
Various Tenements	50	2	12
Ditto (not titheable)	12	1	26
Allt Wen (not titheable wood & rocks)	52	2	4
Tremadoc Church Yard	1	1	9
Portmadoc town green	19	1	12

Total 5346¼ acres

Arable land	1350	acres
Meadows & Grazing land	3273	acres
Land under Forestry	58	acres
Total rateable area	4681	acres
Remainder under water	5346¾	acres

NOTE: Richard Tavistock Price Esq of Rhiwlas near Bala, at the end of the century owned five-sixths of the land of the parish, together with half the parish of Llanfrothen, but he started selling in 1798. The places sold were: Cefnymeusydd, Eisteddfa, Garregfelen, Caegwenllian, Tyddyniolyn, Penyclogwyn y Gest, Llanerch, Glanmorfa Bach, Garregwen, Tyddynyllwyn, Tuhwnt i'r bwlch, Llidiart Ysbytty, and the two Pen'rallts. (Hendregadredd and Tyddyn Adi belonged to Mr Price's ancestors, but were usurped by Madam Jones by treachery). The following farms in the parish were sold from the same estate in the year 1866: Cwm mawr, Drwsdeugoed, Tyn'rhos, Llwynmafon ucha', Llwynmafon isa'. (Mrs Walker of Hendregadredd bought about 11 acres later, part of Twllycae and a field belonging to Y Felin (The Mill) in Pentrefelin.)

A REGISTER OF THOSE WHO LIVED IN TRE'R GEST IN 1843

No attempt has been made to compile a complete register, only those of the chief inhabitants (as far as can be recollected)

Rev W Ambrose (Independents), Porthmadog
Capt John James Barton, Aberia
Rev Richard Brown (Baptists), Porthmadog
Robert Byers Esq, Tremadoc
WB Chorley Esq, Tremadoc
Thomas Christian Esq, Tan'rallt
Rev John Evans (Independents), Tremadoc
JW Greaves, Tan'rallt Hall
George Homphray Esq, Y(n)ystowyn
Rev John Jones (Calvanistic Methodists), Tremadoc
Rev Morris Parry (Curate), Tanygraig Cottage, Pentrefelin
James Spooner Esq, Morfa Lodge
Major Spooner, Brecon Place, Porthmadog
Gill Steadman Esq, Ty Nanney
Miss Wainhouse, Tremadoc
Capt Isaac Walker, Hendregadredd
Miss Ellen Williams, Brecon Place, Porthmadog
WN Solly, Welsh Slate, Porthmadog
John Williams Esq, Manager for the Trustees of the late WA Madocks
Evan Lloyd (Agent for North & Co), Flag & Slate Works, Alltwen
J Kent (Agent for Snowdon Copper Mine, Snowdon
Thomas Hill (Agent for Lewis & Co), Porthreuddyn
William Owen (Agent for Cambrian Copper Co), Bronygadair
William Pasco, Tremadoc (Agent for Hafodyporth Slate Co, Beddgelert)

DOCTORS

Robert Roberts, Porthmadog
John & Rowland Williams, Tremadoc & Llanystumdwy

SOLICITORS

Daniel Breese, Brecon Place
Williams and Breese, Brecon Place
David Williams (Broneryri), Clerk to the Justices, Commote of Eifionydd

CHEMISTS

Edward Jones, Porthmadog
Robert Isaac Jones, Tremadog

BANKS

National Provincial Bank, – Capt Richard Pritchard, Manager
North & South Wales Bank, – Anthony Dillon, Manager

BREWERS

William Jones, 'Sgubor Hen, near Penamser
John Griffiths, Tremadog & Porthmadog

AUCTIONEERS

David Jones and son, Tremadog

POST MASTERS

John Ellis Roberts, Tremadog
Edward Jones, Porthmadog

TOWN CRIERS

David Shon James, also the sexton for the parish of Ynys and Tremadog church

INSPECTOR OF WEIGHTS & MEASURES

Ellis Owen, Cefnymeusydd
Custom House Officer, – Joseph Cox, Painter, Porthmadog

CLERK TO THE BOARD OF GUARDIANS

John Pritchard, Goat hotel, Beddgelert

COOPERS

William Lloyd, Tremadog
John Jones, Porthmadog

HATTERS

James Griffith, Tremadog

BLACKSMITHS

John Evans, Pentrefelin
Evan Evans, Tremadog

John Jones, Britannia Foundry, Porthmadog
William Roberts, Tremadog
Richard Williams (Beuno), Porthmadog
Alice Williams (widow of Thomas Williams), Porthmadog
John Williams (Ioan Madog), Porthmadog
John Henry Williams, Porthmadog

BUTCHERS

Robert Jones, Tremadog
Ellis Williams, Tremadog
Thomas Pugh, Porthmadog

WHEELWRIGHTS

Henry Hughes, Tremadog
Robert Pritchard, Tremadog
(It was with R Pritchard that the famous Nicander started as an apprentice in 1830)
Owen Parry, Tremadoc

CARPENTERS

David Jones and John Roberts, Tremadog
Dafydd Shon James, Tremadog
William Jones, Porthmadog
Robert Efan, Beudymawr, Pentrefelin
Robert Davies, Ty'nyrardd, Tremadog

TIMBER LIME & FLOUR MERCHANTS

William Owen, Tremadog
William Jones, Porthmadog

GLOVERS

Ellis Griffith, Barracks, Tremadog
John Jones, Glanygamlas, Tremadog

MILLERS

William Roberts, Tremadog
William Evans, Tremadog
Evan E Jones, Tremadog

WOOLLEN FACTORS

Robert Ellis, Tremadog

TANNER

Griffith Lloyd, Tremadog

CURRIER

John Jones, Market Square, Tremadog

A LIST OF THE FARMHOUSES THAT WERE LIABLE FOR LIGHT OR WINDOW TAX IN THE PARISH OF YNYSCYNHAIARN IN 1773

	Windows.	£	s	d
William Owen, Cwmmawr	6	0	3	0
Edward Jones, Cwmbach	5	0	3	0
Ellenor Pritchard, Tan'rallt	4	0	3	0
Robert Parry, Llidiart Yspytty	4	0	3	0
Rowland Thomas, Tuhwnt i'r bwlch	4	0	3	0
Humphrey Pierce, Tan'rallt isa	6	0	3	0
Evan Thomas Penyclogwyn	4	0	3	0
Robert Griffith, Tyddynyllwyn	4	0	3	0
Jane Owen, Llanerch	6	0	3	0
Robert Dafydd, y Borth	6	0	3	0
Gruffydd Hughes, Garregwen	6	0	3	0
John Jones, Bronygadair	6	0	3	0
Lowri Pritchard, Tyddynadi	3	0	0	0
Jane Griffith, Garregyfelen	8	0	7	0
Owen Ellis, Cefnymeusydd isa'	5	0	3	0
Ellenor Jones, Cefnymeusydd ucha'	2	0	3	0
John Williams, Tyddynysguboriau	3	0	3	0
John Williams, for Nhyrra	2	0	2	0
Gruffydd Jones, Llwynymafon ucha'	2	0	2	0
Martha Roberts, Llwynymafon isa'	4	0	3	0
William Owen, Drwsdeugoed	6	0	3	0
Henry Parry, Penamser	6	0	3	0
Ann Williams, Tyddyniolyn	4	0	3	0
Daniel Williams, Eisteddfa	6	0	3	0
		£3	16	0

John Jones, Assessor and Collector, Bronygadair
Love Parry, Peniarth (LS)
Zacheus Hughes, Trefan (LS)

AN ASSESSMENT OF LAND TAX IN THE PARISH OF YNYSCYNHAIARN, IN THE YEAR 1791

The following is a list of farmhouses which paid the rates or tax called 'The High Rate', this existed before the Poor Rate, since there was only the Window or Light Rate, the High Rate and the Church Rate in being about 100 years ago. From the Church Rate the poor were assisted if the collection raised at the church was insufficient to meet their needs; together with the voluntary donations of the parishioners. No assistance was given to the able-bodied, neither was any payment made for services rendered at this time, but the parishioners carried out their duties free of Charge.

Tenements	Proprietors	Occupiers	Sums Assessed		
			£	s	d
Coedycefn	Robt. Godolphin Owen	Robert Owen	0	12	0
Borth y Gest	Robt. Godolphin Owen	David Humphrey	1	4	0
Tyddyn adi	Robt. Godolphin Owen	Lowry Pritchard	1	2	0
Tyddyn madyn	Robt. Godolphin Owen	Gaynor Pritchard	0	6	0
Garreg fawr	Robt. Godolphin Owen	Henry Roberts	0	8	0
Hendregadno	Robt. Godolphin Owen	Margaret Rowlands	0	6	0
Gweirglodd y cefn	Robt. Godolphin Owen	John Rowlands	0	4	0
Cefnperfedd bach	Robt. Godolphin Owen	Rev Mr Evans	0	10	0
Penamser	Griffith Parry	G Parry	1	12	0
Cwmmawr	Richard T Price	Owen Williams	4	0	0
Tan'rallt isaf	Richard T Price	William Davies	1	10	0
Tan'rallt uchaf	Richard T Price	Richard Humphreys	1	0	0
Llidiart Ysbytty	Richard T Price	William Williams	1	6	0
Tuhwnt i'r bwlch	Richard T Price	Rowland Thomas	1	14	0
Penyclogwyn	Richard T Price	Elizabeth Evans	1	0	0
Tyddynllwyn	Richard T Price	Griffith Roberts	1	0	0
Llanerch	Richard T Price	Humphrey Williams	3	8	0
Glanymorfa	Richard T Price	Catherine Jones	0	14	0
Garregwen	Richard T Price	Owen Roberts	1	14	0
Garregfelen	Richard T Price	Owen Evans	2	0	0
Bronygadair	Richard T Price	Mrs Jones	2	18	0
Cefnymeusydd isa	Richard T Price	Owen Ellis	2	0	0
Cefnymeusydd ucha	Richard T Price	Ellenor Jones	0	18	0
Eisteddfa	Richard T Price	Griffith Williams	1	4	0
Tyddyniolyn	Richard T Price	John Jones	1	4	0
Llwynymafon isa	Richard T Price	David Parry	1	16	0
Llwynymafon uchaf	Richard T Price	Griffith Jones	2	6	0
Drwsdeugoed	Richard T Price	William Owen	0	14	0
Cwmbach	Ambrose Lewis	John Pritchard	1	16	0
Tyddynysguboriau	Ambrose Lewis	Owen Griffith	0	16	0
Y Nhyrra	Ambrose Lewis	John Williams	0	12	0
Bronygadair bach	Ambrose Lewis	Evan Ellis	0	6	0
Mynydd du	Ambrose Lewis	Griffith Williams	0	8	0

Bachysaint	WG Oakley	Margaret Morris	0	16	0
Church	D Ellis (Rector)	David Ellis (Tithe)	0	16	0

Griffith Roberts, Collector — Z Hughes, Trefan (LS) — R Ellis, Gwynfryn (LS)
GW Hughes, Trefan (LS)

NOTES RELATING TO LAND TAX IN YNYSCYNHAIARN

William Davies moved from Ty'nyberllan, Penmorfa to live at Tan'rallt around the year 1775. Before that it is likely that he lived at Criccieth. According to the following entry found in an old manuscript: 'William, son of William Davies, of Court, Excise Officer, & Gwen his wife, was christened May 9th 1762 at Criccieth Church'. A daughter of his became the wife of Cadwaladr Jones, who went to live at the Chapel house, Tremadoc. The last named died in 1831, aged 76 years. Catherine, his wife, died in the year 1848, aged 90 years. They were both buried at Ynyscynhaiarn Churchyard. His occupation was a clockmaker.

Gruffydd Jones, the weaver (or Gruffydd Shon of Ynysypandy as he was called) lived at Ty'nllech around the year 1774. He moved from there to Ynysypandy, near Cefncoch. It was with him that Shon Elias o Fon (John Elias of Anglesey) started his apprenticeship as a weaver and also started preaching.

Twllycae is not recorded in the register of Land Tax because it was part of Cefnymeusydd at the time. Since then it has separated and set up on its own, as it is at present. As shown, Margaret Pritchard of Cefnymeusydd had three husbands, Ellis Owen, the cattle dealer was her third husband. Her son was Robert Roberts of Twllycae, by her first or second husband. It can be seen that he was half brother (from his mother's side) to Ellis Owen, Cefnymeusydd isa. Robert Roberts' first wife, Ann, died on November 20th 1767, aged 40 years; he died on April 12th 1803, aged 80 years. There were two sons and a daughter from this marriage, one settled at Crugan, the other at PenyBerth in Lleyn. Janet became the second wife of Robert Roberts; she died at Twllycae in 1828, aged 80. They had the following children: William, John, Ellis, Owen Roberts of Twllycae and Ellin Roberts of Garthyrhebog. The last named was the mother of Mrs Roberts of Albert House in Pentrefelin (who is still alive). It is believed that Robert Roberts of Twllycae was the son of Margaret Pritchard by her first husband.

John Jones of Tyddyniolyn, held Caegwenllian at this time; that is the reason that its name is not shown on the register.

Around 70 years ago Morris Llewellyn of Llwynmafon uchaf had 15 children, and Hugh Evans of Caegwenllian had the same number. David Parry of Llwynmafon isa had eight children, five of these were deaf and dumb. The following englyn can be seen on their tombstone at Ynyscynhaiarn (the work of Ellis Owen):

The deaf and the mute in their graves shall hear
The Lord's call at death,
To open his mighty gates,
Closed so long throughout the world.

THE POPULATION OF YNYSCYNHAIARN PARISH DURING THIS CENTURY

1801 – 223;	1811 – 889;	1821 – 885;	1831 – 1075;	1841 – 1888
1851 – 2540;	1861–3059;	1871 – 4260;	1881 – 5506;	1891 – 5097

A decrease of over 400 can be seen in the population during the last decade.

THE BUILDING OF THE CHURCHES

Lleufer ap Coel, called Lleufer mawr, built the first church at Llandaff. This was the first in Britain and gave civil and ecclesiastical jurisdiction and 'Bridduw' (a baptismal vow of one who forsakes the pagan life and adopts Christianity) to all who would be true to the Christian faith.

The early Christians taught in circles and temples as they knew that the attraction to such places was very strong. It enabled them to give their message of the Christian faith and attract those who wished to be converted from their previous style of worship of false idols. The glory and the fame of the old church in Britain, its many 'Bangorau' and the thousands of missionaries during the latter half of the first century and afterwards, all led to an expansion of the faith in these islands – until the massacre at Bangor on Dee in 602-7.

It is likely that the preaching of the Gospel took place in these areas many centuries before the establishment and consecration of the Church of St Cynhaiarn.

THE CHURCH OF ST CYNHAIARN AT YNYS CYNHAIARN, EIFIONYDD (ACCORDING TO AN OLD MANUSCRIPT)

This church or house of worship was established by St Cynhaiarn around the 6th century. He was the son of Hygarfal ab Cyndrwyn; he had been Bishop of Llanbadarn fawr in Ceredigion. The church is on a pleasant island about a mile from the sea called y Nheraig (meaning break of the waves, 'breakers' or the shallow waves). It is on a spur of land standing midway between Criccieth and Tremadog, with Treflys to the southwest and Moel y gadair to the northwest. The place is exceptionally secluded and ideal for meditation and worship. At that time the river Aberdowarch flowed between the Moel and the Ynys, so that the place was virtually an island in the true sense of the word. The original building stood within a few yards of the Lych Gate. The chancel, called Capel Ystumllyn reached close to where the west door of the present building is standing on a completely new site and not on any foundations of the old church. The plot of land for the church (with burial grounds on both sides) was the gift of Mr RT Price of Rhiwlas, the owner of Bronygadair at that time (that is 1832 – when the new church was built). The Rhiwlas family were munificent benefactors of Ynyscynhaiarn Church throughout the years.

The churchyard is called 'God's Acre' and is indeed nearly a Welsh acre, measuring 160 yards by 16 yards making 2560 square English Yards. (A Welsh yard is 40 inches in length, so a Welsh acre was slightly larger than an English half acre.)

The custom of burials at the church and surrounding cemeteries started around 750 AD. In 1538 the registration of births, marriages and deaths was started (by order of the Government); these were recorded in Latin. Prior to this date the inhabitants kept their own careful family records. It was not usual to show the age of the deceased in the parish register until the beginning of this century.

The old church was far larger than the present building and at the eastern end was a chancel-like addition called Ystumllyn chapel, the history of which is as follows: when the princely family of Bronyfoel came to reside in the old mansion at Ystumllyn following the outrage of the burning of the house and outbuildings and the shooting of Gruffydd ab John ab Goronwy, they started building the Island Chapel opposite the lands of Ystumllyn between Ynyscynhaiarn and the sea. Even today this is known as Ynys y Capel (the Chapel Island). The project was soon abandoned, however, and agreement was reached with the Ynyscynhaiarn church authorities which enabled a section to be built on the eastern end of the church – the family of Ystumllyn being responsible for the upkeep and repair. (It was said that, at the same time, Bettws Treflys was changed from a family chapel of Bronyfoel to a parish church). The porch or lychgate is as it was previously, roofed with thick slates of a colour and texture similar to those at Allt wen, Penmorfa. Inside are stone benches and here the needy would wait for the Wardens to distribute offerings and charity after the service was concluded. Parishioners made these contributions for the poor in the days before the Poor Law was passed.

The church is in a very isolated position, and this may be explained by the following note from *Origines Britannicae or Antiquities of the British Churches* by Edward Seelingfleet. 'When they were being harassed and victimised so cruelly by the pagans, they used to retreat to the most difficult and unlikely spots for their own safety and, as a rule, in these places they built a church convenient for their use, where they lived a secluded life.'

BUILDING THE PRESENT CHURCH IN 1832

The old church was demolished in 1832 and there is no record showing when it was first built, but the walls and its construction show that it was very old. The entrance door was in Early Gothic Style, the windows were plain and the pews similar to those at present. The pulpit and lectern were close together and there was no cross-section in the old church, as in the present one. The ceiling was covered in semi-circles and it had an old communion table and a parish chest (both now in the vestry). Apart from these and an old bier and ladder, which were in use in 1792, little remains of the old church, there being no trace of earlier foundations. An adjoining building, Beudy'r Ynys (The Island's Shippon) once belonged to the church and it is highly probable that the beams and roof timbers in this building once came from the old church There was once a mounting stone or steps in the yard in front of the porch, as there was only a bridle path leading over Moel y gadair to the island until 1832. In that year the present road was built, but even this is incomplete and hardly worthy of being the road leading to the Parish Church. There was another bridle path leading from Ystumllyn but this has been terribly neglected and is practicably impassable. It is said that water from the lake flooded round the island until 1760 when John Parry (Mr Price's steward) altered the course of the river to the eastern side. The late Rev John Jones of Mynydd Ednyfed, Vicar of Ynys and Criccieth, had a copy of a petition sent from Ynys Cynhaiarn to Zachary Pearce, Bishop of Bangor, in 1747, requesting a regular Sunday Service at the Church. The Bishop replied, however, that it was an island and that it was not possible to reach it at all times. Two zealous churchmen, Owen Efan of Tyddyniolyn (great-grandfather of the writer) and Owen Ellis of Cefnymeusydd, went on foot all the way to Bangor with the petition. When they were informed of the Bishop's excuses, they undertook to build a causeway, which is now the road over the place where the river used to be. However, services were only held on two Sundays out of three until the death of the Rev John Jones in the year 1863, when they succeeded in getting a service every Sunday. This was when the Rev Erasmus Parry accepted the living, through the efforts of Mrs Walker and her secretary.

Old Ynyschnhaiarn Church in the year 1784

THE CHURCH BELL

THE OPINIONS OF THE ELDERS OF THE BELL'S VIRTUES

In olden times it was generally believed that there was great virtue in the pealing of bells, it being thought that they created holiness in the ears of the listeners; that they cleared or purified the air (warding off storms and tempests), and also scared away evil spirits! Wynkin de Warde described the hatred of evil spirits to the sound of bells thus:

> The evil spirits that are in parts of the air or heaven are greatly worried when they hear the sound of a bell. That is the reason why bells are rung when there is thunder or a great tempest or rough stormy weather about, causing the evil spirits to be shamed and flee and not to encourage the storm.

It was customary about 80 years ago to ring a knell on the death of any parishioner and a vigil was kept each time the incumbent or verger came to a house to start the funeral. Hot drinks and funeral cake would be given to those who had journeyed from afar. The knell bell was also tolled for those who lay sick on their deathbed, this enabled prayers to be offered and the minister would hurry to give the Last Sacrament. (Note: The 6th Canon requests 'that whenever anyone is departing from this life, a bell should be rung, then the minister should hasten to carry out his duties'.)

The inscription on the old bell in Llan yr Ynys (Island Church) is as follows:

THE GIFT of WILLIAM PRICE, Esq, 1683
Vire X, RA X, OF RHIWLAS

The bell is now at Rhiwlas, when the new bell was given in its place. Everyone throughout the parish felt it was their special duty to attend Easter Communion. The heads of families together with the menservants and maids, would all attend Sul y Pasg Bach (Little Easter Sunday) – that is the first Sunday after Easter. The parish sexton would also go round the houses to collect his 'Easter pennies' usually receiving between four and six pence; most probably this is 'Peter's Pence' as we understand it. There was a sundial on the southwestern corner of the cemetery wall in olden times. The stone to which it was fastened, with the holes to secure it, can still be seen. The present dial was placed in the southern corner of the church wall in 1853, by William Jones of y Cwrt, Criccieth.

As previously stated Ynys Cynhaiarn (together with Bettws Treflys) was part of the living of St Catherine's Criccieth, and is attended by the Rector of Criccieth. A service was held on two Sundays out of three at Ynyscynhaiarn; on the third Sunday it was closed and a service held at Treflys! We find that at one time Ynyscynhaiarn was a chapel belonging to St Beuno's Penmorfa, because in a book published in 1728, called *Thesaurus Rerum Ecclesiasticarum* by John Ecton Esq (late Receiver General of the Clergy), 3rd edition with additions by Brown Willis, Ll.D, page 354, it states 'Penmorfa, R, cum Capella Cynhaiarn, D Eifionydd, alias Evioneth'.

The old building had become very insecure and dilapidated, the furniture inside was in bad condition and the roof of the chancel (or 'Stumllyn Chapel) was leaking badly. When the Rev John Jones, MA, was Rector and John Williams of Tuhwnt i'r bwlch and Elizeus Griffith of Bronygadair were Wardens, an appeal was made to R Watkin Price Esq of Rhiwlas for a fresh plot of land at the eastern end of the cemetery so that a new church could be built without disturbing the graves; even after extending the churchyard it was already full as the parish population was increasing enormously at the time. A further plot was received as a gift and it was decided to build the present building. The plans were prepared by Mr John Williams and the building costs were £800. There were six stone-masons working on the building – Harry Robert Parry and his sons, Robert Parry, William Robert Parry, and John Robert Parry, also Shon Griffith Shon and Robert Jones of Caedu, who is still alive in Criccieth. The carpenters were William Griffith of Plymouth, Griffith Jones of Tanlôn and his son William Jones. The slaters and plasterers were Gruffydd Roberts and his son, Robert Roberts of Tremadog, formerly of Efail bach. The glazier was Evan Ellis of Pwllheli and the painters Rhys ap Robert Prys (Price) of Plasdu, Llanarmon. The flooring flags came from the quarry at Tyddynllwyn. Voluntary donations brought in a goodly sum, leaving about £200 to be collected. This was obtained under a mortgage, which was signed by about 20 parishioners. The interest was paid by a small tax at the church, from which also were paid other expenses pertaining to the wardens. In 1850 this tax was abolished when the landowners and the ratepayers agreed to pay the costs through donations, each to pay the same amount. And so during the year, through the efforts of the wardens, Henry Llewellyn of Carregfelen and Robert Isaac Jones of Tremadog, the whole debt on the mortgage was repaid. The mortgage is now in the parish chest. Mrs Walker of Hendregadredd donated the organ to be used for church purposes only; she also gave the bier cloth, the grate and chimney-piece and the chair within the altar rails. This chair was made by Richard Daniel (Joiner) from oak wood taken from the church at Llanfihangel-y-pennant in Eifionydd, and the word 'Ynyscynhaiarn' was carved by John Roberts of Llanystumdwy.

Note: There is an old manuscript stating that there was an old yew tree in the churchyard at the time of the Rev Robert Anwyl, but no-one living today remembers seeing it. There is a small yew tree planted by the porch entrance by one of the wardens (the secretary for the year 1846).

The following inscription can be found on the old chest: *WRHW 1727.*

None of the old 'boxes' can be found today and only one oak chest; the other is of a later date. There is one 'collection ladle' with the inscription RIJ, RR 1846 carved on it.

TERRIER OF YNYS CYNHAIARN CHURCH

There is a copy of this account (shown below) in the parish chest, proven in 1784, during the living of the Rev Robert Anwyl MA This is given in full in the language in which it was written – English.

> A true and perfect Account and Terrier of all Tythes, Pensions, Profits, Rights, goods and implements, belonging to the Rectory, Parish and Parish Church of Ynyscynhaiarn in the County of Carnarvon, and the Diocese of Bangor, taken made and renewed 10th day December 1784 and exhibited before the Worshipful Thomas Beven, Doctor of Laws, Chancellor of the aforesaid Diocese, at the primary Visitation of the Right Reverend Father in God, John, Lord Bishop of Bangor held at Bangor aforesaid, the 14th day of September in the year aforesaid.
>
> There are belonging to the Rector, First a Modus of 2 pence for each Farm in lieu of Tythe Hay, also the Tythe of all Corn in kind. Also the Tythe of Wool being the tenth part, and three half pence for each Wether sold unsheared. Also the Tythe of Lambs in their proper kind, and the custom concerning them is this, if a person's number is one he pays 3d, if 2—6d; if 3—9d; if 4—12d; if 5—15d; if 6—18d; if 7 he pays a Lamb, the Rector, paying back 9d; if 8—6d; if 9—3d; if 10 the Rector hath the lamb complete. And in like manner for every number above 10, and every lamb sold before the time of Tything, 3d the usual time of Tything is some few days before the first day of July, being Criccieth Fair Day. The lambs are all turned together, the owner takes his choice Lamb and his choice Ewe Lamb then the Rector takes his choice Lamb, and so on alternately until the Rector hath his number. Also the Tythe of Kids and Geese, one out of three, one only out of threescore of each kind. Also the Tythe of Pigs, one out of each Litter if there are three or more in the Litter. For every Mare and Colt, two pence. For every Cow and Calf, three half pence, excepting the first Calf, for which a penny is paid. The Tythe of Hemp and Honey in kind, and also Flax. For every wedding five shillings. An oblation of one shilling for every churching of women. Oblations at Funerals at Discretion. The Tythe of Eggs about Easter, two for each Cock, one for each Hen. Easter dues, six pence from each Married couple, two pence from each person of age to communicate. There is also due to the Parish Clerk a shilling for every wedding, for every Funeral oblations at discretion, there is due to him from the Rector, two pence for every churching of Women, and two pence from each married couple as Easter Dues. Belonging to the said Parish are first, the Parish Church containing in length with the Chancel 62 feet, in breadth 13 feet inside. Within and belonging to which are one Communion Table, with a covering for the same of Blue Grey Linsey. Also one Linen cloth for the same, with a Napkin; one Pewter Flagon; one Pewter Paten; one Silver Chalice with a cover engraved underneath, Ex. Dono. WP Arm. 11:11½; two Boxes for the Offertory; two Chests; one with two locks, the other without one; one Pulpit and Reading Desk; one Stone Font with a cover; one Pulpit Cushion; one folio Welch Bible; one folio Welch Common Prayer Book; two 8vo. Welch

Common Prayer Books; one Bier; one Surplice; two Parchment Register books, one beginning in 1692 and ending 1791 imperfect; the other beginning in 1772 and continued to the present time; one Paper Register Book according to an Act of Parliament, made to prevent Clandestine Marriages; one Bell, one Ladder, three Spades, one Shovel, and one pickaxe. There are 14 young Ash Trees growing in the churchyard. In Testimony of the truth of the above mentioned Particulars and of every of them, we the Minister, Church Wardens, and Principal inhabitants, have set our hands, the aforesaid 10th day of September, 1784.

(signed)

ROBERT ANWYL, Rector

ROBERT GRIFFITH, Churchwarden

Owen Ellis, Cefnymeusydd
Edward Jones, Cwmbach
John Jones, Tyddyniolyn
Rowland Thomas, Tuhwnt i'r bwlch

DETAILS OF THE PRESENT CHURCH, THE ORGAN &C.

The organ which has been placed in the gallery, was once in use at Tremadoc Church, Mr WA Madocks having purchased it from D Ellis Nanney, Barrister of Gwynfryn. Councillor Nanney is said to have paid £300 to the makers (Flight & Robson) when it was new. The case is solid Mahogany and the diapason is very valuable. It has a melodious tone and was in use at Tremadoc Church for over 40 years until being replaced by a new instrument. Mrs Walker of Hendregadredd bought the old organ in 1854 for £30, but spent a considerable sum in setting it up and carrying out repairs; it now makes a handsome ornament to the church. In donating it to Ynyscynhaiarn Church, Mrs Walker made a provision that the parishioners had no right to sell it or move it, but could transfer it to another church if it was no longer required.

The present church measures 49 feet in length by 15 feet in width; the transept is 14 feet by 11 feet and the vestry is 11 feet by 11 feet. The length of the present burial ground is 168 feet by 96 feet at its centre. In the transept there are ten pews on a sloping floor with the names of the farmhouses or residences to which they belong, such as Y Garreg wen, Tyddyn-ysguboriau, Penamser, Cefnymeusydd isa, Eisteddfa, Tyddyniolyn, Hendregadno, Cefnymeusydd ucha and WO Gore. There are two long pews, one on each side of the Communion table – one used by Bronygadair and the other by Hendregadredd.

In the body of the church there are eight pews on the right hand side and seven on the left, the name 'RW Price' is shown on those on the right and 'Tremadoc' on those on the left. The pulpit, reading desk and the verger's seat, one above the other, are on the left of the church; a wooden font with cover, very plain and unadorned by the door (it can be seen from the Terrier on a preceding page that there was a stone font in the old church but no-one knows where this is now). There is a gallery with stairs leading up to it on the right hand side of the church where, as previously stated, the organ is installed. The space below the gallery stairs has been adapted to accommodate tools and grave digging implements. The name-plates of many families buried in the churchyard were fixed to the walls and on the front of the gallery, but for some unknown reason these were removed, an action which caused much distress to the families. There are two arched windows on the side, a small one in the transept, with a slightly larger east window with stained glass in the upper half. The Ten Commandments have been carved on a board fixed to one side of the east window and the Creed an the other; these were repaired some years ago by Mrs Ignatius Williams.

On the south wall in the transept there is a memorial (in Latin) to Councillor Walker, as follows:

In Memoriam
ISAACI JOHANIS WALKER
Juris Consulti de Medii Templo
Filii unigeniti de Lieut Col Walker,
et Louise uxori Ejus
de Hendregadredd.
Obeit quinto Maii, AD, 1862
Amii—aœatis 45

Another plaque (in English) for Lieut Col Walker is as follows:

In Memory
Of
LIEUT. COLONEL ISAAC WALKER,
of Hendregadredd,
Who died December 8th, 1865, aged 80.
He was the eldest son of the Rev William Walker of Wisbeach, Cambridgeshire
and Lynstead Priory, Suffolk, by Anna Maria his wife.
He was educated at Trinity College, Cambridge.
Entered the Army in 1805, in the 88 Regiment, or Connaught
Ranger, through the Peninsular War.

Note: re Lieut Col Walker: In addition to his biography, the following further information may be of interest to the reader: He was educated, first at Wisbeach Grammar School and then Trinity College, Cambridge, following graduation he entered the Army. His father was Rector of Terrington, St John's, Cambridgeshire. At the end of the American War he went to Canada in a sailing boat with another Army Officer on 'official business' but bad weather and mist marred the voyage and they were shipwrecked close to Pwllheli. He later resigned from the Army, sending in his papers to the Horse Guards, and settled in Bangor. His partner was Colonel M McGregor, who married the daughter of Sir Love Parry of Llanbedrog. Col Walker was wounded whilst fighting in Spain and he was also decorated with a medal and four clasps. Mrs Walker was the daughter of John Balk Esq of Crowland in Norfolk, and her mother was a descendant of one of the French refugees at the time of the Huguenot outrages in France.

Lieut Col Isaac Walker, Hendregadredd (Late) 88th Regt of Foot (Connaught Rangers)

On the transept wall of Ynyscynhaiarn Church there is a memorial to Captain Jones of Cefnymeusydd Uchaf, as follows:

To commemorate
A candid, upright, honest man,
Capt Thomas Jones, Cefnmeusydd,
Late of the Brig 'Esther'
who died August 19th 1843,
aged 56 years.
Also Elizabeth, his wife,
she died July 3rd, 1861,
aged 67 years.
Erected by his son, JR Jones, 1867.

There used to be memorials on the walls of the old church – that of Henry Griffith (black marble) and Catherine Parry (red slate). These were later removed to the entrance of the present church.

In the Vestry room (above the chimney-breast) are two slate memorials and carved on them is the following:

Here lyeth the body of Henry Griffith of Penamser, who was interred 4th May, AD 1755, aged 85.

Here lyeth the body of Jane Lloyd, the wife of Henry Griffith, who was interred 29th *May, AD 1734, aged 74.*

Here lyeth the body of Catherine Parry, the daughter of Henry Griffith by Jane Lloyd his wife. Heires of Penamser, the wife of John Vaughan, Penmaen (Dyfi), she was interred AD 1750, aged 67.

A LIST OF THE RECTORS OF YNYSCYNHAIARN

The following list (as complete as possible) of the Rectors of Ynyscynhaiarn and Criccieth was found in the Criccieth Register of AD 1538. 'Decantus de Eifionydd, Rectoria de Merthyr vi, marc cum Capella Treflys xls. Ynyscynhaiarn vii, marc et Eclesia Krickieth D — David Lloyd, Rector.'

Rev David Lloyd.................................. 1538
Rev William Jones. 1621
Rev Thomas Meredith........................... 1627
Rev John Gethin.................................... 1638

It is not known whether the rector who held office at the time of the Republican Government of Cromwell was allowed to retain his living

Rev Francis Lloyd................................. 1674
Rev Humphrey Humphreys 1677
Rev John Anwyl (curate) 1692
Rev Edward Lloyd (Rector).................. 1695 died 1727

Rev Richard Griffith, BA .... 1727 died 1746
Rev John Jones, Bronygadair................ 1746 died 1772
Rev Robert Anwyl, MA......................... 1772 died 1789
Rev David Ellis...................................... 1789 died 1795
Rev William Evans................................ 1796 died 1817
Rev Owen Jones 1817
Rev John Jones, MA.............................. 1827 died 1863
Rev Erasmus Parry .... 1862 died 1883
Rev John Lloyd Jones, Rector of Criccieth and Treflys (1883)
Rev David Lloyd Jones.......................... 1884
Rev Llewellyn R Hughes, MA 1889

NOTES CONCERNING THE LIST OF RECTORS

Richard Griffith, who once lived at Garregfelen, later made his home at Eisteddfa, where he died in 1746. His remains lie in the cemetery at Criccieth, and there is a Latin inscription on his gravestone. His family lived at Eisteddfa until 1848 and his grandson died at Penygroes y Gesail in the year 1891, aged 85 years.

The Rev Robert Anwyl, MA, Rector of Criccieth, Ynyscynhaiarn and Treflys, who died in 1789, was the son of William Anwyl, a descendant of the lineage of Hengae of Talyllyn in Meirionydd. (In 1636) He lived at Bachysaint (there being no Rectory attached to the living until 1829). Several children were born to them at Bachysaint and Mrs Anwyl outlived her husband by many years.

The Rev Zacheus Hughes, son of Trefan, was ordained to the living in 1789, but died before he could take up his duties.

The Rev David Ellis, who came here from Amlwch where he officiated in 1782, lived at Ty Newydd in Llanystumdwy, as the Rectory was not attached to the living until later. He was an excellent bard and historian and was born at Hafodymeirch in Meirion. He left an endowment of £200 the interest of which went towards the teaching of the Welsh language to eight children: these to be children of members of the three churches. If no candidates were available the money had to be devoted to repairs to the church and nothing else. The following is inscribed on his gravestone at Criccieth Churchyard,

Here lieth the remains of the Rev D Ellis, Late Rector of this Parish, interred on 11th May 1795, aged 56 years. An excellent linguist and bard, he was diligent in his efforts and conscientious in his calling as a Minister of the Gospel. He heartily hated flattery and hypocrisy in himself as in others.

(These words are said to have been written by Dafydd Ddu Eryri).

Epitaph for the Rev Dafydd Ellis, Rector of Criccieth (the work of Gwallter Mechain):

Worshippers, citizens of God, will love
A man of constant labour;

Hypocrisy in any faction
His soul's instinct desired not.

Through a brave and industrious life a man
Eminent and faithful;
Behold the grave, sweet song's end.
Where Aaron's son is laid.

Though cold earth stoop, and place him
In his lowly grave;
After his sleep, the hand of Jesus Christ
Will raise him from this stony bed. – GWALLTER MECHAIN 1798

The Rev William Evans gave up his post in favour of his son (due to blindness) some years before he died. He was the son of John Jones of Brynhir, Criccieth. He lived at Mynydd Ednyfed Fawr; he built the present building. His wife was the daughter of Nanhoron Isa, one of his descendants is the Rev J Parry Morgan, Rector of Llanrhaiadr DC.

There is an epitaph at Denio Cemetery, Pwllheli:

Gaynor, Relict of William Evans, Rector of Criccieth and Ynyscynhaiarn. She died on 27th February 1828, aged 79. Also, their grandson, William Morris, second son of the late Rev Robert Morris, Rector of Edeyrn. He died April 17th 1833, aged 14 years.

The Rev John Jones MA lived at his own mansion at Mynydd Ednyfed fechan near Criccieth. He purchased a plot of land at Tyn'llan, Criccieth, on which he built a Rectory. He married Miss Massey from Chester; they had one son who died a bachelor. The following is inscribed on his gravestone at Criccieth cemetery.

In memory of the late Rev John Jones, MA, of Mynydd Ednyfed, who departed this life on 8th February 1863, aged 67. Rector of Criccieth and Llanfihangel y Pennant for 45 years, also Rural Dean of Eifionydd. Also Ann, wife of the Rev John Jones, and eldest daughter of the Venble Roger Massey, Archdeacon of Bwmstaple (sic), Devon, Died October 2nd, 1868, aged 75. Also Owen Massey Jones, Esqr., of Mynydd Ednyfed, only child of the Rev John Jones and Ann Jones, died March 20th, 1870, aged 36.

The Rev John Jones held English services at Tremadoc Church (or Chapel of Ease) for 33½ years on Sunday afternoons, free of charge. He was assisted by the Rev David W Thomas (now Canon Thomas, St Anne's), curate in 1856. The congregation gave him a silver salver, worth £33 10s in recognition of his services. He was a peaceful gentleman, kindly and true-hearted. He was also a Justice of the Peace for the commote and attended the Petty Sessions at Tremadoc for nearly 40 years. His home was an 'ever open door' to the poor and during his term of office the church of Llanfihangel y Pennant was repaired and Ynys Cynhaiarn church was rebuilt. He had a curate for services at Llanfihangel y Pennant.

The Rev Erasmus Parry was a native of Llandyssul in Ceredigion. At this time the living of Llanfihangel-y-pennant was separate from Criccieth and Ynys. These were combined from the year 1795 until 1863. His widow is still alive; they had children.

The Rev John Lloyd Jones was native of Rhyl and was Curate of St Beuno's Church, Holyhead, for a number of years. He was appointed Rector of Criccieth and Treflys in 1883. This industrious gentleman was responsible for building the church of St Deiniol (English) in the old but rapidly expanding borough of Criccieth. The new church is a fine and splendid building, an adornment to the town and an essential place of worship for Criccieth's visitors and others. He was also responsible for repairing St Michael's Treflys for the benefit of the parishioners.

The Rev David Lloyd Jones, Ynys Cynhaiarn vicar in 1884, was promoted Vicar of Amlwch.

The Rev Llewellyn R Hughes, MA was appointed in the year 1889. His Curate officiated at Treflys and Ynys as additional services were held in the benefices when the present Vicar took office. Two Curates and two meetings were kept – one at Ynys Cynhaiarn and the other at the School House, Pentrefelin.

Three services were held at St John's Porthmadog and two at Tremadoc. A rectory was built conveniently close to St John's Church, Porthmadog in 1890. The site was a gift from FM Roche, Esq.

THE CHURCHWARDENS FOR YNYSCYNHAIARN FOR THE PAST HALF CENTURY WITH DATES

According to ancient custom in this parish, the Rector chose his warden and the parishioners chose the other. On Easter Sunday, the Rector would announce the name of his warden who would then, in turn, name the parishioners' choice to serve with him. They would both go to Pwllheli to be sworn in and also to hand in the records containing the lists of births, marriages and burials.

Robert Davies, Borth and Robert Owen, Glanmorfa Bach. 1778
Griffith Williams, Eisteddfa and Griffith Jones, Llwynmafon. 1779
Owen Williams, Cwm Mawr and Robert Jones, Mynydd Du. 1781
Wm Davies, Tanrallt and Hugh Pritchard for Mrs Jones, Brongadair. 1782
John Jones, Tyddyniolyn and John Roberts, Brongadair bach. 1783
Richard Humphreys, Tan'rallt and Robert Davies, Tyddynadi. 1784

Humphrey Williams, Llanerch and Owen Ellis, Cefnymeusydd.................. 1785
John Williams, Tyddynysguboriau and Wm Owen, Drwsdugoed................ 1786
Owen Williams, Cwmmawr and Owen Evans, Garregfelen.......................... 1789
Rowland Thomas, Tuhwnt i'r bwlch and Robert Roberts, Twllycae........ 1789-90
Owen Roberts, Garreg wen and Griffith Williams, Eisteddfa. 1791-92
Griffith Jones, Llwynmafon Ucha' and Griffith Williams, same address...... 1793
John Jones, Tyddyniolyn and Evan Ellis, Bronygadair bach......................... 1794
John Jones, Tyddyniolyn and John Owen Tuhwnt i'r bwlch......................... 1795
Owen Ellis, Cefnymeusydd isa and Humphrey Williams, Llanerch............. 1796
Humphrey Williams, Llanerch and Hugh Evans, Caegwenllian.................... 1797
Griffith Roberts, Tyddynllwyn and Richard Jones, Cwmbach. 1798
Owen Ellis, Cefnymeusydd and William Roberts. 1799
Richard Griffith, Eisteddfa and Owen Ellis, Cefnmeusydd................. 1799-1800
Robert Roberts, Efail Bach and Griffith Jones, Llwynmafon. 1801
John Jones, Tyddyniolyn and Robert Roberts, Efail bach. 1802
From 1802 – 1809 there is a gap in the records
Ellis Owen, Cefnymeusydd and Robert Roberts. 1810
Owen Roberts, Garreg wen and John Jones, Tyddyniolyn. 1811
Richard Thomas, Cefnymeusydd and Owen Roberts. 1812
Evan Williams and Richard Thomas, Cefnmeusydd Ucha'.......................... 1813
Robert Lloyd and D Humphreys, Bronyfoel... 1814
The records end here.

Ellis Owen of Cefnymeusydd and Owen Roberts of Twllycae, held the offices of wardens for many years after these last dates. John Williams (Agent) of Tuhwnt-i'r-bwlch and Elizeus Griffith of Bronygadair were in office in 1832. The writer held the office of churchwarden in the parish from the year 1843 until 1864, together with Henry Llewelyn of Garregfelen, Robert Roberts of Bronygadair and J Morris of Tyddynadi.

ASSISTANCE FOR THE POOR

It should be known that the rate known as the Poor Rate was not in force in this parish until 1815. Up to then the parishioners would meet at the church or at Pentrefelin every six weeks (sometimes more often) to discuss the parish problems and to consult the wardens as to the amount of expenses incurred. It was discovered from the old registers that a rate of 2d in the £ per annum would suffice for the years 1778–1810 and that the total sum of the rate would amount to £7 to £10 at that time!

The parishioners were a close-knit community and would know who really required assistance – the very old, the sick, the infirm – although the poor made every effort to help themselves as much as possible. There was a certain stigma to being 'on the Parish' and this was a slur to be avoided. If help was sought it would usually be granted 'in kind' – potatoes, flour, clothing, etc. Before the building of the Embankment the population of the area was quite sparse with relatively few finding it necessary to seek parish assistance, the addition of the 'Vale of Madog' however, made a great change; much more relief work was necessary. The present system of Poor Rate is very costly and is due to high wages, offices, etc.

THE SEXTONS OF YNYSCYNHAIARN

Sylfanus Williams, Garthyrhebog.	1777
William Jones, Cwrt, Criccieth.	1815
John Williams, Plas isa (known as Shon Wm Ellis)	1825
Dafydd Shon James, Tremadoc.	1838
Morris Jones (Meirig Idris)	1855
John Roberts	1859
Griffith Roberts, Mynydd Du.	1866
His wife Margaret Roberts is the present sexton	1892

Those who held this post in olden times were called Parish Clerks. Their duties did not involve tolling the bell, opening graves and burying the dead. Since the Reformation both jobs have been combined in rural parishes. According to canon 91, the choice of sexton is the Vicar's duty; he must be over 20 years of age, be able to read and write, have musical ability, and have the right to be paid for their labours through a Church Court.

In this parish, however, the custom is for the remuneration to be decided by discussion and agreement between the Vicar and his wardens; in olden times the emoluments in this parish were very good. Nowadays the sexton depends on what are called 'offerings' for weddings and funerals for although the parish had the right to decide sexton's wages, when the tythe system was re-arranged in 1838 this apparently was neglected.

FOLK LORE

It has been said by some of the old folk that, at certain times, lights could be seen in the church at night time; this strange occurrence would be followed by the death of a well known or public figure in the parish. One of the parishioners told me that about 30 years ago, whilst accompanied by the curate, for about five minutes they watched a light moving in the church from the chancel to the doorway, illuminating each window in turn and then extinguished as if it was a candle held by a man. His father and mother both died within 12 months. A family at Treflys also say that they have seen lights at night time in the church at Ynys.

This account has been given to illustrate the credulity and superstition of the simple harmless people. An explanation for the phenomenon is that it was marsh gas arising from the nearby lake.

EPITAPHS IN YNYSCYNHAIARN CHURCHYARD OR THE CHURCH OF ST CYNHAIARN IN YNYS, EIFIONYDD

The recording of epitaphs in the churchyard at Ynys (as in other churchyards) has not been an easy task, and those given in this book are the fruits of very diligent and hard labours. I gratefully acknowledge the substantial assistance given by that painstaking and thorough historian, Mr Robert Evans, formerly of Pentrefelin. As the graves and burial places are scattered these records are not in chronological order – the information is taken from each gravestone as we came to it. In some cases erosion of the lettering has made it impossible to record the details completely.

It was found that more than half of the graves are unmarked – only the green turf and a slight mound marking the site. It is possible that no other cemetery in the area is as badly neglected as that of Ynyscynhaiarn for, although a few are neat and tidy, many are in a disgraceful state and neglected by the families of those who are buried there. This is proof of the disrespect shown for the departed. Perhaps after reading this book there may be an improvement.

THE EPITAPHS

The names and dates are correct, but the remainder of the inscriptions have been omitted due to lack of space.

Here lyeth the body of Jane Lloyd, who dyed 24th July 1721, aged 79.

Here lyeth the body of Daniel Roberts, who dyed 28th December 1717, aged 80.

Catherine, daughter of David Williams, dyed 25th December 1734, aged 9 years. Also the above named David Williams, dyed 3rd August 1776, aged 89 years.

(It is believed that the above named DW was the son of S Williams of Brondanw. It is said that he once lived at Ystumllyn, but it was at Bach y Saint that he died).

Here lyeth the body of John Parry, Garregfelen, late agent of William Price of Rhiwlas, who departed this life on 17th January 1765, aged 82. Also here lyeth the remains of Jane, his wife, who departed this life on 19th July 1781, aged 80.

(The above J Parry came from Llangybi. Jane Parry's maiden name was Griffith and after the death of her husband her niece, Mary Jones, came to live with her at Garregfelen. Mary Jones became an executor when her aunt died and later married Owen Evans, son of Evan Thomas of Penyclogwyn y Gest by his first wife, Margaret Morris. A sister of Mary Jones lived at a place called Glanllyn, on the right of Tanyclogwyn, on Garregfelen land. She was the mother of Owen and Morris Owen of Garregfelen, as they were called; the first named was the father of Mr Robert Owen of Portmadoc, formerly agent of the Rhiw Quarry. They, that is his father and mother, went to live at Llanfrothen, and there they were buried.)

GW, 51, 1766 KW, aged 24, 1732
WW aged 37, 1774

Griffith Williams, Eisteddfa, who was buried January 4th 1799, aged 58.

Here lyeth the body of Margaret Jones, of Drwsdugoed, widow of the Rev Rowland Jones, late Rector of Edeyrn, who departed this life 5th May 1762, aged 75. Here also lyeth the remains of Rowland Jones, son of John Jones, of Bronygadair, Gent. by Mary his wife, who departed this life on 12th May 1799, in the 39th year of his age.

Here lyeth the body of Mary Roberts of Bangor, who departed this life 9th June 1767, aged 75. Also, Margaret Roberts, daughter of the above mentioned dyed September 29th 1820, aged 78.

HP, Æ, 50, 1709 RR, formerly of Beudy mawr

Underneath this stone are interred the remains of John Jones, Bronygadair, Gent, who dyed much esteemed and respected on 30th April 1778, aged 51. Here also, are interred the remains of Mary Jones, wife of the above named John Jones, who dyed on 30th March 1817, aged 92. Also, Mary, daughter of the above-named John and Mary Jones, second wife of the late William Williams, Esq, of Bryngoleu, Abererch, who died on 12th October 1838, aged 75.

John Jones is reputed to have obtained some relief to his eyes after visiting St Cybi's Well in Llangybi. W Williams of Bryngoleu, was a widower in 1788; he had three sons, William, Lewis and Lieut John Williams. He died at Bronygadair on December 3, 1837, aged 58, and was buried at Abererch. He had estates at Llandecwyn, Merioneth. Around the year 1788 he was on his way home after collecting rents when his horse stumbled just below the shippon of Bronygadair Bbach on the old road. He sustained a broken leg in the fall and was found shortly after by William Williams of Pwllbudr, Glanbyl. William carried the injured man on his back to Bronygadair, and there he stayed under the care of Robert Isaac Roberts, the bone setter, until his leg got better. Later Mr Williams married Mary, daughter of John Jones, Gent, and his wife Mary, of Bronygadair. John Jones was a solicitor and steward to Richard Tavistock Price, Esq of Rhiwlas. He was the son of the Rev Rowland Jones, Curate of Llanfihangel y Pennant. His father became Rector of Edeyrn and there he died.

William, son of Elizeus Griffith, and Mary, his wife of Bronygadair, died March 12th 1827, aged 2 years and 4 months.
Owen Lloyd Griffith, son of the above named died January 11th 1864, aged 40. Mary, wife of Elizeus Griffith, died 14th February 1863, aged 76.

The grave of AH aged 53, 1719 and JC aged 56, 1720.

Richard Thomas, Tyhwnt-i'r-bwlch, 1751, aged 12 years. And also Elizabeth Evans of Breubwll, Meirionydd, first wife of Rowland Thomas of Tyhwnt-i'r-bwlch, who died 20th May 1764, aged 24 years. Also the above mentioned Rowland Thomas, who died September 22nd 1829, aged 88 years. Also to the memory of John Thomas, MA Head Master of Beaumaris Grammar School, who was burried near the altar at Llandegfan, Anglesey, March 27th 1769, aged 33 years. Also to the memory of the Rev Richard Thomas, BA, who was burried at Ruthin, April 23rd 1780, aged 27. Also to the memory of Ann Thomas, Cefnymeusydd, buried in this churchyard December 24th 1841, aged 92. And also to the memory of Gaynor Thomas, Fferam Bailey, Trefdraeth, Anglesey, who died February 3rd 1811, aged 89 years. Four sons and two daughters of Thomas Rowlands, Tyhwnt-i'r-bwlch, by Jane Jones, his wife.

In memory of Thomas Rowland, aged 55, 1757. Here also, lieth the remains of Thomas Rowland, who departed this life the 21st day of July, 1789 in the 10th year of his age. Ann Humphreys, second wife of Rowland Thomas, late of Tyhwnt-i'r-bwlch, who departed this life on 1st May 1817, aged 74.

HJ : JH

Jane Jones, Tuhwnt-i'r-bwlch, died 30th July 1750, aged 44, after giving birth to Humphrey and Evan Thomas who died both infants.

Ellis Owen, Cefnmeusydd, noted Cattle Dealer, aged 65, 1757. Also his son, Owen Ellis, of the same place, who was buried March 22nd 1803, aged 70 years.

Margaret Pritchard, wife of Ellis Owen, and mother of Owen Ellis, died July 27th 1784.

Ann Thomas, Cefnymeusydd (mother of 11 children) who died December 18th 1841, aged 93. Her daughters were Jane, Elin, Gaynor, Margaret, Ann, Mary and Catherine. The seven sisters were married, but Ellis Owen was not. The following died in infancy, Catherine in 1784, Thomas in 1781 and Ellis in 1775.

Robert Ellis, and his wife, Jane Jones, of Hendre-ddu in Dolbenmaen had the following children; Ellis, Owen, Rhys and Margaret. Ellis Owen, the eldest (cattle dealer) was the third husband of Margaret Pritchard, Cefnmeusydd Isaf. Owen married the daughter of Morris Parry (formerly of Cefnmeusydd Isaf) and went to live at Brychyni and from there to Rhedynog, Abererch. He was the grandfather of the Rev Owen Jones, Plasgwyn, and Shon Cawrdaf, Abererch. Rhys did not marry but joined his brother Owen as a cattle dealer. A white bullock of enormous size came into his possession and this was exhibited in many places in England and Scotland. There is said to be an English book which gives the history of 'Rice Owen with his white bullock'. The family claim that he died in Scotland between 1760 and 1780, leaving behind valuable property for which they searched far and wide. It is not known whether Robert Ellis and his wife, Jane Jones, had more than one daughter (the above Margaret), neither is it known whether they reached marriageable age.

Here lyeth the body of Harry Edwards, who died 7th February 1712, aged 77.

E G Æ. 90, 1727.
R P XXXII, 1698.

(This is the oldest inscription in the cemetery.)

Here lyeth the body of Owen Humphrey, who dyed XNI 14th 1714.

Lowry Parry, wife of David Parry, Llwynymafon isaf, died June 1822, aged 69. Also the above named David Parry, died August 6th 1827, aged 78.

(They had three sons and five daughters, Harry, Griffith, Ellen Jane and Mary were deaf and dumb.)

Underneath lie the remains of Richard Thomas, Gent, of Cefnymeusydd ucha', who died 22nd February 1814, aged 69 years. Also Ann, his wife, who died 16th March 1828, aged 68.

Underneath are the remains of Capt Thomas Jones, Cefnymeusydd, who died August 19th 1843. Elizabeth, his wife, died July 3rd 1861, aged 67 years.

In memory of Capt John Richard Jones, Cefnymeusydd, who departed this life 17th March 1870, aged 44 years.

Richard Humphreys, Tanyclogwyn, who died August 10th 1836, aged 62 years. Also Mary, his wife, who died August 4th 1847, aged 70 years.

Sacred to the memory of James, third son of Charles Forbes, Esq of the Island of Jamaica who died 1st April 1830, aged 22.

He went to Clynnog, lodging at Bryn Cynan, on the night preceding the accident. The following morning he went to a high place by Llyn Gele and ran and threw himself over the edge – a drop of around 25 feet. Farm labourers working in a nearby field ran to the spot where he had fallen and heard him say the word 'dead' three times. He died shortly afterwards and when the body was searched a note was found in his pocket in which he wrote that he intended to commit suicide, thus giving proof of the nature of his death. He had been staying at Ystumllyn, with his brother and a Mr Neil, and it was from here that he went to Clynnog to die. He was brought back to Ynys for burial.

Cadwaladr Jones, Ty'r Capel, Tremadoc, who died April 12th 1831, aged 76 years. Catherine, his wife, who died July 23rd 1846, aged 90 years.

(She was the daughter of Wm Davies, Excise man, Tan'rallt.)

Catherine Owen, Trwyntywyn, died October 9th 1868, aged 76. Hugh Owen, her husband, died January 18th 1875, aged 89.

(Parents of the late Owen Owen Esq, Llwynrhudol.)

Morris Griffith, Llwynmafon, died November 24th 1869, aged 67.

Harry Llewelyn, Garregfelen, died February 13th 1878, aged 67.

Robert Hughes, Morfa Bychan, died June 14th 1823, aged 45 years. Ellin, his daughter (wife of Owen Lewis, Manchester), *who died July 25th 1844, aged 34. Also, Margaret, wife of the above Robert Hughes, who died June 12th 1876, aged 88 years.* (Parents of the Rev Hugh Hughes, Gelli dara, Lleyn.)

Ann Griffith, Beudy Glas, who died May 1874, aged 75 years. William Griffith, her husband, who died December 8th 1877, aged 72 years.

Here were buried two children of Samuel and Ann Griffiths, Tremadoc. Elizabeth, who died January 28th 1833, aged 2 years. Robert, who died August 15th 1831, aged 7 years. Samuel Griffith, their father, who died October 6th 1835, aged 40 years.

Samuel is sealed in earth,—his son
And daughter together;
One day the three shall rise
From this place into joy. – BARD OF TREFLYS

Ann Griffith, his wife, who died April 26th 1871, aged 69 years.

Robert Williams, Miller, who died January 21st 1876, aged 79.

Catherine Ellis, wife of John Williams, Penystumllyn, who died in 1790, aged 51 years. John Williams, her husband, who died in 1812, aged 76 years.

The Lord when it is time, at the end
Will raise me from earth;
And when the doors of the world's graves
Open at one word.

Catherine Ellis was the daughter of David Ellis, Bodychain, and grand daughter of the lawyer, David Ellis Nanney, of Gwynfryn. Her husband, J Williams, was the son of Berth, Llanllyfni. John Williams had been living at Tyddynysguboriau and rented Nhyra from the same landowner before he moved to Penystumllyn. That is the reason why Nhyra is still attached to Penystumllyn. John Williams was father of Janet Williams, second wife of Robert Roberts, Twllycae. Their children were William Jones of Penystumllyn, David Jones of Penbryn mawr, Llanllyfni, John Jones of Caerdyni, Margaret Jones of Nhyra uchaf, and Mary Jones of Cwmbach.

William Jones, Penystumllyn, their son, who died in 1821 aged 55.

John Jones, Penystumllyn, who died November 9th 1853, aged 43 years.

To the right of his father and grandfather he lies
To this place where he wished to be buried,
Confident that on Judgement Day
He would be at the right hand of the Saviour.

Thomas Williams, Garthyrhebog, who died November 27th 1841, aged 79 years. Ellin, his wife, who died January 30th 1849, aged 74 years.

Ann, wife of Robert Roberts, Twllycae, who died October 20th 1767, aged 40 years. Also, RR, her husband, who died April 12th 1803, aged 80 years. Jannet, second wife of Robert Roberts, who died February 6th 1828, aged 80 years.

Owen Roberts, The Goat (Twllycae) who died October 16th 1847, aged 63 years. Jane, his wife, who died October 1861, aged 88 years.

Every moment, every breath,
In the passage of sad life
Will bring you to some grave,
Through the minutes that are numbered. – EO

Owen Jones, Glazier (Tremadoc), who died March 13th 1846, aged 34 years. Elizabeth, his wife, who died July 3rd 1846, aged 30 years, also their infants who died.

So strange their heavy slumber, where they lie
Not a word they speak,
The light of day they see not,
They wait through a long night.

One light morning, they will see each other,
And arise from sleep
Then into Glory,
Swiftly from Ynys they will depart. – EO

Catherine Roberts, second wife of Griffith Prichard (the Baker), who died July 11th 1812, aged 59 years. The above named Griffith Prichard, who died November 15th 1823, aged 89 years.

He planted a sycamore tree in the garden of Penybryn, saying 'if I live maybe the tree will grow large enough to provide my coffin timbers'. His son was Owen Griffith, Penygarnedd. Jannet Jones, Griffith Prichard's first wife, was the mother of the above Owen Griffith, who died February 17th 1801.

Ann Griffith, wife of Owen Griffith, Penygarnedd, died April 2nd 1833, aged 75 years. Owen Griffith, her husband, died December 27th 1850, aged 85 years.

John Jones, Caerdyni, who died June 7th 1851, aged 73 years.

S LL, aged 62, 1761. EI, aged 64, 1762. Owen Hughes, Cae'rhengaer (Llanllyfni) who died March 23rd 1789, aged 60 years. He lived and died at Drwsdugoed. His father lies at Llanfihangel-y-pennant. Hugh Owen, Cae'rhengaer, father of Owen Hughes, who died in 1757, aged 46 years. They belonged to the family of Ynys maen.

Ann Thomas, Cefniwrch, who died November 18th 1815, aged 60 years.

To the hand and pain of death we move
Swiftly through a brief journey,
And doubtless will go at the end

To follow Ann to the second life.

Also, William, her husband, November 5th 1818, aged 61 years.

To the memory of Lowry, wife of Joseph Parry, of Ty'ndwfr, who died on the 6th of December 1819, aged 85 years. Also of the said Joseph Parry, who died 1st January 1821, aged 81. Also Ellin Parry, their daughter, who died October 18th 1837, aged 65.

Sacred to the memory of William, son of John Jones, Schooner 'William Alexander', of Portmadoc, by Margaret, his wife, died October 21st 1857, aged 5 years. Also the above named John Jones, aged 49 years, and his eldest son, John, aged 16 years, who with their vessel and all hands were lost in the North Sea in the memorable and awful gale on 3rd October 1860.

Oh, the loss of three; Oh, the blow
to the wounded feelings,
For dear sons, and their father,
Long will be tears of loss.

In memory of the blameless, separated
Between earth and the deep,
From land and sea will come the dead,
To the same court will happily return. – EMRYS

Also Mary, the beloved wife of William W Lloyd, Portmadoc, Draper, and the only surviving daughter of the above named John Jones and Margaret, his wife, who departed this life on 24th February 1866, aged 26.

'The flower fadeth'

Griffith Jones, Draper, Tremadoc, who died February 13th 1839, aged 58 years. Also Elizabeth, his wife, who died July 15th 1854, aged 70 years.

Her main feast was constant peace, and Jesus
Was her life's comfort,
With ease she would attain
From all burdens a million times better world.

The Grave of Wil Ellis of Porthmadog, who died April 18th 1875, aged 65 years.

Here lyeth the body of Evan Humphreys, who dyed 4th of August 1731 aged 29 years. Also the body of Margaret Roberts of Bronygadair, who dyed 25th of August 1764, aged 72. Also the body of Robert Griffith, late of Tyddynyllwyn, buried 17th January 1788, aged 66.

G P, 1724, aged 47.

Underneath also, lyeth the body of Catherine Cadwaladr, the wife of Robert Griffith, of Tyddynllwyn, who was interred April 7th 1784, aged 48 years. Here likewise the remains of Margaret Roberts, daughter of the above named RG and Catherine, his wife, who departed this life 20th May 1796, aged 28 years.

Without warning death will take
All ages to rot like ourselves,
Thou of frail dust, consider,
See thy journey, thy plight too will be low.

John Roberts, Penclogwyn, September 18th 1840, aged 73 (eldest son of Dr Robert Isaac Roberts, Ystumllyn). Elizabeth, his wife, who died 3rd March 1850, aged 91 years.

Their good Lord till late in life was their succour
And strength in all weathers,
They both fled through faith
To the joy of Mount Zion. – IOAN MADOG

Underneath lye the remains of Morgan, son of Griffith Hughes, late of Garregwen, by Margaret his wife, who died 29th June 1787, aged 26. Also Ellin Owen, first wife of the said G Hughes, buried 28th July 1741, aged 26. And also the above Griffith Hughes, and Margaret Humphreys, his second wife. He died January 5th 1770, aged 50 years and she died September 28th 1779, aged 77 years.

Also the remains of Jane Griffith, wife of Owen Griffith, late of Garregwen, who was buried 11th January 1797, aged 53 years, Also the said OG was buried 11th June 1798, aged 60 years. Also the remains of Humphrey Owen, Saddler, who was buried the 13th day of December 1819, aged 62.

Margaret Williams, second wife of Griffith Jones, of Llwynmafon ucha', was buried August 13th 1806, aged 25 years. Also her husband, who died August 13th 1822, aged 81. (She was a sister of Cadwaladr Williams, Glanbyl.)

Ann Ellis, wife of Humphrey Williams, Llanerch, who died December 1804, aged 67 years.

Humphrey Williams, who died August 18th 1823, aged 80 years.

William Williams, Llanerch, who died January 15th 1856, aged 78. Also Margaret Williams, his second wife, who died December 15th 1874, aged 86.

Elinor, wife of Robert Roberts, Slater, Tremadoc, who died February 11th 1843, aged 33.

A true and honest wife, best of thousands
And sweet tempered,
Virtues sink to the grave,
But she will be remembered.

Robert Roberts, Cefnperfedd bach, was buried April 4th 1807, aged 84 years.

William Roberts, Drwsdugoed, son of the above, died February 23rd 1853, aged 85.

Susan Kitching, widow of Joseph Kitching, Streatham, Surrey, born May 28th 1797, died May 15th 1877. (She lived at Tan'rallt, Tremadoc.)

Samuel Evans, who dyed 5th June 1762, aged 53.

Ellin Samuel, aged 27, 1799.

Jennet Hughes, who died March 15th 1820, aged 60 years. Evan Ellis her husband, who died August 16th 1837, aged 79 years.

> *Praise there was for the farrier, to seek him*
> *Was the task of many Welshmen,*
> *He rests below the furrow*
> *With a word to tell where he lies.*
>
> *Evan Ellis was meticulous to trace*
> *The cause of illness,*
> *To the sick he gave health*
> *With goodwill to his utmost.* – MOELWYN FARDD

The above named Evan Ellis and Jennet married in January 1786. Their children were: Hugh, John, Robert, Jane and David. Hugh died around 1832, he was a dock-gateman in Liverpool, in which city he died and is buried in the cemetery of St John's Church, Liverpool. John died in 1866, Robert in 1850, Dorothy (his wife) died in 1862, Jane in 1869 (William Roberts was her husband), David in 1878. They were all buried at Ynyscynhaiarn except Hugh as mentioned.

Here also lies Ellin Ellis, she died in 1836, and her husband Henry Humphreys in 1840.

Ellen Ellis was the sister of the above Evan Ellis. John her only son lies at Dolbenmaen. He died in July 1841, aged 47 years, Jane, their daughter, died in London around 1847.

Note: Evan Ellis was the only farrier in this area at that time and lived at Bronygadair bach. He was one of the earliest smiths of his age and was father of John Evans (smith and farrier of Pentrefelin, and grandfather of Mr J Ellis Evans (farrier of Pwllheli), the historian Mr Robert Evans of Beddgelert, and the late Evan Evans of Pentrefelin.

To the memory of Daniel Morris, Harbour Master in Portmadoc, a strong, active, useful man who died December 29th 1840, aged 51 years.

> *If ever truth in epitaph was told*
> *Look on his Tomb his character behold;*
> *To live upright was throughout his plan,*
> *He lived and died an honest man.*

Also of Mary, relict of the above said, beloved by her family and highly respected by a large circle of friends, she gently fell on the 20th of November 1865, aged 69 years.

Sacred to the memory of Catherine Evans, wife of David Evans, Master of the Barque 'Gwen Evans' and second daughter of the late Daniel Morris, Harbour Master, who departed this life on 4th October 1842, in the 22nd year of her age.

When age is call'd to pay the general debt,
Great many feels the loss with deep regret,
But when fair youth that every promise gave
Sheds her sweet blossoms in the dreary grave,
All eyes o'erflow with many a steaming tear
And each fond bosom heaves a sigh sincere.

Here lyeth the body of John Ystumllyn, who died July 27th 1791, aged 46,

Erstwhile in India I was born –and brought
To Wales to be christened;
Here beneath the grey stone
In the cold earth I lie. – DAFYDD SHON JAMES, PENRHYNDEUDRAETH

Mary Lloyd, Tremadoc, who died March 23rd 1871, aged 67 years.

From a world of lamentations and its sorrow
Suddenly she fell;
When the great call comes to earth,
Unfettered she will rise again. – ALLTUD EIFION

Also for William Lloyd (her husband), *who died May 16th 1890, aged 74 years.*

John Griffith, Tyddynllwyn, who died November 13th 1876, aged 83 years.

John Griffith was a man we loved,
And the true care for the beauty of his faith;
On Mount Zion he found balm of heaven for his soul,
To worship there was his joy;
After long life he fled, with his faith, beyond fear.
From the land of woe to God forever.

Richard Owen, Garregyfelin, who died May 26th 1853, aged 73 years. Grace, his wife, who died August 5th 1860, aged 81 years.

Catherine, wife of John Griffith, Tyddynllwyn, who died February 2nd 1888, aged 86 years.

Laura Llewelyn (wife of Henry Llewellyn), Garregfelen, who died January 29th 1859, aged 39 years.

(The husbands of both the above have already been recorded.)

Here lyeth waiting in hopes of a joyful resurrection and forgiveness the body of Jane Daniel, second wife of David Williams, who departed this life the XXVIII day of August AD, MDCCLXI, aged LXXVIII.

NUNDUS IN HUNC NUNDIUM UENI QUOQUE NUNDUS ABIBO

Noeth i hwn Noeth y daethym, Hefyd noeth yr af ymaith.

Naked to him, naked I came also, naked shall I depart.

Grave of David Owen or 'Dafydd y Garreg wen' (David of the White Rock), the excellent harpist, who was buried in May 1749, aged 29 years.

NOTE: In 1693 lived Humphrey Owen of Garreg Wen, his children, Humphrey, Owen and Ann. Humphrey married and had a son, Owen, who married Gwen Roberts of Isallt. Owen married a branch of the Borth family. Owen Humphreys and Gwen had children, David their son was the talented harpist known as Dafydd y Garreg Wen. David Owen, who married Elizabeth Roberts of Tymawr, Treflys, was a nephew of OH and G Roberts. Jane, their daughter, was the wife of Owen Robert of Gwernddwyryd. Ann Humphreys of Garregwen married John Griffiths of Tuhwnt i'r bwlch, son of Griffith Owen of Fronoleu, Penmorfa, who was a cousin of Richard Humphreys of Penrhyndeudraeth (father of Bishop Humphreys of Bangor and later of Hereford). Thomas Edwards of Tyddynllwyn married Jane Jones, daughter of the above JG and AH.

They had several children. The eldest was the Rev John Thomas, MA who was born at Tyddynysguboriau. All the other children were born at Tuhwnt i'r bwlch. Ann Humphreys, died in 1719, aged 53 years; John Griffith her husband died in 1720, aged 56 years. Thomas Rowlands died in 1757, aged 55 years. Jane Jones, his wife, died in 1750, aged 44. The last named were grandparents of Ellis Owen of Cefnymeusydd on his mother's side.

William Owen, died August 24th 1807, aged 30. John Owen, Miller, Felin Uchaf, died July 18th 1824, aged 24. Catherine, his wife, died 1st April 1829.

Likewise to the same mute place
At the same age we return home.

Owen Jones, son of the above John and Catherine Owen, was interred December 29th 1834, aged 34.

Robert Jones, Felin Uchaf, was born in the year 1813, and died in March 1818.

John, nephew of the sister of the above named John and Cath. Owen died May 9th 1835, aged 2 years.

In the flower of morning he was cast to a cold grave
And his Journey ended;
Fair child, thou art buried,
but we doubt if you are there.

Elizabeth, his sister, wife of Griffith Parry, who died March 24th 1878, aged 67 years.

Catherine Evans, wife of John Evans, Farrier, who died May 18th 1866, aged 77 years. Also the above named John Evans, who died July 24th 1866, aged 77 years.

> *Foremost of Farriers, his methods were praised,*
> *Giving skilled proof of his life's work,*
> *The good to his country through his fine treatments*
> *Raised his name in the view of his fellow-men.*
> *And faithfully he gave his long life*
> *To the work of Jesus, to whose servants he was a source of strength.*
> *From the world he went in a chariot of fire.*
> *With the words of heavenly Light giving joy to his thought. – IOAN MADOG*

Hugh Parry, Garregfawr, who died June 5th 1805, aged 7 years. Henry Roberts, Garregfawr, who died July 21st 1836, aged 74 years. Jane, his wife, who died August 7th 1847, aged 78 years.

Griffith Evans, Garregfawr, who died July 16th 1853, aged 49 years. Jane, his wife, who died February 6th 1873, aged 80 years.

William Daniel, Cobbler, Twllycae, who died August 19th 1879, aged 91 years.

(He was a soldier for five years when Napoleon the Great was marauding Europe. Col. Edwards of Nanhoron, and Captain Parry of Madryn were in the same Regiment and Dr Edward Carreg, was MO for the same Regiment, in which were those named above.)

Edward Carreg Esq, Surgeon and Coroner for the Co. of Carnarvon, died at Tan'rallt uchaf, February 18th 1842, aged 57.

To the memory of Margaret Dorothea Carreg, died 5th October 1859.

R E, 1729, aged 25 years.

Owen Efan, Tyddyniolyn, was interred here May, 1767, aged 67 years. Also the body of Ann William, his wife, who died May 1768, aged 75 years.

(There is a remarkable will pertaining to her.)

Also Ann Jones (formerly Tyddynllwyn) who was buried here March 21st 1841, aged 74 years. (She was the daughter of John Jones of Tyddyniolyn.)

Here also lyeth the body of the abovesaid John Jones, who was burried November 9th, 1816 aged 70 years.

Here lyeth the body of Jane Owen, the wife of John Jones, Tyddyniolyn, who died 1st May 1816, aged 81 years.

Here also was buried Owen Lloyd Jones, son of R Isaac Jones, Tremadog (great grandson to the above) December 13th 1856, aged 15 years.

Here was buried Owen Jones, Tyddyniolyn, who died 15th April 1838, aged 64 years. Also here was buried Gainor, his wife, who died July 6th 1862, aged 73 years.

In remembrance that here were buried the sons of Owen and Gainor Jones, Tyddyniolyn, who died as follows:
John, February 3rd 1819, aged 5 years.
Griffith, February 25th 1830, aged 2 years.
Henry, March 24th 1842, aged 16 years.

The grave of Elizabeth, wife of RI Jones, Chemist, Tremadog. Who died February 8th 1840, aged 28 years, together with her baby, Owen Hughes Jones, who died January 5th 1840, aged three months.

(She was the second daughter of the late Dr Thomas Hughes, Plasyward, Pwllheli.)

Here with my little babe, we are
Never more to roam
Under Heaven. May she be well,
And move to happier climes.

The two of us asleep in one day, in the grave
We shall be together,
Until our Saviour comes,
To raise and set us free. – ALLTUD EIFION

Close to a yew tree planted in 1856 is the grave of three of the children and inscribed on the headstone is the following: Here were buried three of the children of R Isaac Jones, Tremadog, by Martha, his wife; – Edward, who died February 22nd 1848, aged 10 days. Edward, who died October 5th 1855, aged 6 years. Mary Ellen, who died October 13th 1856, aged 5 years.

To the grip of the dark grave, death sent
Three children in sorrow,
Past this life, to them shall be
An ageless life in heaven.

Here also lieth Martha, second wife of R Isaac Jones, who died March 26th 1875, aged 52 years.

(She was the eldest daughter of William and Mary Roberts of Farmyard, Tremadog.)

To a still grave their pious mother, beloved
And her husband's succour;
To her dear ones her virtue
Made the home a house of peace. – TJ (CYNHAIARN)

On a stone close to the eastern end of this chest are the following letters; *HE, aged 21, 1721*, and on another stone underneath; *In memory of Gainor, daughter of Owen and Ellen Jones, Tyddyniolyn, who died September 27th 1860, aged 8 months.*

As a flower it will emerge, When cut away it will perish.
Also Martha, her sister, who died January 24th 1871, aged 6 weeks.

(There is a grave at the foot of this one with a stone lying in the ground, making it impossible to decipher further.)

On the seaward side of this grave is that of Dr John Jones of Dolwyddelen. On the side nearest the path is the grave of Mary, wife of G Jones of Tyddyniolyn (Grand-daughter of J Roberts of Penyclogwyn y Gest)

ET 1762. : TP 1763.

John Morris, Tyddynadi, who died August 24th 1886, aged 64 years.

(He was churchwarden of the parish for years.)

Robert Evans, Blacksmith, Criccieth, who died January 20th 1850, aged 56 years. Dorothy, his wife, who died April 6th 1862, aged 64 years.

W Jones, Penystumllyn, who died in 1821 aged 55 years. Ellin, his wife, who died November 13th 1864, aged 82 years.

Ellin, wife of Richard Williams, Blacksmith, Tremadoc, who died March 18th 1843, aged 71 years. Richard Williams, her husband, who died October 30th 1851 aged 79 years.

Thomas Williams, son of the above (blacksmith), who died February 13th 1841, aged 34 years. Alice, his wife, who died March 21st 1874, aged 66 years.

Mary, wife of Richard Williams 'Beuno' (blacksmith) who died February 21st 1873, aged 56 years.

Ellin, wife of Richard Thomas, Cefnymeusydd bach, who died February 17th 1849, aged 72 years. Richard Thomas, her husband, who died October 14th 1853, aged 72 years. John, their son, who died March 28th 1844, aged 27 years. (Grand-parents of John Thomas of Eifionydd, Carnarvon.)

Griffith Roberts, Tabor, who died November 1877, aged 83 years. Elizabeth, his wife, who died May 14th 1881, aged 78 years.

Robert Jones, Tanyclogwyn, who died December 10th 1869, aged 65 years. Catherine, his wife, who died December 4th 1883, aged 80 years.

Robert Jones, Cross Keys, who died April 10th 1877, aged 33 years.

Caroline, eldest daughter of James Spooner, Esq, Morfa Lodge, died 31st December, 1829, aged 13 years. Elizabeth, his wife died February 9th 1850, aged 63 years. The above J Spooner Esq died 19th August 1856, aged 67 years. Mathew Wrench, the eldest son of the above James and Elizabeth Spooner, who died at Bordeaux, November 9th 1834, aged 20. Louisa Matilda, second daughter of the above, died 5th December, 1885, aged 65 years.

(The last named was the writer who used the nom de plume, Gladys Harlech.)

Bertram Steadman Greaves *1859*

died *aged 2 years*

Henry Whitehead Greaves *1860*

(This grave is surrounded by railings and a cross-shaped stone with the words 'Of such is the kingdom of Heaven' near the headstone.)

Elizabeth, wife of Major Pilkington, died July 8th 1842, aged 65. Also Mary Ann Wainhouse, sister of the above, died February 2nd 1856, aged 80.

George Homffray, Esq, who died in 1848, aged 70. Caroline, his sister, died February 16th 1875, aged 58.

Robert Harrison, CE (a native of Lancaster) who died April 15th 1874, aged 58.

(He was the Architect of the Pentrefelin N School and the Llwynon Church, Prenteg.)

Hollis Solly, of Walthhamston, Essex, Esq, born 31st October 1777, died 30th July 1851.

Margaret McLean, who died December 7th 1880, aged 81. George McLean, her husband who died August 4th 1872, aged 90 years.

William Roberts, Nhŷra, who died February 23rd 1853, aged 84 years. Margaret Jones, his wife, who died August 31st 1872, aged 85 years.

Griffith Roberts, Slater, who died January 12th 1844, aged 64 years. Ellin, his wife, who died October 4th 1852 aged 70 years.

Richard Williams, Llwynymafon ucha', died 21st October 1762, aged 49. Jane Hughes, his wife, buried July 7th 1804, aged 79 years.

William Williams, Garthyrhebog, who died April 18th 1847, aged 30 years.

Ellis Williams, his brother, who died March 6th 1875, aged 78 years.

James Roberts, Albert House, who died February 24th 1875, aged 61 years.

> *Wise and kind father, diligent*
> *And calm constantly,*
> *Gracious and full of feeling,*
> *He was loved in the hearts of his people. – AE*
>
> *He was kind and true, a man*
> *Honest in his actions,*
> *Sincere, a father beloved,*
> *Of his family and neighbourhood. – RR*

Mary, wife of Capt Meyrick Ellis, who died November 21st 1866, aged 36 years.

David Owen, Cefnymeusydd ucha', died the 7th December, 1796, aged 48. Elizabeth, his wife, died July 23rd 1824, aged 73. Owen Owens, Ty Coch, died July 13th 1825, aged 73.

Joseph Jones, Ty'ndwr, died January 8th 1840, aged 84. Catherine Joseph, died December 18th 1850, aged 69.

(Jane Jones and Catherine Joseph were daughters of Joseph Jones of Ty'ndwr.)

David Pritchard, Llanerch, died 1717, aged 73. Richard Ellis, ditto, died 1722. Ellinor Ellis, ditto, 1748, aged 20. John Ellis, ditto, 1761, aged 21.

(Jane Owen, widow, lived at Llanerch in 1774, Francis and Gaynor Humphreys lived at Llanerch in 1774.)

Morris Parry Edward (Cefnymeusydd Isaf), who died May 28th 1732, aged 49 years. Margaret Pritchard, his wife, who died July 27th 1784, aged 89 years.

(Margaret Pritchard was Morris Parry Edwards' second wife. It appears that her first husband was Robert Roberts of Twllycae. She was the daughter of Richard Williams of Ty mawr, Treflys. She married also Ellis Owen, Drover, son of Robert Ellis of Hendre ddu, Dolbenmaen; therefore he was her third husband, and they were the grand-parents of Ellis Owen of Cefnymeusydd. The above MP Edwards was one of the four brothers who, in 1721, carried the 'Long Stone' to the mill pond at Pentrefelin.)

Richard Jones, of Cwmbach, who died April 1805. Also Mary, his wife, who died 3rd January 1849, aged 75 years.

William Pritchard, Pencraig, who died March 8th 1837, aged 71 years. Also Jane, his wife, who died September 20th 1845, aged 81 years.

In memory of Peter Pugh, Snowdon Street, Portmadoc, who died June 1880, aged 50 years. Also Thomas, son of the aforesaid Peter and Ellen Pugh, his wife, who died November 18th 1860, aged 5 months.

In memory of two daughters of Thomas Pugh, Portmadoc, by Mary, his wife, viz., Ann, died September 11th 1846, aged 18 years. Elizabeth, died September 21st 1845, aged 5 years.

In memory of Thomas Pugh, Penmount, who died June 6th 1862, aged 57 years. Also Mary, his wife, April 2nd 1878, aged 80 years. Also Thomas, their son, who died in New Zealand March 11th 1866, aged 31 years.

Also the children of William Jones, Butcher, Portmadoc, and Jane, his wife. – Thomas Pugh Jones, who died June 6th 1864, aged 6 years.

The pleasures of a harmful world we recalled not
For earthly comfort,
So early, deathless love,
Drew us back to Jesus.

(These are all encircled by iron railings close to the wall on the left hand side.)

William Jones, died 15th June 1864, aged one year and nine months old.

After them weep no more, they are
Today in fair plenty,
They shall pluck the tender strings,
And the sound heard beyond the stars.

Also William Thomas Jones, who died July 20th 1870, aged 5 years. Also Winifred Mary, who died March 12th 1875, aged 8 months old.

Here lieth Jane Roberts, wife of Hugh Evans, Caegwenllian, who died May 14th 1826, aged 54 years. Also the aforesaid Hugh Evans, who died January 3rd 1843, aged 82 years.

In memory of Laura, wife of Morris Jones, 25 Lombard Street, Portmadoc. Born December 3rd 1839. Died July 7th 1882.

In memory of Ellin Evans, only daughter of Evan Evans, and Jane his wife, Manafon, who died 5th March 1873.

A lissom girl, she left the suffering
Of the world and its sorrow,
To dwell with Jesus Christ,
Whose word was her delight.

Richard Roberts, Penycafn, who died April 12th 1857, aged 69 years.

When he succumbed in death, in the grace
Of Jesus he slumbered,
And through him to the one that gave
He fled to the land of Angels.

Also Margaret, his wife, who died February 12th 1864, aged 77 years.

(They used to live at Hen dy, Hendregadredd before the mansion was built.)

In loving memory of the dear children of the Rev William and Gwen Jones, Trawsfynydd. Also Edmund Jones, brother of Gwen Jones, who died in Melbourne Hospital, Australia, May 30th 1861, aged 17 years.

In memory of Thomas and Laura Lloyd, Portmadoc, who died March 6th 1867, aged 4 years and 4 months. Also the abovementioned Laura Lloyd, who died April 9th 1891, aged 55 years.

William Thomas, Cwmbach, who died April 1st 1871, aged 67 years. Also Jane, his wife, who died February 23rd 1879, aged 69.

Griffith Ellis, Union Tavern, Tremadoc, who died June 13th 1847, aged 81 years. Ann Ellis, his wife, who died January 21st 1850, aged 82 years.

The mountains and hills of our land will leap
At the time of agitation
And Gruffydd will escape from earth,
The great time of his awakening.

What avails it to complain? all people
All names, grades and ages,
Will soon depart from life,
As certainly, to Ann's condition. – EO

John Griffith, Tremadoc, who died August 24th 1846, aged 61 years.

The Lord will restore him from earth, with joy
To praise in blessedness;
Free of pain in a higher world,
In the element of heaven. – JRG

William Owen, Pilot, who died May 11th 1832, aged 70 years. Catherine, his wife, who died June 21st 1839, aged 81 years.

In memory of Hugh Ellis, Lletty, who died June 16th 1869, aged 55 years.

Our gentle Hugh lies in peace, his pain changed
For eternal rejoicing.
His virtue extols his name,
And his good life honours his grave.

With sober heart he kept his great repute, without break
Without pride or vainglory;
The God of his faith heard his cry,
The reach of his anxious prayer.

His careful honest course is ended
On Zion's bosom of love,
And on His Cross and His Crown,
He carved the strength of his Lord's faith. – IOAN MADOC

Here lieth Sarah, wife of James Owen, Tremadoc, who died February 15th 1889, aged 79 years old.

Through her long life she treasured the better half
this was her sustenance;
In old age she slumbered,
And went to her favoured country. – AE

Humphrey Williams, Penamser, who died February 1st 1871, aged 60 years. Also, Margaret, his wife, who died January 6th 1892, aged 86 years.

John Thomas, Wharf, Portmadoc who died March 1st 1887, aged 63 years.

(He was a shipping clerk for Messrs JW Greaves & Sons, for about 40 years and he was also one of the founders of the Church Movement in Portmadoc.)

SOME OF THE GRAVES WITHOUT A MEMORIAL STONE

William Augustus Riddell Maxwell (Major), Esq Born 2nd August 1796, died 24th January 1846, at Tanygraig Cottage, Pentrefelin.

Mary Jones, Garregfelen, who died September 6th 1819, aged 67, Owen Evans (Excise man) who died November 16th 1819, aged 39. Owen Evans (husband of Mary Jones) who died January 3rd 1824, aged 78. Evan Owen, their son, who died February 4th 1864, aged 79. Dorothy Owen, his wife, who died March 2nd 1871, aged 75.

Hugh Jones, Dafarn Loyw (Cross Keys), who died May 25th 1824, aged 46 years. Jane Jones, his wife, who died January 21st 1829, aged 42 years.

Ambrose Lewis, Esq Ystumllyn (a native of Anglesey), buried July 18th 1792 (second husband of Mrs Montague Wynn).

Margaret Griffith, Eisteddfa, wife of William Jones of Erw Suran, who died September 25th 1817, aged 43 years.

David Humphreys, Borth y Gest, who died August 15th 1820, aged 74 years.

Ellis Pugh, Gent, of Talyllyn, Merionethshire, buried February 25th 1802.

(The above Ellis Pugh had started from home with the intention of getting married to Jane, daughter of Owen Evans of Garregfelen. He was drowned whilst crossing the Traeth Mawr, and that is the reason why he is buried at Ynyscynhaiarn. Seven years later Jane married Griffith Roberts of Tymawr, Treflys.)

Ellis Owen of Cefnymeusydd (the bard and historian), *who died in the year 1868, aged 79 years.*

John Williams (Ioan Madog) Portmadoc, who died May 5th 1878, aged 66 years.

(The graves of the last two are on the left by the church door.)

Dr John Jones of Dolwyddelen, who died February 17th 1878, aged 59 years.

[Here we have to end the recording of epitaphs at Ynyscynhaiarn for the moment as space is required for other valuable records which cannot be omitted from the book. – Ed]

[There are stones on Ellis Owen and John Williams now; it is understood that they were raised by public subscription. – JK]

FUNERALS IN OLDEN TIMES

On the evening preceding the funeral, a prayer meeting or 'wake' would be held – some maintain that this was a Catholic practice – and it was very effective. Because of its name and origin it could be likened to the Irish wake, but there was a vast difference between them as regards purpose or character.

The Irish ritual was full of paganism and was terribly immoral. Although mourners would moan 'Why did'st thou die, O brother?' and other pious words, the whole thing looked more like a carousel for the living rather than a mourning for the dead. In contrast, the Welsh 'wake' aroused the deepest feelings of reverence and occasioned heartfelt prayers. It would have been considered a sacrilege to show feelings of merriment in a house of sorrow and outrageously ungodly and hypocritical to be joyful under the same roof as the dead.

Reference to the deceased would be made in truly moving exhortations. They made a 'pulpit of his death' to warn the living of the vagaries of life and the length and depth of eternity. Appeals would be made to the conscience of those listening in the name of the holy place in which they stood to sincerely recognise those facts and to prepare themselves for death so that they would meet it unafraid and joyfully.

Before starting for the church, friends and relatives would gather round the body, over which they would sigh and grieve. After bringing out the coffin from the house and placing it on a bier near the door, the deceased's relatives would carry bread and cheese over the coffin and give it to the poor. This practice was called 'Diodlas' but has been abandoned for the past 100 years or more. In this parish the recipients would have been those who had collected flowers and fruit to place on the coffin. Sometimes a loaf of bread with a piece of silver in it would be added.

The whole gathering would bow together and the priest (if present) or the sexton would recite the Easter Prayer or the Lord's Prayer and a cortege would be formed. The same prayer would be repeated at each crossroad until the church was reached.

NOTES OF VARIOUS INTERESTS

The following gentry lived at Hendregadredd, Pentrefelin: Sir John Kingston James, Bart. (former Mayor of Dublin). Mr Lee, Captain Barnes and Lieut-Col Walker.

Those who have lived at Tanygraig Cottage include: Mr Stokes (Agent to the Cambrian Mining Co), Mr W Owen (formerly of Amlwch), Manager of the Cambrian Mining Company (Bronygadair copper mine). Major Maxwell, Sir Edward Poore Bart., Lady Dowager Poore, the Rev George Phillips (Incumbent of Penmorfa), the Rev Morris Parry (Curate of Llanfihangel-y-Pennant).

Whilst digging a grave on the site of the old church in 1865 a mint coin similar to a farthing was discovered; it bore the impression of Charles II.

THE PEDIGREES OF HENDRE DDU, &c.

Robert Ellis and Jane Jones, his wife, Hendre ddu. Their children were Ellis, Owen, Rhys and Margaret. The son, Ellis Owen of Hendre Ddu and Cefnmeusydd. Obit. 1757, Eta 65.

The grand-son, Owen Ellis of Cefnymeusydd, Obit Martii, 1803, Eta 70.
The great-grand-son, Ellis Owen of Cefnymeusydd, Obit 1868, Atatis 79.
The great-grand-daughter, Ann Williams of Bryngoleu, Obit 1877.
William Williams, her son.

Owen Owens of Bodnithoedd, son of Griffith Owen of Penarth, Clynnog, son of Owen, son of Robert Ellis, and Jane Jones, his wife of Hendre ddu. Owen ap John lived at Plâs, Clynnog, about 150 years ago. His son, Owen, married Elizabeth, daughter of Richard Owen of Tyddynmawr. Her mother was Jane Glyn of Elernion; through her marriage with Ellis Evans of Breubwll, Meirion.

Robert Owen went to live at Maesog and from there moved to Penarth, Clynnog. From him descended the prolific family of Penarth. One of Robert Owen's daughters went to live at Pencaenewydd, Llangybi, and there she gave birth to a son, Owen, who in time went to live at Quirt, Llangeinwen. He was called Owen Jones, Y Quirt.

Mary, daughter of Owen Jones y Quirt, was the mother of the late Sir Hugh Owen Esq, London.

DOG TONGS

A relic of 'Cymru Fu' (Bygone Wales) are dog tongs, which were used to remove dogs which had followed their masters into church. One of the wardens, whose duty it was to keep order during the service would use this instrument to grasp the neck of the unwanted animal and take it outside. They were made of solid material, usually of solid and tough oak, though others were made of iron. Once held in its grip the dog had absolutely no chance of wriggling free; the section was formed like the back of a dog. It was jointed, and when opened to release the victim, it extended to the length of a pitchfork, so there was no chance of the dog attacking its captor.

They were used frequently in olden times, but there is no use for them today, as dogs seldom enter churches, especially in towns and villages. Examples could be found at Llaneilian Church (made of black or bog oak), Trefdraeth Church in Anglesey, and Penmynydd Church in Anglesey (made of iron).

This item was made to recall the use made of them by our devout fore-fathers who believed that the church was sacred and should not be defiled.

THE TIMES OF THE BUILDING OF THE CHURCHES AND CHAPELS IN TRE'R GEST

St Cynhaiarn's Church probably dates from the year 600, but how many times it has been renovated or rebuilt we have no knowledge, as nothing was recorded until the year 1832.

Tremadoc Church was built in 1806 by Mr WA Madocks. It is sited on a small hillock called Ynys y gwartheg (Isle of the Cattle) and in 1810 an Act of Parliament established it as a chapel of ease to the parish church. It is still owned by the heirs of the Madocks Estate.

Brynmelyn Chapel (Methodist) 1806. A lease was obtained on this place for a period of 99 years from the late Hugh Lloyd of Chester (he was the owner of Bronyfoel at the time). Before the chapel was built, the Rev Daniel Evans of Llangeitho, when journeying through the North, preached in the hall of Bronyfoel.

Peniel Chapel (Methodist), Tremadoc, 1810. This chapel was opened on February 17th 1810, and among those present were: Revs T Charles MA of Bala, John Roberts of Llangwm, Michael Roberts of Pwllheli, John Jones of Edeyrn, John Elias, Robert Jones of Tybwlcyn and John Jones of Tremadog. William Alexander Madocks Esq, with Thomas Edwards known as 'Twm o'r Nant' by his side, sat in the deacons' pew amongst the congregation. Mr Charles (in his robes) read a Church of England service in English in the morning, with John Roberts of Llangwm as his clerk. The Rev Charles preached in English and for the remainder of the day the services were conducted in Welsh.

Tabor Chapel, Pentrefelin (Independents)................................ 1826
Salem Chapel, Portmadoc (Independent)................................ 1827
Ebenezer Chapel, Portmadoc (Wesleyan)................................ 1840
Zion Chapel, Portmadoc (Baptists).. 1841
Moriah Chapel, Garth, Portmadoc (Methodists)...................... 1845
Sandinan Chapel (Baptists).. 1854
Morfa Bychan Chapel (Methodists)... 1856
Siloam Chapel, Morfa Bychan (Independents)......................... 1856
Cambell Baptists Chapel, Portmadoc...................................... 1860
Tabernacl Chapel, Portmadoc (Methodists)............................. 1862
Bethel Chapel, Borth y Gest (Independents)............................ 1867
Cedron Chapel, Pentrefelin (Methodists)................................. 1867
Borth y Gest Chapel (Methodists)... 1874
St John's Church, Portmadoc.. 1875
English Wesleyan Chapel, Portmadoc...................................... 1877
Coffa (Memorial) Chapel, Portmadoc (Independents)............... 1879
Ebenezer Chapel, Borth y Gest (Calvanistic Methodist)........... 1880

TREFLYS OR TRE'R LLYS (TOWN OF THE COURT)

An earlier name for this area of land now encompassed by the parish of Ynyscynhaiarn was 'Gwely Wyn ap Ednewyn'. It formed the estate or 'tref' (later shortened to 'tre' and meaning 'township') of the minor princes of Llys Bronyfoel. When the old family moved to Ystumllyn, a number of farmsteads were joined together to make a small parish. These included Penrhyn-y-pryfaid, Porth-y-rhirfaen, Cefn Cae Shon, Coed-y-llyn, Cae shon, Garth-y-morthin, Cefn cyfanedd, Bron-y-foel, Tyddyn einion, Ty mawr and Glanymorfa mawr.

This parish is particularly irregular in shape; it terminates at the northern end at Coed Cefn and extends to grochan y Greig-ddu (the Cauldron of Black Rock) to the westward side of Morfa Bychan, along the beach to a place called Mount Pleasant (one of the most splendid bathing places in the British Isles and named by the English visitors as Black Rock Bathing Place); nearby are the noted caves of which mention has previously been made.

The boundary follows through parts of Morfa bychan, towards Tyddyn adi, and from there between Glanymorfa bach, y Llanerch and Bronyfoel. The parish ends on its western side with Llyn Ystumllyn and Nheraig, on the land of Garregfelen. There was once an old road from Criccieth to Treflys Church and Morfa bychan but only a few traces of it can now be found. No care was taken of its foundations when the Cambrian Railway was built and there is now only an inaccessible footpath that follows the tidemark along the beach from Abergeraint through Nheraig, Y Penrhyn, and Morfa bychan to Borth y Gest.

The time and the occasion when the small parish was formed is not known, but the farms in Treflys are much intermingled, giving rise to the belief that at one time they were in the ownership of one person and run an a community basis.

ST MICHAEL'S CHURCH (OR BETTWS TREFLYS)

It has been stated earlier in this book that the word 'bettws' can be interpreted in a variety of ways. The following is an explanation by a well known historian, so the reader may judge as he pleases.

THE WORD 'BETTWS'

Relating to the origin of the word 'Bettws' there are many varying suggestions. According to the historian, GHF Nye, in his *A Popular Story of the Church in Wales* it appears that the word has connections with the English word 'Baptism'. He states, therefore, that the name Bettws y Coed translated in English into 'Baptismal Chapel in the Woods' (Capel Bedyddiol yn y Coed). Another opinion is that it springs from the Latin ward 'Abastis' – denoting a bettws attached to a monastery.

From 'Beattus' could be derived the name 'dead house' but others hold the view that 'bettws' is a Welsh word denoting a bridge between two hills. It is a common name for many churches in Wales.

Most probably the word 'Ys-bwd-ty' was the original: it means hospital, 'yspytty' in Welsh. It is known that at the time of the Crusades, a monastic Order, the Knights of the Hospitalum, came to this country in order to give succour to soldiers and pilgrims who were going to, or had returned, from the Crusades.

One writer shows satisfactorily that 'hospitum' is the parent of 'ysbyty' or 'bettwysau' – all being traced to the time of the Crusades – and that the source or origin of the word is not of an earlier date.

So we are led to the belief that it was originally 'ysbyty' and for this reason – between the church and Llys Bronyfoel – many old graves called 'Beddau Milwyr' (soldiers' graves) were discovered and it is possible that a garrison had quarters on a shoulder of land between Bronyfoel and Black Rock.

There was an ysbyty by Alltwen, close to where Tremadoc now stands, although there is a possibility that another was sited at Treflys, as places nearby were ports or anchorages at that time.

Sir Howel of the Battle-axe and his family are connected with Criccieth and Ystumllyn, as well as Bronyfoel, and this leads to the belief that the hospitum was later changed to a family prayer house. Sir Howel, of course, was created Constable of Criccieth Castle by the Black Prince and there he resided with his family and some soldiers. There is a record that he had twelve hand-maidens in silk finery and also many men-servants.

Here in Cruccaith of fine work,
An ancient building it is,
And the pale handsome breaker of spears
Is Sir Howel, cannon of lightning.
Sir Howel, lord of battle in our need,
And his lady of the golden girdle
With her gay handmaidens,
Twelve of them together
Weaving the beauty of coloured silk
By the full light of coloured glass.

Measurements taken of the old church in 1834 were: 47 feet long by 12 feet wide up to the chancel, which measured 15 feet by 11 feet. A rather odd thing can be seen from the Terrier and that is that the landowners of Treflys had subscribed voluntarily one-tenth part of their land's products towards the cost of the services and keeping the church in good repair – not because of an Act of Parliament. It is apparent that the heirs of Coedyllyn had a closer affinity towards the church than any of the other farmhouses.

For a period of about 20 years the church was left in a state of disrepair and services ceased to be held for a number of years. When they recommenced a service would only be held on one Sunday in three, as there was only one cleric to serve the three churches of Criccieth, Ynyscynhaiarn and Treflys! The clamour for repairs to be carried out continued over the years and an appeal was made to Mrs Jones-Parry of Aberdunant for a portion of land to enable the churchyard to be extended. The original one was overfull and land belonging to the church had been lost due to the carelessness of the wardens.

However, repairs were not started until the present industrious incumbent, the Rev J Lloyd Jones MA of Criccieth, took over the living in 1888. He started in earnest to carry out this necessary task and the church is now one of the neatest and tidiest of the smaller churches in the deanery, with a regular service there every Sunday. There is still a great need for an extension to the churchyard.

On September 31st 1888, the first stone was laid by that generous lady Mrs Jones-Parry, the owner of Coedyllyn. The occasion was attended by a vast multitude which had congregated from Criccieth, Tremadog, Portmadog, Morfa bychan, Borth etc. A service was held and many speeches were made both by clerics and laymen. Thanks were expressed to Mrs Jones-Parry, who was handed a trowel and a hammer to set the foundation stone of the chancel. She had proved a generous contributor to the costs incurred and had also provided a splendid repast for all who wished to partake. Mr Thomas Roberts, of Porthmadog who planned and supervised the whole work free of charge, was also warmly thanked.

Rebuilding was done on the old foundations and what was known as Bronyfoel chapel on the eastern end was converted into a chancel. The floor was raised, the windows were surrounded with free stone but the old door and Gothic arch were left as they were.

Hearty support was given by the parishioners and generous donations towards the expense were contributed by ladies and gentlemen from neighbouring areas. On October 10th 1889, the church was reopened for divine service every Sunday – for the first time as far back as can be remembered.

The Venerable Archdeacon Evans took part in that service and gave an excellent address, in which he referred to the antiquity of the area and its connections with early Christianity. He made reference to the late Bardd Treflys (Bard of Treflys), whose remains were buried close by. The sermon was given by the Rev HE Williams of Llanaelhaiarn, and a splendid collection was taken by the churchwardens, Mr Owen Evans of Broom Hall and Mr William Owen of Cefn. The church is served by a Curate in conjunction with

Ynyscynhaiarn, who also share his services; this at the expense of the Vicar of Criccieth (to whom the living belongs) and the Vicar of Ynys Cynhaiarn. The whole amount of the tythe is only £34 per annum; they are also assisted by the Curates Aid Society.

NOTE: Admiral Robert Lloyd of Tregayan, Gesail Gyfarch and Mynachdy Gwyns (Clynnogfawr), to which last estate the Chapel of Treflys belongs, until lately kept it in repair. The living of Llangelynin is in the gift of this family. MSS.

The church was presented with a reading desk and a pulpit of beautiful oak wood by Mrs Jones-Parry; it was also furnished with chairs. If someone was to present a Christening-font the church would be well equipped. There is need also for a more convenient entrance from the main road – the present one is far too narrow.

PARISH LANDOWNERS AROUND THE YEAR 1789

W Ormsby Gore of Brongyntyn; — Cefn cyfanedd, Ty mawr, Tyddyn adi, Cae shôn and Cefn.

Col. Wynn of Ystumllyn; — Porthyrhirfaen, The Mount and Garth-ymorthin.

Sir Watkin Williams Wynn; — Tyddyn einion, Trip and Penrhyn-y-pryfaid.

Owen Thomas; — Glanymorfa mawr.

Hugh Llwyd of Chester; — Bronyfoel and Bryn Melyn, in 1799.

The name given to the lands of Sir William Morris, Clennenau (one of the ancestors of Mr W Ormsby Gore, now Lord Harlech), in this parish in the year 1567 was Cefn Keyvanith (Cefn cyfanedd) and 'Dryll Madyn Llwyd', ancestors of the family of Gesail and Clenenney. It can be seen that these lands have changed hands many times by today; many cottages have disappeared although a number are still in existence along the length and breadth of the parish of Treflys. It is not easy to find in the commote of Eifionydd a spot which has more extensive views than those obtained from Treflys.

SOME OF THE OLD FAMILIES OF TREFLYS

The following record of some of the old inhabitants of Treflys, who lived during the past century and in the early part of the present one, will, I hope, be of interest to the reader. Harry Owen, around the year 1777, was buried at Criccieth, he was aged 74. Robert Williams and his wife, Margery Ellis (father and mother of the old patriarch William Roberts of Coedyllyn) lived 102 years ago – that is in 1790. Humphrey Pritchard came there after him, having lived previously at Beudy'r Moelfre (Moelfre Shippon), on the land of Llanerch y Gest. He had also lived at y Garreg fawr, and was a descendant of the 'Costoglwyth y Gest' (the Surly tribe of Gest), to which reference has been made earlier in the book. You will remember that they were forced to carry timber for the King's mills as a punishment for refusing to obey the laws; their descendants are numerous in Tre'r Gest even to his day.

William Evan of Lleyn and Elen Jones, his wife lived at Cae shôn, Treflys, in 1733. He later married Ann Owen, daughter of Harri Owen of Bronyfoel, who died at the age of 86 in 1793. Ann's sister, Jane Owen of y Llanerch, became the wife of Ellis Davies of the same place; she died in 1774. They were grandparents to William Williams of Llanerch, and great-grandparents to the present William Williams.

On the descending line of Harry Owen of Bronyfoel was Jane Owen (Siani Owen o'r Gest) who, when I knew her as a youth, was a well-known elderly spinster. She brought the first tea-leaves to the area but neither she nor her neighbours had any idea how to prepare them. It is said that they first boiled and strained the leaves, put them on their plates and tried to eat them with salt.

A brother of the above Harri Owen was Owen Owens of Hendre'r Penrhyn, who was the grandfather of Lowri Roberts of Tyddyn adi. He was also a cousin of Owen Williams of Cae shôn, and grandfather of William Owen of Cefn, Treflys. Therefore, Jane Owen of LIanerch and Ann Owen (wife of William Owen of Cae shôn) were sisters of Harry Owen of Bronyfoel.

The mother of Eben Roberts, 'Y Calchiwr' (the Limer or Lime man) of Portmadoc, and mother-in-law of William Roberts, lived in one of the two Coedyllyn houses. She was a sister to the father of William Owen (Merchant) of Tremadoc. William Roberts of Coedyllyn was a cousin of John Parry, who once kept a school at Pwllheli, Caernarfon, etc.

Thomas Prys, a former cattle dealer, was a brother of Morgan Prys of Llech Oronwy in Llanfrothen, and of the family of Arch-Deacon Prys. When increasing age prevented Thomas Prys from carrying on his former trade, he used to visit the farmers with whom he had formerly done business – having a regular round of the main farms. So it was that he came to Cae shôn in the early summer of 1831 and met a tragic end. It was surmised that he lost his way when darkness overtook him and that he accidentally fell into a peat bog at Pwllgloewlas, Tremadoc. On the Sunday morning local people noticed that dogs and pigs were gathered at the marsh and, on further investigation, found parts of a human torso strewn all over the place. From his belongings which were close by they were able to identify the remains as those of the old Cattle dealer.

Dr Evans of Dolgelley, the son of Cefn cyfanedd, Treflys, was a former pupil of 'Llwyd the School' at the Church School, Penmorfa, at the end of the last century.

An old saying in the Treflys area is: 'A fearful noise in Treflys, would split the rocks of Ynys'.

There was an old rural character living at Garreg fawr about 50 years ago, named Harri Roberts. This quiet humorous little man had to go to Lundain as a witness in a law case and could not speak a word of English. Tiring of the city he started for home on foot, asking all and sundry that he met, 'which is the way to Garreg Fawr'.

Margaret, daughter of Hywel Meredydd of Bronyfoel, was chosen as nursemaid to the first English Prince born at Caernarfon. Hywel was a cousin of Owen Tudur, father of Henry VII (see Wynn's *The History of the Gwydir Family*).

VARIOUS NOTES

Cefn cyfanedd was one of the places chosen by the Prince of Eifionydd in which was kept a 'brwydas'. This was an ancient system under which various known places were charged with the duty of keeping a fire constantly alight and other members of the township had the right to go there to rekindle their fires if they had gone out.

In the great election between Sir Robert of Nant and Wynn of Wern, Owen Efan of Tyddyn iolyn and his manservant carried a load of peat and timber to the top of Moel y Gest in order to make a bonfire to celebrate Sir Robert's victory. He was later given a cheap lease on his cottage.

The first farm cart in Treflys came to the farm of Coedyllyn.

There was an old oak chest at Cefn cyfanedd with the inscription *'AE 1731'* carved on it. The initials stand for Ann Ellis, grandmother of the late Efan Meredydd. An uncle of Efan Meredydd was a pupil at Penmorfa School under 'Llwyd the School'. Another pupil was Dewi Wyn who became a servant to a doctor in Dolgellau. The doctor discovered that this lad was very talented and brought him up as a doctor; this entailed very little effort at that time. Dewi's sons, in turn, also became doctors and served on 'men of war'. Their father built himself a house, which was later left to one of the sons.

There was once a 'llwybr llan' (Church or public footpath) between llyn Ystumllyn and Treflys, as some of the cottages at Treflys (Garreg fawr etc) belonged to the parish of Ynyscynhaiarn. The restoration of this path is essential for Treflys and it would be a great acquisition for the parishioners of Pentrefelin. There are still some living who remember the position and bed of the path.

Morus Jones was an old man who lived at Ty capel in Brynmelyn, and, after reading a book on providence called *Trugaredd a Barn* (Mercy and Opinion), decided to stop work and start praying in the hope that providence would provide him with a sack of flour. He persisted for some weeks until overcome by a great hunger – no flour appeared, so he was glad to resume work.

THE TERRIER OF TREFLYS PARISH

A true copy of a renewed Terrier, exhibited at a Visitation held at Abererch, September 6th 1826.

> A true Account and Terrier of all the Lands, Goods, Implements, Tythes and other Rights belonging to the Rectory, Parish and Parish Church of Treflys, in the County of Carnarvon, and Diocese of Bangor, taken, made and renewed on the 4th day of September 1826; and exhibited before the Worshipful Charles Warren, AM, Chancellor of the Diocese aforesaid, at the Primary Visitation of Right Rev Father in God, Henry William, Lord Bishop of Bangor, held at Abererch the 6th day of September, in the Year aforesaid.
>
> There are belonging to the Rector, First a Modus of Two pence in lieu of Tythe Hay, for each farm. Also the Tythe of all Corn in kind. Of Wool the tenth part, and three half pence for each Wether sold unsheared. The Tythe of Lambs in their proper kind, and the custom concerning them is this, if a Person's number is one he pays three pence; if two—six pence; if three—nine pence; if four—one shilling; if five—one shilling and three pence; if six—one shilling and six pence; if seven, he pays a Lamb, the Rector paying him back nine pence; if eight—six pence; if nine—three pence; if ten, the Rector hath a Lamb complete. And in like manner for every number above ten, and every ten. The Lambs are all turned together, the owner takes his choice Lambs, and choice Ewe Lamb; then the Rector takes his choice Lamb, and so an alternatively until the Rector has his number. Also the Tythe of Kids and Geese, one out of three, one only out of three score of each kind. Also the Tythe of Pigs, one out of each Litter, if there are three in a Litter. For every Mare and Colt, two pence. For every Cow and Calf, three half pence, excepting the first, one penny only. Also the Tythe of Hemp, Flax and Honey in kind. For every Wedding, five shillings. An oblation of one shilling at each churching of Woman. Oblations at Funerals at discretion. The Tythe of Eggs about Easter, two for each Cock, one for each Hen. Easter dues, six pence from each Married couple, two pence from every person of age to communicate. There is also due to the Parish Clerk, a shilling for every Wedding. For every Funeral at discretion. There is due to him from the Rector, two pence for every churching of Woman, two pence for every Married couple as Easter Dues.
>
> Belonging to the said parish are, first, the Parish Church, containing in length 47 feet with the Chancel; in breadth 12 feet inside. The chancel in length, 15 feet; in breadth 11feet. Belonging to which are one Communion Table with a covering for the same of Black Cloth. Also one Linen Cloth for the same with a Napkin; one Silver Chalice; one Silver edged paten; one Chest with one lock; one Reading Seat and Pulpit; one 8vo. Welsh Bible; one folio Welsh Common Prayer Book, two quarto Welsh Common Prayer Book, one in the old black letters; one Bier, one Surplice, one Parchment Register Book, beginning 1772 and continued to the present time; a Paper Register Book according to an Act of Parliament, made to

prevent Clandestine Marriages; one Bell. The Church is kept in repair as followeth, the South side of the Church by the owner of Coedyllyn, in the Parish of Treflys. The South side of the Chancel by the owner of Ystumllyn, in the Parish of Criccieth; The North side of the Church, one half by the owner of Coedyllyn, aforesaid, the other half by the owner of Glanmorfa mawr, in the Parish of Treflys; The Eastern half by the latter; the western half by the former; the North side of the Chancel by the owner of Ty mawr, in the Parish of Treflys, towards which expence they have as—Tradition goes—Quillets, or portions of Lands—commonly called Llatheni, viz yards—that go by the name of Caeau'r Eglwys (Church Fields), the bounds or Limits of the several Quillets are well known and ascertained, of which Quillets are ten belonging to the owner of Coedyllyn. Five to the owner of Ty mawr, and one to the owner of Glanmorfa Mawr. Tradition says that all the Seats in the South side of the Chancel, were given to the Esquire of Ystumllyn by the Esquire of Porkington (Shropshire), to whom all the Chancel belonged as owner of Ty mawr, on Condition he (the Esquire of Ystumllyn) kept the South side of the Chancel in repair. In Testimony of the truth of the above mentioned Particulars, and of every one of them, we, the Minister, Churchwarden and Principal Inhabitants, have set our hands the said fourth day of September, in the year of Our Lord, 1826.'

Owen Jones, Rector, Mynydd Ednyfed
Thomas Owen, Churchwarden, Glanymorfa
Griffith Roberts, Ty mawr
Evan Jones, Porthyrhirfain
William Owen, Cefn Caeshôn
John Pritchard, Tyddyn Einion

(A renewed Terrier from this copy was sent to Pwllheli on 17th September 1834.)

There is a note that the church was previously repaired in 1762.

EPITAPHS IN TREFLYS CHURCHYARD

Mary Jones, wife of William Roberts, Coedyllyn, who died October 1827 aged 51 years. Also the above William Roberts, who was buried November 19th 1859, aged 89 years.

In memory of Robert Morris, Shop Newydd, Beddgelert, who died March 6th 1867, aged 73 years.

Beneath this tomb a Christian, his dark grave
But like small feathers,
There is some comfort here
Within the sound of Zion's angels.

Catherine, wife of Captain W Watkins, Born November 18th 1845, died September 18th 1869.

If it were part of all her kind, to be
Such a beloved woman,
A gift would be for all husbands,
A second Paradise like heaven to live.

In memory of Humphrey Prichard, Bronyfoel, who died March 30th 1872, aged 75 years.

He was a pleasant singer, the charm
Of his voice like an organ;
Below in earth is no song –
The clay now silences the nightingale.

(The above was an excellent singer and one of the best Bass singers of his time.)

Margery Ellis, wife of Robert Williams, Bronyfoel, who died June 28th 1789, aged 44 years. Also the above R Williams, who died May 27th 1800, aged 57 years.

(Father and mother of the old William Roberts, Coedyllyn, who died at Bontfaen, in November 1859.)

Humphrey Prichard, Bronyfoel, who died February 12th 1829, aged 77 years. Also his wife, Mary, who died March 31st 1841, aged 93 years.

Ann Humphrey, Bronyfoel, who died May 8th 1820, aged 36 years. Also her brother, Humphrey Humphreys, who died 29th June 1866, aged 80 years.

David Humphrey, Bronyfoel, who departed this life 31st March 1870, aged 81 years. Catherine, his wife, who died 5th June 1876, aged 70 years.

Catherine Jones, wife of Griffith Dafydd, Gorllwyn who died June 14th 1824, aged 75 years.

Robert, son of Robert and Jane Roberts, Ystumllyn, died the 30th April 1863, aged 55.

Richard Roberts of Rhydygwystl, who died 1st May 1834, aged 80. Thomas Roberts, Garthymorthin (his brother) who died May 25th 1834, aged 68.

Not for ever the place for Thomas, he will come
To possess a kingdom.
Jesus will see his servant's loss,
And will hold him in honour. – RR

Jane, wife of Griffith Roberts, of Ty mawr, who died November 30th 1830, aged 58. Also Griffith Roberts, who died October 30th 1848, aged 84.

Enjoying all comforts in peace, through his life
In his home of Ty mawr,
Now we are made to lie
In a little house in a shallow grave.

Let angels keep and watch
Their dust under this stone. – RR

Mary, wife of Thomas Roberts, Garthymorthin, who died January 19th 1856, aged 78. Also Jane, their daughter, wife of Joseph Williams, Erw, Morfa Nefyn, who died September 13th 1861, aged 49.

William Pierce, Garreg wen bach, who died May 12th 1828, aged 28. Elin Pierce, his sister, who died January 1st 1877, aged 89.

Elizabeth, second wife of William Owen, Cefn Cae shôn, who died August 2nd 1840, aged 63.

Elin, wife of John Jones, Cae shôn, who died June 29th 1856, aged 41.

Rowland Williams, Glanymorfa bach, who died November 17th 1883, aged 64.

Rowland Humphreys, my bosom friend,
Kindly and good he was, ever pure;
One truly loved as a son of excellence,
He led a life of proper virtue,
From the grave rises a warning cry to each man
In the sudden lesson of his fearful death.

Tremadoc *Madog*

William Humphrey (Father of the above) who died May 28th 1850, aged 70. Elin, his wife, who died December 24th 1861, aged 75.

Griffith Jones, Tyddyn einion, who died November 14th 1885, aged 67. Ann Jones, his wife, who died October 17th 1890, aged 70.

Griffith Lloyd, Tanner, Tremadoc, who died October 4th 1876, aged 72 years. Jane, his second wife, who died December 12th 1877, aged 70 years.

Ebenezer Roberts, Porthmadog, who died June 20th 1868, aged 73. Laura, his wife, who died December 11th 1873, aged 81. Pierce Roberts, Ship Builder, who died September 22nd 1873, aged 31.

John Owen, Borth Farm, who died July 8th 1887, aged 74 years.

Owen Ellis, eldest son of Ellis and Jane Owen, Coedyllyn, who died March 22nd 1868, aged 31. Also Ellis the youngest son, who died January 13th 1871, aged 15.

Owen Ellis from wilderness was drawn
To the city of blessedness
Here in the dust his place
Deserving of honour and peace – RR

Margaret, wife of the following (daughter of Cadwaladr and Catherine Jones, Bachysaint) Born January 23rd 1825. Died April 30th 1876. William Jones, Castle House (her husband) who died March 1st 1885, aged 73.

Robert Parry, Penrhyd fechan, who died June 4th 1849, aged 57. Catherine, his wife, who died December 17th 1857, aged 66. Evan Roberts, who died February 23rd 1892, aged 62.

Elin, daughter of Robert and Elizabeth Owen, Penrhyn Treflys, who died April 8th 1875, aged 18.

Mary Jones, Garreg wen, who died January 18th 1880, aged 75. Richard Jones her husband, who died April 28th 1892, aged 76 years.

Ellis Evans, Coedycefn, who died July 14th 1874, aged 50. Also Mary, his wife, who died December 30th 1883, aged 55. Catherine, their daughter, who died May 2nd 1892, aged 21.

Griffith Morris, Trip, who died July 5th 1865, aged 74. Margaret, his wife, who died February 23rd 1873, aged 82 years.

In memory of Capt Ellis Roberts, of 3 Osborne terrace, Portmadoc. Who died on 2nd June 1881, aged 77 years; and of John, his eldest son, aged 32 years, Commander of the Ill-fated Steamer 'Borussia' which foundered in the Atlantic, on the 20th of December, 1879, and of Edward, his son, 3rd Officer of the Ship, 'Duleep Singh', who died at Calcutta 1st June 1875, aged 21 years.

William Owen, second son of Ellis and Jane Owen, Coedyllyn, who died April 12th 1882, aged 42. Ellis Owen, father of the above, who died at Gallt y balch, Anglesey, July 23rd 1885, aged 79. Also Jane, his wife, who died December 20th 1890, aged 78.

Mary Jones, daughter of Robert and Eliza. Jones, Glanrafon, Tremadoc, who died March 9th 1863, aged 9 years. Also the above named Robert Jones, who died March 13th 1887, aged 62 years.

In memory of the dear child, Mary Jane, the beloved daughter of John and Jane Lewis, who died January 9th 1878, aged 9 years and 4 months. In memory of the said John Lewis, Roche terrace, Portmadoc, who departed this life on 15th July 1889, aged 63 years. [These inscriptions are on a square column of multi-coloured marble. – JK]

John Jones, Glanymorfa, who died April 5th 1852, aged 50. Dorothy Jones, his wife who died December 19th 1883, aged 79.

Pierce Samuel, Garreg wen bach, who died May 9th 1848, aged 88. Also Catherine, his wife, who died June 11th 1854, aged 87.

In memory of Mary, wife of Richard Roberts (Pilot), Borth y Gest, who died March 23rd 1869, aged 60. Also their daughter, Elizabeth Roberts, who died June 3rd 1860, aged 7 years. Also of the aforementioned Richard Roberts, who died of an accident at Ffestiniog, January 12th 1890, aged 70 years.

In memory of Griffith, son of William and Jane Jones, Ty newydd, who died December 18th 1857, aged 17. Also William Griffith, son of the above, who died April 17th 1883, aged 21. Also Mary, who died August 18th 1884, aged 21.

> *Griffith came from his brief stay to his bare grave*
> *And the most gentle William,*
> *With dear Mary laid so close,*
> *In the cold bed of death. – BEUNO*

Here was buried Robert, son of Evan and Margaret Humphreys, Ynys cyngar, November 10th 1855, aged 9 years.

Here was buried Robert Prichard, Pilot, Borth, who died September 1st 1865, aged 66.

> *He was diligent in all life's journey, frugal,*
> *Honest and sincere,*
> *And the purest of companions,*
> *To Jesus in a long life.*

Also Ann Prichard, his wife, who died May 23rd 1887, aged 84.

In memory of Evan Roberts, who was buried February 5th 1845, aged 33. Also Margaret Roberts, his wife, who was buried April 29th 1868, aged 72.

In remembrance of Jane Owen, Ty'n'rardd, Tremadoc, who died June 26th 1873, aged 68.

Robert Roberts, Ty mawr, who died October 29th 1804, aged 79. Mary, daughter of Griffith and Jane Roberts, Ty mawr, who died in 1810, aged 11 months.

Robert Roberts, Ystumllyn, who died 1st of December 1839, aged 78. Also Jane, widow of the above-mentioned Robert Roberts, who died February 18th 1864, aged 82. Ellis Roberts, their son, who died June 8th 1889, aged 80.

Catherine Richards, wife of Richard Roberts, Ty mawr, who died October 22nd 1785, aged 31. Psalm cii. 23. Catherine, their only daughter, who died April 28th 1789, aged 4.

Underneath lyeth the body of William Jones, Bookbinder, Portmadoc, who departed this life the 29th January 1842, aged 62 years. Here also lyeth the body of Ellen Jones, widow of the above named, who died on the 5th October 1860, aged 91½ years.

> *Through the world and its struggles she was industrious*
> *Until the hour of death,*
> *After a great age she went*
> *To a place without grief.*

In memory of Thomas Owen, Hen dy, Caernarfon. Born at Muriau bach, Criccieth February 3rd 1805, and departed this life October 6th 1872, aged 67 years. Also Jane Owen, the beloved wife of the above, who entered into her rest May 23rd 1891, aged 77 years. Also of their son, Thomas Owen of Plas Llanwnda near Caernarfon, who entered into his rest May 2nd 1891, aged 46 years.

> *'Precious in the sight of the Lord is the death of one of His saints.'*

This burial place is in an enclosed corner an the southeastern side.

Mary Daniel, aged 46, 1783. Richard Jones, late of Tyddyn Einion, died April 23rd 1788, aged 57 years.

MR 6. 1775

Drowned in Dublin, Capt John Richard Jones, Eagle, Portmadoc, aged 40 years, July 7th and was interred on the 13th, inside of the Church, 1837.

In remembrance of Richard Roberts (Bard of Treflys), Ty mawr, Treflys. He died June 19th 1876, aged 58 years.

Beloved man, long will his excellence be remembered,

> *He was faithful and of great kindness;*
> *For him from Zion rises the sound of grief,*
> *For its true patron literature mourns,*
> *For the fair countenance and wit of Bardd Treflys,*
> *Through Eifion the longing will not cease. – GWILYM ERYRI*

Mary, wife of John Evans, Porthyrhirfaen, who died December 31st 1790, aged 39. Also the above named John Evans, who died February 7th 1824, aged 77 years.

Thomas, son of John Evans, Porthyrhirfaen, and Ann, his second wife. He died August 18th 1834, aged 46. Also the above Ann, who died March 12th 1842, aged 84.

A0. 86. 1793 John Owen, Cae shôn, aged 33, 1808.

Sacred to the memory of Henry Derepas, a native of Drogheda, Ireland, who was drowned at the mouth of the Boyne on 6th July 1832, aged 28 years.
This stone was erected by his deeply afflicted wife, Maria Derepas.

John Pritchard, Tyddyn einion, died 5th December, 1851, aged 86 years. Ellin Owen, his wife, died February 2nd 1858, aged 86. (Interred inside the church.)

Dorothy, daughter of John and Dorothy Jones, of Glanymorfa, who died September 30th 1847, aged 10, and a younger sister of hers, who died at birth in 1848.

> *A summons will come to Treflys, to call*
> *Christ's beloved unto him,*
> *To fair heaven from grave of earth,*
> *To appear in his like.*

Morris Jones, Brynmelyn, who died August 26th 1825, aged 83. Margaret Jones, his widow, who died January 17th 1838, aged 86 years.

> *They took Jesus for their friend*
> *In spite of the trouble they bore,*
> *And heaven with him shall be*
> *Their reward when they arise.*

Morris Griffith, Efail Llewellyn, Penmorfa, who died January 24th 1847, aged 30 years.

> *To the holy there is honour and glory in the world,*
> *And in the sad cold grave,*
> *Then also at the resurrection,*
> *And forever, what is their claim?*

Griffith Morris, Garth, Portmadoc, who died January 17th 1855, aged 36.

The graveyard is my dwelling, this long time
God has placed me to lie,
And His, the wondrous Lord's command
Will call me living from my poor grave.

In loving memory of Laura, beloved wife of Edward Evans, Master of the Brig 'Geraldine', Portmadoc, who died January 2nd 1879, aged 31 years.

'The Lord giveth and the Lord taketh away'

Also the above named Edward Evans, who died March 31st 1888, on his voyage from the West Indies, as Captain of the Brigantine 'Ida', Portmadoc. He was buried at sea April 1st, aged 43 years.

Our brother went from the land of the living,
But blessed is he in death;
He left the strife of the world
To rest in Jesus.

In memory of Tryphena, daughter of John and Jane Davies, Portmadoc, died February 20th 1876, aged 4 years.

In remembrance of Thomas Owen, Tremadoc, who died August 25th 1860, aged 60. Also Jane, his beloved wife, who died March 29th 1885, aged 85. Also Margaret Owen, their daughter, who died March 25th 1889, aged 52 years.

She was never neglectful and always
Fulfilled her appointed tasks,
Virtue was her wealth, but behold,
She was cast into cold depths.

In loving memory of Jannet, beloved wife of Capt Edward Evans, who died January 2nd 1872, aged 31 (daughter of Borth farm). Also the aforesaid Edward Evans, who died March 31st 1888, aged 42.

Thomas Griffith, Cross Keys, Pentrefelin, who died 24th October 1844 aged 42. Also Elin Griffith his wife who died 14th September 1866, aged 61.

Note: This concludes the recording of epitaphs in both churches, the time having come to move on to other items of interest. As previously stated it was not possible to place them correctly in the order in which they appear in the churchyards – priority being given, wherever possible, to record the most ancient; if some have been overlooked, it was due to lack of space and also the time to record them.

THE OLD CHURCHYARD OF OUR FATHERS

When I approach the mortal resting-place,
Encircled by antiquity it stands,
The dwellers shadowed, calm and silent still,
In their old churchyard, all asleep in peace.
A mournful spot, its very boundaries
Mark the corruption that must come to all.
Death is the king that grimly wears the crown,
The dread black crown; his place in the grave.

The earth, dear graveyard of our father's church,
Covered great saints, the godly men who were
Worthy ancestors, matchless in their time,
And mighty columns of the church above.
I honour in my heart the land that kept
The bodies of the heroes of God's truth,
The 'mobile martyrs' who suffered unto death
To keep alive the holy Christian faith.

The fine carved tombs, the marble columns fair,
Memorials to the gentry of the world,
While golden letters tell upon the graves
Of high born noblemen of other times.
As beauteous ornaments upon the mossy Ground,
Of the old Church, older among them now,
A place of worship for the host at rest
Who sang the praises of the Three-fold God.

O ancient graveyard of our Fathers' Church,
May all thy dead in peaceful silence sleep,
While little birds above chant plaintive notes
In grief and mourning while man's world remains,
And may the clouds of heaven slowly move
For the old churchyards honour and respect,
Above the resting-place the whispered breeze
Shall gently stroke the coverlet of green.

Hail to the morning when the graves are seen
All empty of their tenants here below,
The day the books are opened, and is heard
The full and rightful judgement on the world.
O awful vision! every sun extinguished,
When heaven's glowing planets turn to dark,
And fearful earthquakes make the graveyards tremble,
Let me that day in Jesus find my rest. – PELICAN MON

CANTRE'R GWAELOD (THE HUNDRED OF THE DEEP)

As this historical cantref terminates with the cantref of Y Gest and because it is the subject of many varied opinions, I have included in this book what little information is known. This will enable those with an enquiring mind to resolve for themselves any conclusions that may be derived from old traditions and ancient history on this subject. Some historians may well believe too much whilst others, on the other hand, believe too little.

The position of Cantre'r Gwaelod is the plain on the southern side of Carnarvonshire, opposite Merioneth and in the direction of the northwestern boundaries of Cardiganshire. This vast plain is now inundated by the sea.

In the many discussions, arguments and written articles by historians and bards there is obviously a wide diversity of opinion. Some hold the view that it is only fiction and is unsupported by any convincing proof; others believe that the history is true and endeavour to prove their point by quoting place names and traditions connected with this strange territory. They hold the view that the area now under the sea was once a habitation of people and a place of populated townships

When one looks at the position of the surrounding lands and the names of places along the shores, the impartial may well come to the conclusion that there was something there that is not visible today. Apart from what little evidence is available in one's mind and records, it seems likely that the cantref stood on the side nearest Arfon, with the bed of the sea between it and Cardigan. The lowland would be protected by a steep embankment running from the westward side of Merioneth (opposite Harlech) to Penryn Dû (Black Headland) in Lleyn, near Abersoch.

The seawall or causeway would be many miles in length, perpendicular on the seaward side and fairly level on the northern side. Along the line indicated are large free-standing rocks on the seabed and other parts comprised of solid rock. The local name for this is 'Sarn Badrig' (Patrick's Causeway), a reference to the Irish saint, although others believe that the name is derived from the word 'Padrwyg'.

There are many gaps between which ships can proceed over the Gest Bar on their way to Portmadoc. It is a most complex area. More ships have been lost close to shore here than anywhere else known to us, scores, if not hundreds of large vessels have been wrecked and completely destroyed by 'taro ar y Bar' (by striking the Bar). Vessels unfamiliar with this area headed in this direction (called St Tudwal's Roads) by confusing two lights. But to return to the story, there is another causeway off the Cardigan shore called 'Sarn y Bwch' (the Buck's Causeway). It is possible that this defended the estate of Gwyddno

Garan Hir, since it is called 'Caer Wyddno' (Gwyddno's Fort). There is an old saying that in Cantre'r Gwaelod were sixteen large populated townships that excelled all Welsh townships apart from Caerlleon on Usk.

Dewi Wyn has the following to say about Cantre'r Gwaelod:

> ......As we are told,
> Dwellers of Tre y Gwaelod
> There was a wondrous province,
> That sank many ages since;
> Below might lie forgotten.
> Silver halls, we know not when,
> The gold of mighty heroes,
> And gold-torqued warriors in force;
> The time that high born ladies,
> On myriad ways took their ease,
> Twelve would walk in evening's glow,
> Or two would slowly follow,
> Men of valour riding tall,
> Where now sea-horses gather,
> Companies of maidens there,
> This day the lampreys slither.
> In Dyffryn y Gog* truly
> A spired church for all to see,
> From Persia, brass and iron,
> Trumpets, circlets, swords and crown.
> And in their joyful palace
> Virgins sang religious praise,
> The land with water covered,
> In the deep the harp is dead.

*Where is Dyffryn y Gog (Cuckoo's Valley)? Is it the lowland below Penmorfa which is now called the Vale of Madoc?

As the best explanation of the above saga, the following is a copy of a letter sent by the venerable bard, Dafydd Ddu Eryri to his bardic friend, Ieuan Lleyn, which was posted at Llanfair Bettws Geraint, Anglesey, on January 24th 1793.

Dear Friend.

Relative to your enquires about Cantre'r Gwaelod, which is now covered by the sea. I have not happened to come across many actual facts, but what little I know I will tell you freely and willingly, therefore, study the following.

I believe that, according to history, the sea flooded the area around the years 540 to 550 or 560 at the most. That is at the time at Gwyddno Garanhir, father of Elphin who, according to legend, found the bard Taliesin lamenting the father's tragic loss thus.

The lament of Gwyddno Garanhir
When the wave came over his land.

Gwyddno, king of Cantre'r Gwaelod, married Ystradwen, daughter of Cadell Deyrnlleyg, king of Powys. Gwyddno sired Elphin; Elphin sired Belyn; Belyn sired Tudur; Tudur sired Dyfnwal.

Belyn died in the year 729, Tudur died in the year 750, Dyfnwal was killed by the English at Hereford during the time of Rhodri Molwynog, in the year 757.

I believe that a wall similar to the one built at Malltraeth lately was constructed to prevent the sea over-running the rich lowlands of Cantre'r Gwaelod. Perhaps Sarn Badrig is part of the remains of the wall, about which you and the other inhabitants of Lleyn will know better than I.

It is also believed that the sea breached the area due to the carelessness of the flood-gates keeper, but the best thing to throw light on the subject is the following sonnet which was copied from the Llyfr Dû Caerfyrddin (The Black Book of Carmarthen), by the late historian, Mr Lewis Morys. This, in turn, was copied by me, and here it is:

Seithenyn, stand forth,
Look upon the land's fury,
The sea has overlaid Gwyddno's land.

Accursed he on the water's edge
Who, when drunk on wine, opened
A gap for the rush of water in the sea wall.

Accursed be the maiden
Who let in after the deed
The foaming sea through the gap.

The sound of the waves on the fortresses,
The surface reaches wide
After violence, dissolution.

The sound of the sea on fortress wall,
Today until you worship God,
After violence, remorse.

The sound of the sea on brown earth,
God's bounteous throne reigns;
After excess, want.

The sound of the sea overcomes me
Tonight and over-eagerness fails
After violence, vexation.

The sound of the sea imprisons me.
Tonight by my room.
After violence, long dissolution.

The following englyn is among the Englynion Beddau Milwyr Prydain (stanza of the Graves of Britain's Soldiers)

The grave of Seithenyn the foolish
Between Caer Ceredig and Glan
Surrounded by mighty seas.

From the words 'A'i hellyngawdd gwedi gwin' (who, when drunk on wine, opened) in the second verse, one may believe that it was because of his drunkenness that the keeper of the sluice gates allowed the overflow to happen. I think 'Cadair Cedawl' was a defensive position; possibly one should read the fourth verse, 'Oddiar fur caer hyd ar Dduw y dodir' (Off the fortress walls to God is raised, etc.)

'Môr y Werydd yw Môr Werddon' (the Atlantic Ocean is the Irish Sea). Who was Seithenyn, and where was Caer Ceredig? Perhaps the inquisitive will search, but there is a place called 'Caer Wyddno' (Gwyddno's Fort) between Sarn Badrig and Aberystwyth.

A stone was found close to the sea near Barmouth with Latin letters inscribed on it, but in an unknown language.

I am yours truly

D Ddu Eryri

Llanfair Bettws Geraint in Anglesey. January 24th 1793

Note: Seithenyn ap Seithyn Seidi, also called 'Seithenyn Feddw' (Drunken Seithenyn) was a prince of Dyfed who lived in the latter part of the fifth century. Both he and Geraint and Gwrtheyrn were noted drunkards. It was while he was in a drunken state that he allowed the sea to flow though the sluice gates that protected Cantre'r Gwaelod and which resulted in the overflowing of the whole area with water. This province now forms the anchorage at Cardigan. Those inhabitants who escaped the disaster fled to the higher regions of Meirion and Arfon (at that time an uncultivated region). Seithenyn had many sons who, after being left destitute after the destruction of their lands, embraced a religious life at the college of Dunod. Their names were Tudglyd, Gwnodyl, Merini, Tudno, Teneio and Senewyr. – IOLO MSS.

Both the historian and the observant may well see a vast area for further research. Although the prospects for a factual explanation of Cantre'r Gwaelod are, at the moment, somewhat remote in view of the scant evidence available. The old poem from the Black Book and a study of the place names around the lowlands of the cantref on the banks of Ardudwy, Eifionydd, Lleyn and Dyfi, may lead to further light being shed on the subject. It is possible that eventually a story will be created that is both credible and based on a solid foundation of fact.

It was mentioned in the poem on Cadair Cadawl that there is a palace or heirdom carrying the name Gors y Gedawl (Marsh of Gedawl) in Ardudwy, opposite the head of the causeway. In the churchyard of Llanfihangel y Traethau can be seen a memorial stone with an inscription showing it to be the grave of a king or prince of a place that does not appear on the surface of the sea or on land many miles from the Vale of Ardudwy towards the sea. This fact may convince some people that Cantre'r Gwaelod was once a fertile land.

A DROWNING AT CRICCIETH IN 1838

On Friday, October 19th, 1838, the captains of three ships, viz; John Watkins of *Blue Vein*, William Williams of *Eifion*, and Richard Jones of *Linnet*, were together in a small boat that put out from Criccieth with the intention of making towards Portmadoc with stores for the two first named vessels. As they approached 'The Bar' a huge wave struck the boat, which capsized and the three captains were drowned.

Watkins left a widow and six children to mourn their loss; Wm. Williams was married but had no children and Jones was unmarried. The following excellent englynion were composed after the calamity by the venerable bard whose name is attached.

The three who served together, three sailors
Sad rites for Criccieth;
Three who ended the journey
Through desolate seas, three together.

The boat in a moment overturned beneath them,
The great waves already,
So were lost in ocean's flood
Three loved ones, their three lives.

While their kinfolk live there will be grief,
And tears will fall;
For a long time will be heard
Their sighs and lamentations.

We hope for them a perfect land,
Without fear or adversity,
Where their pure souls shall be,
A place beyond loss in a better land.

Though we suffered and died in youth,
Sailing the salt sea,
We are placed and protected
In a grave without fear of drowning. – ROBERT AP GWILYM DDU OF EIFION

THE VALE OF MADOG

The following is a shortened version of the history of this valley and relates only to that section that lies in Tre'r Gest (apart from a few details about the boundaries).

The Vale of Madog stands partly in the parish of Penmorfa, partly in the parish of Ynyscynhaiarn in Tre'r Gest, and partly in the parishes of Llanfihangel-y-pennant and Beddgelert. On the eastern side is the commote of Ardudwy, Meirionydd. It is not easy to find an area of land the size of Dyffryn Madog connected to so many parishes, with boundaries so tortuous and changeable.

The boundary runs from Wern, Penmorfa, to Pwllgloewlas in the parish of Penmorfa, then Ynyscynhaiarn to Bwlchymoch; to the borders of Aberdunant in the parish of Llanfihangel-y-pennant; from there to Cerrigyrhwydwr in the parish of Penmorfa once again; thence to Glandon in the parish of Llanfihangel-y-traethau, Meirion, and then on to Beddgelert; across the valley to the centre of the Embankment; from Bwlchymoch to Aberglaslyn on the eastern side of the river Glaslyn in the parishes of Llanfrothen and Llanfihangel-y-traethau. It will be noted, therefore, that the area lies in six parishes and two counties.

The Vale of Madog (or Traeth Mawr as it used to be called locally) was, at times, a very dangerous place to cross. This was due to the overflowing of the encircling rivers and the influence of high tides on the river Glaslyn, the course of which was subject to frequent changes. Indeed, at certain times, the Traeth was impossible to cross and many were drowned whilst attempting to ford it. The following englyn quotes the times when the tide was wild and dangerous.

> The moon in the east or happy west
> Makes to black stormy tide.
> North and south, it is said,
> Turn the streams of common tides.

A traveller from Lleyn and Eifionydd journeying to Maentwrog, Harlech or Barmouth would, if there were adverse tides, have to wait at Penamser. Tradition says that a 'station' or refuge was located here for the convenience of those waiting for conditions to be more favourable for a safe crossing. If they saw other people coming towards the place, they knew it was 'penamser' (high time to cross) and the guide would shout to say that it was 'amser' (time). That was how the place was given that name.

Penamser, too, was the only place where a man could take his animals from a dealer; if he failed to pay he was liable to punishment. The reason for this most probably is that the location is on the boundaries of two counties.

There is common land between Penamser and Pontfaen, near to the Wern, Penmorfa and here drovers could keep their animals until the Traeth was in a fit state for them to cross in safety – sometimes they would have to wait a week or even a fortnight. The alterative route for them would be along the tiring and dangerous old road up by Gesail Cyfarch, past Oerddwr to Pont Aberglaslyn, where there was a branch of an old Roman road past Cwmcloch and down to Beddgelert.

For the traveller from Anglesey and Arfon wishing to cross to Merionethshire, it would be necessary for him to cross by a narrow road (or Snowdon Pass) between two huge mountains and then over Aberglaslyn Bridge, winding along through Nanmor or (Nantymor), where the famous bards Rhys Goch Eryri and Dafydd Nanmor were brought up together.

There is one road going through Nanmor to Croesor and another crossing the marshes to Peurhyndeudraeth; this starts at Llyn Glâs, crossing the river Cwmcaeth. This road used to go ahead through the Morfa, crossing the river at Nanmor, then along the river to Carreg-hylldrem (this being the boundary berween Llanfrothen and Beddgelert). No-one can remember seeing a road beyond Carreg-Hylldrem bridge because the sea and the tides covered the whole area.

Before the Embankment was built the tide probably came to Aberglaslyn Bridge, thus enabling small vessels and boats to reach this point. The following englyn, the work of Dafydd Nannor, was both recorded and memorised and showed the times of high tide in the upper reaches of the Traeth:

At the new moon, at nine o'clock
The highest tide will reach,
With the full moon the tide will come
To the same mark of change.

When following the road mentioned, the traveller would see a large gulf appear in front of him which resembled those of Polynesia – a parish of islands. The Gulf, once called Traeth Mawr is now named The Vale of Madog or Cuckoo's Valley (Dyffryn y Cogau). Between it and Cardigan Bay is Moel y Gest, and on the northern side lie another range of mountains viz; y Graig wen, y Foel ddu, Moel hebog and many others. On the eastern side, between it and the rising sun, stand Cnicht, yr Arddu and the rich Moelwyns. They are like splendid sentinels continuously guarding these small islands, which are garlanded with beautiful greenmantles. On the other side lies Penrhyndeudraeth, a shapely section of land separated from another gulf called Traeth Bach (the small beach or little strand).

The length of the Vale of Madog from Clogyberth to Aberglaslyn Bridge is seven miles; its width between Clogyberth and Trwyn y Penrhyn (that is, the length of the Embankment) is approximately one mile. It varies in width from one to one and a half miles as one proceeds towards Aberglaslyn Bridge. Thus says the old bard, Glaslyn:

> Protected by the causeway, challenging ocean's might,
> The widespread fertile lowland extends within my sight;
> This land retrieved by Madocks from the rapacious sea,
> While grass make green the meadows, famous will ever be.

LLIDIART YSBYTTY – This was one of the oldest cottages in the district, being within 300 yards of Tremadog. Ys-bwyd-ty is an old Welsh name for hospital. A monastic order, bearing the name Knights of Hospitalus, came to this country during the time of the Crusades; their aim was to provide succour to the soldiers and pilgrims going to or returning from the Crusades. A writer in Notes and Queries shows plainly that 'Ysbytty' is a derivation of 'hospitum', this fact being further strengthened by the knowledge that any 'ysbytty' or 'bettws' can be traced to the times of the Crusades, and are not of earlier origin. This was a strange and remarkable period of history because of the conflict in Europe caused by the Crusades. The Knights of St John of Jerusalem set up many establishments and it is certain that this was one of them.

YNYS FADOG – This lies within 400 yards of Tremadoc, the name 'Madog' has survived from ancient times. It is known that Owain Gwynedd had twenty children. He was married to Gwladus, daughter of Llywarch ap Trehaeren, ap Caradawg, and from her sired Iorwerth Drwyndwn, Cynan, Moelwyn and Gwenllian. He was also married to Grisiant, daughter of Goronwy ap Owain ap Edwin and from her sired Dafydd, Rhodri, Cadwallon (ap Enlli) and Angharad (who married Gruffydd Maelor). Besides these there were his 'natural children': Cynan, Llewellyn, Meredydd, Idwal, Rhun, Howel, Cadell, Madawg, Einion, Gynrig, Philip and Rhirid. Of the above twenty children, three, Rhun, Llewellyn and Cynfrig, died before their father.

Giraldus Cambrensis states that the cantrefs of Lleyn and Eifionydd were in the possession of the children of Owain Gwynedd when he (Geraldus) was on his journey through the country and he noted that they had two castles, one at Penrhyndeudraeth and the other at Garnfadryn. There were two dominant family lines living in this area in olden times; one family were the descendants of Collwyn ap Tango in whose ownership were houses and lands at Chwilog, Bronyfoel, Gwynfryn, Tal hen bont (Plas Hen) and Penardd.

The other families came from the line of Owain Gwynedd and lived at Gesail Gyfarch, Bryncir, Ystumcegid, Clennenau, Glasfryn and Cwmystradllyn. There was continual fighting and spilling of blood between the two families.

Many farms in the area bear the names of Owain Gwynedd's sons: Bron Cynan (Bwlchyfedwen), Wern Rhirid (or Gwernddwyryd), Caegwenllian, Hendrehowel, Tyddyneinion and Caerfadog etc.

As Madog was illegitimate, there was no chance of him succeeding to his father's seat. He also lived in the midst of his enemies and so, being attracted to the sea, he had built some very strong ships.

According to history, these were constructed at Wern, Penmorfa, where ample stocks of timber were available at Coedycefn. In the year 1170 he sailed away towards the west, returning in 1172, giving high praise to the lands he had seen. He anchored off Ynys Fadog, the present site of Tremadoc (the place was called Ynys Fadog generations before Mr Madocks was born). He sailed away again for a second time, accompanied by his brother Rhirid and the elite of the area (approx 300 men and women in 10 ships). They encountered very stormy weather when returning home as they passed through Bardsey Sound, where they nearly lost their ship.

Great Madog of noble countenance,
True son of Owain Gwynedd;
Gentle was he, desiring no land
Or great wealth, save for the sea.

THE PURCHASE OF THE LANDS AND THE START OF THE FIRST EMBANKMENT (TURF AND SOIL)

In the year 1798 William Alexander Madocks (whose coat of arms bore the motto 'Not man for himself only') bought up many of the surrounding farms, as well as the leasehold of some of them. These included Tanrallt, Tuhwnt i'r bwlch, Clogyberth, Llidiart Yspytty, Penyclogwyn and many others; formerly they were owned by RT Price of Rhiwlas, near Bala.

After Mr Madocks had cleared off the terms of the purchase with the owners and cottagers of the area, he started work on the earthen sea wall that extends from Trwynygraig, Prenteg to Clogyberth, Portmadoc. This was semi-circular in shape, approximately 2 miles in length, and enclosed some 2,000 acres of good fertile land. In its second season of cultivation the reclaimed land produced abundant crops of excellent wheat, barley and rye.

For the local people it was a period of great hardship – food was dear and wages were small. Oatmeal cost £3 a peck and there was no convenient market, the nearest being either at Pwllheli, Caernarvon or Llanrwst. One old man who worked on the sea wall once travelled to Penmachno to buy a stone of flour, which he had converted into bread, this he carried on his back all the way to Traethmawr.

Sometimes two or three partners, with a horse or pony, would travel through the night to Pwllheli to make their purchases, but they always faced the danger of being robbed by others who would treacherously lie in wait for them. Even the oldest of the inhabitants could not recollect a leaner or poorer time than this. However, when Mr Madocks came to the area a new dawn broke and the area was rejuvenated. There was now plenty of work available in the area, and many were able to say in later years that they had worked on the sea wall when they were young.

One old woman living at Tremadoc drove her father's horse and sled when she was only 9 or 10 years old. Her job was to cart turf to the sea wall. The tide would often create trouble to the turf walls, so there was ample work continuously repairing the damage. Others would be engaged cutting canals the length and breadth of the Traeth in all directions so that the tidal waters would be able to come up to Penmorfa and Prenteg. This was not only to cultivate the land but also helped to prevent damage to the wall; it also helped to purify the area from the unhealthy damp and choking mist that came from the wet earth. This had proved very unhealthy for the inhabitants, and in earlier times the parishioners of Penrhyn had also suffered from its effect.

They were also building Tremadoc at the time (1805) and work was proceeding on the house Tan'rallt. Mr Madocks was anxious to come and live there and leave Dolmelynllyn in Ganllwyd near Dolgelley. Ty Nanney was built by David Ellis-Nanney, Barrister, from Gwynfryn, and Morfa Lodge by Dr Morris, but all the other buildings were erected by Mr Madocks at his own expense. This included a beautiful church on a hillock called Ynys y Gwartheg (Isle of the Cattle) as the parish church was too far away.

This church, especially the porch, was acclaimed as one of the most beautiful buildings of that time. It was 32 yards in length by 14 yards in width; the bell tower reached a height of 34 yards. It was intended to place a peal of bells in the tower, it being said that they were already loaded on a ship when it was recalled by the owner after he had been informed of Mr Madocks' misfortune. In their absence, therefore when vespers were being held in the church, the town crier would ring a bell at the porch. In the year 1842 Mr J Williams of Tuhwnt i'r bwlch, fitted the bell which is there at present.

Mr Madocks obtained an Act of Parliament concerning Tremadoc Church in 1810; this gave him many extra privileges connected with it and also land worth £30 per annum at the time (£100 at present day values). These are the church meadows close to the Factory, which are not subject to tithe. The porch in front of the church is a source of admiration by visitors. It was originally in front of a palace in Italy and cost Mr Madocks £500, it being made of some composition held together with screws. Children have disfigured it compared to what it was when originally erected. In any case the Act of Parliament has not been enforced up till now because of a misunderstanding between Mr Madocks and the Bishop of the time.

W Alexander Madocks, Esq, MP
Tan'rallt, Tremadoc

It has been mentioned previously that the organ cost Mr D Ellis-Nanney £300. This was a barrelled organ but another one was obtained during the time of Mr Mathew of Wern. The ceiling of the church had been painted with stars of the best quality but these were covered over with limewash in later years. Mr Madocks built a spacious Market Hall and a Woollen Factory (large enough to accommodate 60 weavers), together with a Fulling Mill, a Dye House and ample storage space, a Corn Mill, together with all the houses around Tremadoc Square, those by the Factory, and also the row of small houses that stand along the road to the toll-gate, which are called Dublin Street.

The houses by Llidlart Ysbytty were built by John, Robert and Ellis Griffith. They were stonemasons and were foremen in the building of Tremadoc, but not of the church.

Mr Madocks succeeded in arranging for a twice-weekly distribution of mail. The mail coach was met at Pont Aberglaslyn on its way from Caernarfon to Maentwrog. Thousands of trees of all species were planted and a large nursery was created with apples, pears, plums and all types of fruit that were considered suitable for conditions in this part of Wales.

In spite of all his achievements and his success with the first sea wall, Mr Madocks was far from being satisfied. He now envisaged building a solid wall of stone right across the Traeth from Ynystowyn (on the Caernarfonshire side) to Trwyn y Penrhyn (on the Meirionydd side). If this could be successfully completed he would not only gain for himself thousands of fertile acres, but it would also provide a safe and convenient highway connecting the two shires. Additionally, such an embankment would also protect his present sea wall which, on one occasion, had been badly breached by a heavy storm combined with a southwesterly wind and high tides. This breach had caused hardships to the inhabitants and had proved costly to repair.

His earlier venture had been completed without any argument and was effective, but he now sought the consent of neighbouring land owners from Trwyn y Penrhyn to Pont Aberglaslyn and, on the other side of Ynys Cyngar, up to the Traeth. Eventually he presented a Bill to Parliament which would enable him to construct this new embankment which would exclude the sea entirely from Traethmawr and give him ownership of all the land from Penyclogwyn y Gest to Pont Aberglslyn. This property was to be his and his heirs forever, plus a fifth of the adjoining lands. In 1807 the Bill was brought before Parliament under the sponsorship of Lieut. General Thomas Parry Jones-Parry of Madryn.

To complete preparations for the proposed work, Mr Madocks bought the farm of Penrhyn isaf in order that ample supplies of stone would be available to build the wall on the Merioneth side. Permission given to proceed with the work, and all preparatory details completed, saw the enterprise commencing in earnest in March 1805. Within a few months some 300-400 workmen (English, Welsh and Scots) were busy breaking rocks and transporting them to the site, carpenters and stonemasons were also provided with ample work.

Boston Lodge, the site of the present foundry, was originally constructed to house the forges of the blacksmiths, the workshops of the carpenters and also the stabling. Here, too, were the 'barracks' for the workmen employed on this adventurous undertaking. It was called Boston Lodge because Mr Madocks was the Member of Parliament for Boston at the time.

Work on the Caernarfonshire side made much slower progress than that on the Merioneth side because there was a greater depth of water. This was caused by tidal water as it flowed swiftly against Ynys Towyn meeting the waters of the river Glaslyn. The action of these two bodies of water created a deep pool by Ynys Towyn which was called Llyn y Cob (Cob Pool).

None of the older people remembers the sea covering the land on which the town of Portmadoc now stands. There was a road past Trwyn Cae Iago with houses alongside, which led towards Borth. The area called Brecon Place was once a high sand-dune covered in gorse which reached a height of three to four yards. It was estimated to be about 3 feet higher than ground level at Tremadoc.

John Roberts of Penyclogwyn and old Betty Evan have both said that they had never seen water covering the above mentioned places. There was a small cottage on the spot where the bridge now stands called Pant yr Ynys (Island hollow) but this was demolished to make way for the bridge and enable a cut to be made to form the course of the river. Making the bed for the river was work undertaken predominantly by English, Irish and Scots, for very few Welshmen could follow the task of taking wheelbarrows along the stout planks to the shore. The bridge was completed before the river bed was finished.

The house at Ynystowyn was built for Mr J Williams, who also used it as his office. Mr Ellis Owen of Cefnymeusydd was his secretary.

As the gap narrowed between the two approaching arms of the embankment, the hardships and difficulties increased; and because of the low water in the Glaslyn and the tidal ebb and flow, the work of many people over many months could be destroyed in an hour. Many believed, as Dewi Wyn did:

> Greater peril than victory or exploit
> Will be the siege of the ocean;
> No wall will halt the flood
> Of the deep sea, we can but fear.

> Though wise men plan constantly, and heroes
> Have schemes of Genius,
> And all the building of walls
> Water will find its boundaries.

An old ship was filled with stones and sunk in the gap; this lessened the enormous torrents. The bridge was opened and this allowed part of the flood through, thus enabling work to proceed fairly easily, but the problem was of great concern to Mr Madocks. However, all difficulties were overcome at last, and in 1811 a roadway was established between the two counties. This, of course, gave great satisfaction to Mr Madocks and his friends, and was celebrated by the whole country in general.

A dark cloud dashed their hopes in 1812 for, on 14th February of that year, a tremendous storm came up from the southwest. Gale force winds and a very high tide caused the sea to batter the Embankment, which was breached close to its centre. The sea running through the breach caused considerable havoc sweeping everything in front of it over a wide area. Mr Madocks was not in the area at the time so the whole brunt of the disaster fell on his Agent, Mr John Williams, as Dewi Wyn quotes:

> Backing the gifted Madocks – a brave leader
> When the wall was breached;
> All men with one mind
> Throughout the land supported him.

Meirionydd, Arfon and Anglesey were greatly disturbed and overawed by this catastrophe, for the eyes of the whole country had been on this achievement when the tide had been stemmed and a convenient roadway made to connect the two shires. Beside the assistance given by the tenants of the various land owners, a meeting was held on 28th September at Baron Hill in Beaumaris, under the chairmanship of Lord Bulkeley, when the following resolutions were passed;

1) It was resolved that the Tremadoc Embankment is of great public advantage in facilitating the intercourse between the counties of Carnarvon and Merioneth, and the traffic of the Principality.

2) That seal and liberality were shown upon the late occasion when the Embankment suffered from the extraordinary high Tide.

3) That for the purpose of the meeting the wishes of numerous persons in different parts of the principality, who are in favour of this undertaking for the necessary expenses of completing and repairing the injury it has sustained.

4) That the thanks of the meeting be given to Mr Madocks, not only for the public spirit he has manifested in a work of such extensive enterprise, but one connected with the prosperity and improvement of the Principality.

5) That the Subscriptions be paid to Messrs Williams and Grenfell, for the Carnarvon Bank, to the names of Lord Viscount Bulkeley, Sir Robert Williams, Bart. MP, David Ellis, Esq; and R Middleton Bidulph, Esq, MP.

Lord Bulkeley having vacated the Chair. It was resolved that the thanks of the meeting be given to Lord Viscount Bulkeley for the prompt support he has already given to the Embankment disaster, and for presiding at this Meeting.

Here follows the names of the subscribers, together with the amount of their subscription at that meeting, but the full list is very much longer.

	£	s	d
Warren Bulkeley, Baron Hill	100	0	0
David Ellis, Gwynfryn	100	0	0
William Glynne Griffith, Bodegroes	100	0	0
Edward Lloyd, Rhagatt	100	0	0
Edward Price Lloyd, Pengwern	100	0	0
Joseph Madocks, London	100	0	0
John Madocks, Berkeley Square	50	0	0
Robert Morris, MD, Tanrallt Isa'	50	0	0
Watkin Thelwell, Chester	50	0	0
Percy B Shelley, Tremadoc (The Poet)	100	0	0
John Evans, Carnarvon	50	0	0
Kirkwall, Deganwy Castle	50	0	0
Robert Williams, Friars	50	0	0
R Middleton Bidulph, Chirk Castle	50	0	0
John Heaton	30	0	0
William Williams	5	0	0

NOTES ON SOME OF THE ABOVE SUBSCRIBERS

Thomas Warren Bulkeley (Lord Bulkeley), who died in the year 1822, was the son of James Warren Bulkely, Viscount Cathels, who married Emma, heiress of Thomas Rowlands of Nant Esq. Emma later married Sir Hugh Williams of Penrhyn and Marle; they were the father and mother of Sir Robert Williams Bart. MP, The Friars, and father of the late Sir Richard Bulkely Bart. MP of Baron Hill and grandfather of the present Sir Richard Bulkely Bart..

Edward Lloyd Esq was the father-in-law of RJ Price of Rhiwlas, and grandfather of the present Mr Price.

David Ellis, or David Ellis-Nanney, Barrister at Law, Gwynfryn.

John Evans, was a Solicitor at Llanllyfni, Nantlle and Carnarvon.

William Williams of Garnedd wen was the brother of John Williams, the Agent.

Doctor Robert Morris MD, built Morfa Lodge Portmadoc in the year 1809.

There is a tablet to both him and his wife's memory in Beddgelert Church. He died at Liverpool in 1825, and was burried at the above church.

Percy Byshe Shelley, the English Bard, is known world-wide. He was born in Sussex in the year 1792, the son of a Baron. The special qualities of his cultured poetry have been marred by his agnostic ideas. He drowned in the Gulf of Spezia in 1822.

Rather than succumb to the disaster Mr J Williams responded bravely and surprised many by his wisdom. He immediately wrote letters to gentlemen and farmers in the area from whom he thought he might receive support. Scores of people from all parts of the country, with horses carts and wagons came in droves from Anglesey, Arfon, Denbigh and from every farmer in the locality.

In the meantime, PB Shelley came to live at Tan'rallt in Tremadog. He was of great assistance at this crucial time, not only by calling on certain gentlemen but also by holding meetings throughout the counties of Arfon, Anglesey and Denbigh and he pleaded for support from the country in general – both cash and kind. He stressed the benefits and improvements to the whole country which had resulted from the great efforts and ideas of Mr Madocks. Mr Shelley was successful in his endeavours, which was fortunate since large sums of money were required for such an enterprise.

The cost of food and also wages had to be paid to the workers and hundreds of pounds worth of timber etc were required, but by the end of 1814 the breach was closed yet again. This was achieved by sinking a vessel full of stones in the gap, which made the wall safe and sound. The achievement was over a mile long, 100 feet in height in some places and 400 feet wide at the base: the cost totalled £100,000.

The bridge cost £1,200, the foundations at the eastern end being on the rocks of Ynystowyn. Rock was not available at the other end, so timber baulks (piles) had to be driven in to create a suitable foundation.

The next enterprise that Mr Madocks wished to undertake was the provision of a harbour at Porthmadog to facilitate the loading and unloading of ships. In a letter from Aberystwyth sent to Mr J Williams, he said he was 'thankful that the seawall was safe because this is the mainstay of the whole of our aim, our safeguard and our victory'. Porthmadog was only an area of sand dunes at that time, covered with tall gorse – all trade and traffic in ships being carried out at Ynys cyngar.

After safeguarding the wall and opening the bridge gates, the ebb and flow of the tide was controlled by the sluice gates, with the river Glaslyn also flowing through them, this system remains to the present day. There was deep water below the bridge. This had been created naturally by the new course of the river and it became evident that it would be possible to build a convenient harbour there.

Mr Madocks submitted a Bill for this which went through the House with very little opposition and it received the Royal Assent on June 15th 1821. The boundaries of the port extended to the far end of the Embankment (that is, from Trwyn y Penrhyn to Trwyn y Garth, Penyclogwyn) and from there to the far extent of Garreg wen y Gest. Every ship or vessel unloading in any part of Traethmawr between these points was liable for payment of harbour dues. Mr Madocks was busy working out the needs of the Parliamentary Act of 1821 to make the port a convenient place to load and unload ships, as well as other improvements.

By the end of 1824 the first quay had been established, with ships entering regularly to load and unload. At this time there were only five or six houses at Portmadoc – blacksmiths, cobblers, carpenters' shops, the tailor and shopkeeper were at Tremadoc.

The brave gentleman had exhausted all his capital by this time, so he was forced to take out a mortgage to obtain money to pay for the new works. His visits to the district became less frequent, and when he came he stayed at Morfa Lodge. In the meantime he had married and lived at Hay in Brecknock. In 1829 he crossed to the Continent and in that year he died in France being buried near Paris.

Where long the seas stormed, are glades
And fertile pastures,
A memorial for our hero
Who made a living for thousands.

Where he formed his foundation
Let a monument be raised;
A tower of lasting memory
Where he trod, for evermore.

After building the Factory at Tremadoc, the woollen mill was taken over by a company under the name of Scott & Wardle – two wealthy, adventurous gentlemen. This company carried on at the mill for a number of years with 60 looms at work producing material of a quality equal to any town in Yorkshire. Two ships were laden and sent to France with materials for soldiers' uniforms (at this time there was war between England and France) but the vessels were arrested by an English gunboat and the sailors imprisoned for carrying goods to the enemy. There was a lawsuit between the Duke of York and Colonel Wardle (one of the mill's directors) over an alleged slander; Wardle lost the action. This court case and the loss of the two ships created financial trouble and work had to be halted for a while. After this the mill was taken over by a gentleman named Mr Barnes, that is, the father of John Barnes, who had married the daughter of Cefnymeusydd ucha', a sister of the mother of Capt JR Jones and the Rev T Jones of Eisteddfa.

Mr Barnes continued the work for a number of years and then it was taken over by a Mr Bidwell. He engaged William Williams (the father of William and Richard Williams) as his foreman. Mr Bidwell was a well known merchant who dealt in shipments of corn, flour, beans and many other commodities in addition to his interests at the factory, fulling mill, corn mill and a large warehouse close to the Mill. He also held Farmyard for a time, but something went amiss between him and Mr Madocks, so he had to leave. After this, Robert Ellis of the Fleece, Tremadoc took control followed later by Richard and William Williams.

Tremadoc Market opened with much official pomp and ceremony, as can be seen from the following (taken from an old manuscript found at Tuhwnt i'r bwlch):

On the 8th day of November, 1805, the first Market was held at Tremadoc; the following officers were sworn in:

William Williams, Merchant................Mayor
Robert Morris Esq, MD........................Chamberlain
John Edward Madocks Esq ....Alderman
Charles Mitchel Esq ....Alderman
William Amos Esq ....Alderman
Horace Wyche Billington Esq..............Alderman
John Ellis, Gentleman ....Deputy Recorder and Sergeant

NOTES on the above officers: William Williams was the first merchant in the town after it was built and died around the year 1840. Many of his family can still be found around the district – Mrs Mary Williams of the Smithy, and her sons, William, Robert and John Williams, her daughter Mrs Jones of Tremadog, and Mrs Lloyd of Llechwedd du, etc.

On the 3rd of December, 1837, that is, the first Sunday after the burial of John Madocks Esq of Glanywêrn, prayer meetings were held at Tremadoc Church and all the Non-conformist chapels in the town and neighbouring area were full to capacity of listeners. He had died at Glanywern, near Denbigh on November 20th 1837, aged 52.

Charles Mitchel was Mr Madocks' secretary.

William Amos was a flour and timber merchant. He was followed by William Morris and then by William Owen (Elizabeth Owen & Sons).

Horace Wyche Billington was the husband of Mrs Billington, the actress.

John Ellis of The Union Tavern was the son of Ellis Griffith of Ystumllyn bach.

A market has been held at Tremadog every Friday from then up to the present day (unless there were some special reasons to change the day to another one). Over the years it grew to be a lively market, especially in oatmeal and pigs, setting the standard for the price of oatmeal for the whole county. As there was no market in the north of Merioneth closer than Dolgellau or Llanrwst, the residents of Ffestiniog, Trawsfynydd, Harlech, and all of North Meirionydd would congregate at Tremadog Market. However, as Portmadoc increased in importance, larger warehouses were built there to hold large quantities of corn, flour, beans etc and consequently the market at Tremadoc deteriorated badly.

Before Porthmadog was made into a convenient harbour, merchants used to get their goods from Wrexham and Chester. These were transported in huge wagons which had to cross over the mountains and were often delayed. This method proved very inconvenient to the public in general, since they were often waiting for weeks for the stores to be delivered.

Boats of approximately 15 to 20 tons were used to convey coal, lime and seeds in the district, but these consignments were very erratic. Around the year 1824, a regular service was established between Porthmadog and Llynlleifiad (Liverpool). This used a small ship of about 40 tons bearing the name *Experiment*. It was owned by Mr Holland, father of Samuel Holland Esq. Prior to this there were no regular trading ships, but many vessels engaged in 'trade' long before the steamer service was introduced. The Liverpool trade became very poor for sailing ships because the steamer was able to maintain a regular timetable; this being of great advantage to the merchants.

It can be seen from a letter sent by Mr Madocks to Mr Williams as early as 1814 that the former's main objective was to connect Portmadoc and Festiniog by means of a railway. Apart from the benefit that would accrue to all quarry owners, this project would also be a safe and very manageable method of conveying the slates straight from the quarries directly to the port; it would also establish a solid exchange of other goods between the two places. In the year 1824 we find that Mr Madocks had seen the plans and measurements of the track, but that was all.

In 1826, Samuel Holland, Esq MP contacted a Mr Henry Archer (the same gentleman who had designed the machine for perforating postage stamps) and requested him to come over from Ireland to Porthmadog to plan a railway between the latter place and Ffestiniog. With the assistance of Mr Spooner of Morfa Lodge it was surveyed, measured and planned. A Bill was presented to

Parliament in 1831 but was strongly opposed by the merchants, the hauliers with their boats and carts, and all the cottagers of the parishes of Maentwrog and Ffestiniog, and by all others who profited from the quarries. Such was the antagonism that some even went to London to voice their objections, fearing that their livelihood would suffer. The Bill was initially thrown out but in 1832, an Act of Parliament on May 3rd authorised the project.

In February 1833 the first foundation stone was laid at Tanybwlch Station, and work progressed so rapidly that by 20th April 1836 a 'slate train' travelled from Mr Holland's quarry at Ffestiniog to Porthmadog. Mr Archer formed a company named The Festiniog Railway Co. Agreement with other quarries, such as Rhiwbryfdir, were not reached at the time, but Samuel Holland Esq carried on faithfully. In the year 1837 the Welsh Slate Company joined in, seeing the advantages gained by Mr Holland in getting his slates down from the quarry and exporting them straightaway. The capital laid down by the company was £25,000, and £1,400 was borrowed to complete the arrangements. The loans given to the company realised Interest of 6, 7, and 8 per cent in the £. Among all the improvements there is not one that has benefitted more from all the hard work and determination than agriculture.

It is a fact that the lands that Mr Madocks bought for 2s 6d to 4s 0d per acre are now being rented at between £2 and £3 per acre. One has only to look at places like 'Farm Yard', Ynys Hir, Tyddyn Madog, Pensyflog, and other holdings in the Vale to see that they are like gardens bearing abundant crops. A bard has said:

> Where fish leaped, great sea creatures
> Is now an abundant vale,
> A pasture for sheep, rams and goats.

It can be said without fear of contradiction that this is indeed, a blossoming vale.

> The lowlands we can see, the pools
> Are glades of clover;
> The dwellings of men are raised
> Where once were water and waves. – ALLTUD EIFION

POSTSCRIPT TO THE EMBANKMENT

Today, we cannot contemplate the labour difficulties in the construction of the Embankment. It was only recently that a method of drilling stones and blasting them with explosives had been discovered, but at that time only about one workman in every hundred was capable of doing this work. Considerable time was also taken to train navvies to take wheelbarrows along narrow planks. Rails and wagons were not in use, only sleds. Iron and timber were costly and craftsmen were in short supply.

It was at this time that 'Hwntw mawr' as he was called, perpetuated the dastardly deed of murdering the little maid-servant of Penrhyn isa'. ('Hwntw' is an appellation given to a man from South Wales.) He was executed at Dolgellau Prison for his misdeeds. I knew the man who captured him by going into the waters of the traeth up to his neck; it was stated that 'Hwntw' was a giant of a man

There was great rejoicing when the Embankment was completed and to commemorate the occasion a whole ox stuffed with potatoes was roasted on a huge fire of peat and wood close to Ynystowyn. Dafydd Ddu Eryri wrote the following about the sluice gates that are under the bridge:

On the sea's rim are sluice gates
To open and close above it,
For the work stands firm,
Letting go and holding too.

In the year 1851 a new Bridge and Basin were built with the intention of making a safe haven and anchorage for ships. It was intended to repair the old bridge and make it into a drawbridge, but this project remains uncompleted at the present time.

Many notable and high class personages were present when the foundation stone was laid and the day declared a public holiday in the area. There were hundreds off sightseers on the top of Ynystowyn. The learned bard, Nicander, sang thus:

See the tower'd crag of Criccieth's ancient castle
Above the foaming deep, a wonder to behold;
Above the ocean's wrath and the stormy depths,
This view makes for poets a wonder to be told.
To Treflys and Ynys, my fancy leads me,
Madoc's town well placed with the sea at hand;
The muddy depths where the waves rolled
Are fields of clover, an abundant land.

FURTHER NOTES ON THE VALE OF MADOG

According to the letters that passed between Sir John Wynn of Gwydir and Sir Hugh Middleton in the year 1536, it is believed that the first named was the owner of the lands surrounding the Traethmawr. In his letter Sir John invited Sir Hugh to undertake the venture that was completed roughly 200 years later. It is said that this correspondence between the two gentlemen (included in Pennant's *History of Wales*) gave Madocks the idea of building the Embankment and enclosing the Traeth. At that time, also, neighbouring farms were coming under the hammer.

A rather humorous story is told concerning a Dolbenmaen housewife and Shôn the blacksmith. John was busy heating a large piece of iron and the wife said when she greeted him; 'what are you going to do with that?' 'Oh' said John, 'I am going to make a large staple to pull Moel y Gest into the large gap to close the Traeth.' 'Really,' she said, 'I have heard of this when I was a little girl.' Is it possible that Sir John Wynn's idea continued as folklore in the area for this length of time?

Due to lack of space it is not possible to give in detail the growth in trade in the area and the gradual increase in importance of Porthmadog as a port. A Post Office was established there in the year 1842, but there had been one at Tremadoc since 1805, with Postmen carrying letters to Beddgelert, Garn Dolbenmaen, Criccieth, Porthmadog, etc. Banks were established in Portmadoc in 1837 as branches of the Banks at Pwllheli. First was the North and South Wales in High Street (in a house close to the 'Ship & Castle'), then the National Provincial (set up in the house of the late Hugh Hughes the baker). In 1834 the Custom House was moved from Glandon to Pencei; the officer was Mr Paynter. Many different societies were inaugurated in the area. In 1838 (Christmas) Mr John Williams of Tuhwnt i'r bwlch, Ellis Owen of Cefnymeusydd, Daniel Morris, William Owen (merchant), Robert Isaac Jones and others set up a Friendly Society which lasted for over 40 years; the last named was its secretary from start to finish.

In 1825 the Petty Sessions were moved from Criccieth to Tremadog, at which place they were held until 1860, when a police station was built at Porthmadog. In the year 1846 a small market hall was built at Porthmadog on the spot where the present one now stands. Mr Madocks had built a splendid Market Hall, with a spacious Assembly Hall above it, at Tremadog, with no charges at all except the weighing and storage of flour and corn.

It should be mentioned that a very slack period was experienced after the death of Mr Madocks until his Heiress came of age, and because of the complexity of the estate it was impossible to obtain a lease to build with certainty for 30 years. In 1838 the Annual Hunt Ball was established in the Assembly Rooms at Tremadog, which was suitably decorated for the occasion. Here, also, was held the first daily school, as we shall see later under that heading.

The estate was managed by Trustees, comprising Mr Martin Williams of Bryngwyn and Mr J Powell of Brecon. The entire estate was under the trusty agent, Mr John Williams of Ynystowyn (later he moved to Tuhwnt i'r bwlch). He was looked upon as a minor king by everyone in the area. In 1843, Mr Madocks' only daughter came of age, and great rejoicing took place; celebrations included the roasting of a fat ox, which was shared with the poor.

Later a cloud came over the area when it was known that a Solicitor from Caernarfon (Mr W Lloyd Roberts) had kept alive many mortgages in Chancery on the property of the late Mr WA Madocks. He tried to obtain possession of the estate and there were stormy lawsuits, with Mr David Williams defending. This caused the estate to fall into difficulties, but the slate trade gradually improved and fresh life and activity came to the whole area; this lasting in some measure until the present day.

The construction of a railway from Bala to Blaenau Festiniog and from Bettws y Coed, generally affected and paralysed the trade once seen in the Vale, but who knows what lies in the future?

Someone has mentioned that 'The Ruler of the world does not open the world's treasures to one generation' and all we can say in completing these notes is that someone should erect a memorial to Mr Madocks. He was the man who set the foundation stone of many incomparable improvements to the district and sacrificed his whole resources and energy 'in the Vale' (as he says) that he created and gave it a name.

Note: Most of the above history of the Vale of Madog has been taken from the winning essay of John Jones (Ifor Eifion) of Tremadog, at the Gwynedd Chair Eisteddfod in 1872.

THE EISTEDDFODAU AT TRE'R GEST

Since the National Eisteddfod is an essential part of our education, it perhaps may be expedient to give a short summary of those held in Tre'r Gest during the past 100 years. From this it will be seen that the residents of Tre'r Gest were lovers of learning, although the advantages were very small in the past. Five Eisteddfodau have been held.

The first known was at Wern, Penmorfa, in 1796, under the patronage of the historian and bardic incumbent, the Rev Dafydd Ellis, Vicar of Criccieth and Ynyscynhaiarn. Literary men and bards such as Hywel Eryri and Rev R Jones of Wern attended and the victorious bard was Richard Powell.

In 1811 the Tremadog Eisteddfod was held under the patronage of Mr WA Madocks, at which Dewi Wyn won with his essay on 'Agriculture' and Dafydd Ddu Eryri with his poem entitled 'Embankment' (this he read at the opening of the Eisteddfod). Gwyndaf Eryri, Gutyn Peris, Owen Gwyrfai, Twm o'r Nant and Shon Lleyn were among the bards.

At the beginning of October 1851, Eisteddfod Madog was held under the presidency of Ardalydd Mon, Sir Love Parry, KG, and five gentlemen as vice-presidents. There were over 100 patrons and a committee of 80; the Rev E Andrews, Vicar of Llanfrothen, Samuel Holland of Plas Penrhyn and Ellis

Owen of Cefnymeusydd were secretaries, with Mr (now the Rev) Thomas Jones of Cefnymeusydd as working secretary. Mr David Williamson of Bron eryri was chairman of the committee. The Bard Talhaiarn was compère or presenter of the meetings, with the Arch Druid, Dr James Kirkdale, as president of the 'orsedd' (throne) – a name given to the circle of bards. The first day 30 members were honoured as 'Bards', seven as 'Druids', five as 'Ovates' (female) and 15 (male). On the second day the president of the Orsedd was Carn Ingli (the Rev J Hughes) who deputised in the absence of the Arch Druid. Three were honoured as 'Druids', three as 'Bards' and 20 as 'Ovates'. Among them was Trebor Mai of Carnarvon, later to become a renowned bard. The Hon Lord John Russell, Prime Minister at the time, was one of the patrons. The idea of this Eisteddfod started with the heiress, Mrs Gwynne (who was a widow at the time) corresponding with Eben Fardd and Alltud Eifion.

The third Eisteddfod was called 'The Eryri Chaired Eisteddfod' and was held in August 1872. There were 12 patrons and many committees. The Lords Penrhyn and Mostyn and Sir Watkin Williams Wynn were presidents. This was one of the most renowned and influential eisteddfodau held in Gwynedd within memory and to give all its details would take a complete volume of great size. Although it is only 20 years since it took place, very few of the people who were its leading figures still survive.

The fourth eisteddfod held in the Vale of Madog took place at the end of August 1887 and was called 'The Gwynedd Provincial Eisteddfod'. It had 38 patrons and the presidents were JE Greaves Esq (Lord Lieutenant of the County), Sir Love Jones-Parry of Madryn and FWA Roche Esq. This proved an excellent eisteddfod as regards the subjects and production that ensued. The organisation was excellent under a keen and wise committee but, because there was another following close on its heels and one had just been held in London, it was not as successful as it merited. Inclement weather and many other unforeseen factors caused the committee much grief as they incurred heavy debts and had to fall back on the guarantors – in spite of assistance from many generous gentlemen.

Most probably this generation will pass before the area will once again respond to the staging of another eisteddfod.

EDUCATION OF THE YOUNG

Given here are brief details of the position and the opportunities available in education in Tre'r Gest during the past century. We find that a school was held at Penmorfa at a very early date, this, of course, being run by the gentry in conjunction with the church. No endowments had been made until the death of the Rev David Ellis, Vicar of Criccieth, who left the interest of £200 for the education of a few children from the three parishes in his living. If no children were available, according to the terms of the will, the money was to go towards the upkeep of the church.

When Mr Madocks built the church and the town hall, he earmarked a place for a schoolroom and arranged for land for endowment, but its construction has been delayed (this has not been brought into being yet). A schoolroom on the Lancaster plan was opened in the Town Hall, Tremadoc, in 1810. The first schoolmaster was Owen Williams from Anglesey, then David Morris and Richard Davies (who lived at Llanystumdwy). A native of the south, he was an excellent schoolmaster. Next, in 1816, came John Wynn who had charge for many years and he was followed by a young man from Pwllheli, DM Williams.

The school at this time (around 1824) was one of the most popular in North Wales. DM Williams went to Leicester and was succeeded firstly by Joshua Williams and then by W Jones. In 1837 the Town Hall was renovated and furnished with the intention of holding Balls there, so the school first moved to the church and then to the chapel. John Richards was in charge at first, followed by Mr Stovin.

In 1839 Pontynyscalch was built under the British system but the building was converted into a hotel on the advent of the Cambrian Railway. Many excellent schoolmasters were in charge, such as Morris Davies, Rees Roberts, Mr Jones, Mr Good and others.

In 1855 the National School was built at Portmadog, this being run on a voluntary subscription basis plus pupil payment. It was served by some very good masters. The last before it ceased to exist was Mr R Grindley. Fortunately he labours there again and is one of the most successful teachers in Wales. There can hardly be a son or daughter over the age of 30 living in Portmadog who was not educated by him. A school was held at the Town Hall, Tremadoc in 1856, run by a Miss Jones from Caernarfon; she married Mr David Evans of Church Street. In 1875 the British School was built there and also another in Porthmadog in 1869, a National School was built at Pentrefelin in 1871, which also served as a mission chapel. Many small private schools served the area from time to time, among them being one run by William Griffith (an old injured sailor). An infants school was run by Miss Eagles, an Irish lady, who later married Mr Robert Owen, Tinman, of Porthmadog.

It would be possible to add much more about the history of education in Tre'r Gest, but lack of space prevents it. What has been written may help the rising young generation in the area to see the gradual increase in educational advantages over the years.

THE CONSTRUCTION OF THE ROAD FROM PORTDINLLEYN TO CAPEL CURIG THROUGH TRE'R GEST

We, at the end of the century, have little idea of the difficulties experienced by earlier generations who used the inaccessible and dangerous roads in this part of Eifionydd, say between Criccieth, Penmorfa, Beddgelert and Llanfrothen; roads that sometimes climbed the hillsides to avoid the dangerous floods of the Traeth.

The following is the summary of an Act which was passed in 1803, when Parliament decided to construct a highway from the chief city of London to Dublin. Residents of western Arfon and Anglesey were aware of the advantages and were eager to determine which would be the harbour on the Irish Channel. The notables and the residents of Lleyn and Arfon maintained that Porthdinllaen was the most suitable site, saying that nature had already prepared this location and very little skilled help would be necessary to complete it. A Petition was sent from both Anglesey and Caernarfonshire each praising its own harbour. Objections were raised against Holyhead on the grounds that thousands of pounds would have to be spent before a safe harbour could be provided and added to that would be the cost of building a bridge over the Menai Straits. On the second reading of the Act there was a majority of one in favour of Holyhead, but by the time of the third reading this slender majority had increased.

In the meantime, the gentry of Lleyn and Eifionydd and also parts of Arfon put their shoulders to the wheel and presented a Bill to Parliament seeking authorisation to construct a highway from Porthdinlleyn to the Ceunant Llanfrothen in Meirionydd, then to the Bala road, with a branch to Capel Currig.

The Act was passed on the 17th May 1803, the title being 'Anno Quadragesimo Tertio, Georgia III, Regis, Cap.38'.

The purpose of the Act was to construct and maintain in good repair from Porthdinlleyn to the Ceunant, in the parish of Llanfrothen, Merioneth and from Tanygraig in the parish of Bodfean to Pwllheli and from there to Llanystumdwy, Cricceith and Penmorfa to Cerrigyrhwydwr with a branch towards Beddgelert and Nantgwynant to Capel Currig, to the highway that leads to Bangor Ferry. To build a bridge by Cerrigyrhwydwr and a sea wall from there across the traeth to the turnpike road that leads to Bala., close to the place called Ceunant, with the right to widen and straighten it and move it as required, and to build a seawall from the bridge at Cerrigyrhwydwr and to move the river Glaslyn or Gwyant in order to get rock foundations tor the bridge.

It is apparent that the Act splits the existing roads into two sections, that is, First and Second District roads – one going through to Capel Currig and the other to erect a bridge over the river Glaslyn to make a road to the Ceunant and then to the Bala road. The Act provided for tolls on the bridge and the roads. From the following list of trustees, it will be seen who were the most influential people in the country 90 years ago, two lists of trustees are named in the Act.

TRUSTEES FOR THE FIRST DISTRICT

Rt Hon Thomas Lord Newborough. Hon. Richard Lord Penrhyn. Sir Robert Williams, Friars. Sir Watkin Williams-Wynne. Sir Thomas Mostyn. Robert Thomas, Carreg. Richard Edwards, Nanhoron. Zacheus Hughes, Clerk. Thomas Ellis, Glasfryn, ditto. Richard Ellis, Dinas, ditto. Hugh Ellis, Carnarvon. Robert Evans, Bodfean, Clerk. Wm. Evans, ditto. The Hon. Charles Finch. John Griffith, Llanfair. William Griffith, Carnarvon, Clerk. Ed Griffith, Carnarvon. Hugh Griffith, Pwllheli, Clerk. William Griffith, Bodegroes. W Glynne Griffith, Carnarvon. D Griffith, Methlem. Richard Griffith, Middlesex. William Griffith, Cefncoch. William Harvey, Bodvel. Jeffrey Holland, Dolbenmaen, Clerk. Robert Meyrick Humphreys, clerk. Henry Jones, Carnarvon, Clerk. Owen Jones, Criccieth, Clerk. Griffith Jones, Cwrt, Clerk. Thomas Parry Jones, Madryn. Thomas Parry Jones (jun.) Madryn, Rowland Jones, Weirglodd fawr (Broom Hall). Thomas Thomas Jones, ditto. John Jones, Brynhir. John Jones, Gelliwig, Evan Jones, ditto. Humphrey Jones, Ystumllyn. Richard Jones, Cefncoed. Wm. Jones, Ty Mawr. Griffith Jones, ditto. Thomas Lewis, Mount hazel. John Lloyd, Trallwyn, Clerk. Richard Lloyd, Bodvel. William Alex Madocks. John Edward Madocks. John Madocks, Glanywern. John Mander, Bampton. Robert Morris, Sygyn, Beddgelert. Richard Nanney, Bachwen, Clerk. William Oakeley, Tanybwlch. Edward Owen, Llaniestyn, Clerk. Richard Owen, Edeyrn ditto. William Owen, Bronheulog, ditto. Owen Ormsby, Clenennau. Love Parry, Penarth. Hugh Reveley, Bryngwin. Thos. Roberts, Abererch, Clerk. William Roberts, Hendre wen, do. John Roberts Cefnamwlch, do. Hugh Rowlands, Ty Mawr. Edward Williames Vaughan Salisbury, Rhug. Thomas Assheton Smith, Vaenol. Thomas Assheton Smith (jun.), do. Rice Thomas, Coed helen. Rice Thomas (jun.), do. John Thomas, Llanfrothen Clerk. Griffith ap Howell Vaughan, Hengwrt. Gwilyn Lloyd Wardle, Wern fawr. William Williams, Plashen. William Williams, Rhiw. David Williams, Saethon. Thomas Wright, Knutsford. Peter Williams, Llanbedrog, clerk. Owen Gethin Williams, Bottwnog, do. Evan Williams, Carnarvon, do. The Hon Thomas John Wynne. Charles Watkin Williams Wynne. William Wynne, Llandegwning. Robert Wynne, Llanerch, Llannor, Pwllheli.

All the above are also members of the second list of trustees but the following names are members of the second list only.

TRUSTEES FOR THE SECOND DISTRICT

Sir Edward Pryce Lloyd. Sir Robert William Vaughan. Sir Hugh Owen. Charles Nelson Cole, Quellyn. Robert Currie, Carnarvon. David Ellis, Gwynfryn. William Evans, Trefeilir. Richard Garmon, Llanwnda. Rd. Garmon (jun.), do. John

Griffith, Treyfan. Thomas Jones, Bryntirion. Thomas Jones, Surgeon, Carnarvon. Thomas Lloyd, Glangwna, do. John Lloyd, do., Clerk. Evan Lloyd, Porth yr Aur, do Clerk. Hugh Owen, Surgeon, Carnarvon. Owen Anthony Poole, do. Richard Parry, Meillionen, Beddgelert. William Ll. Roberts, Oakland, Llanrwst. Robert Roberts, Carnarvon. John Roberts, Bangor. Daniel Vaudrey, Hafodtanygraig, Beddgelert. Joseph Williams, Glan'rafon, do. John Williams, Dolwyddelen, Clerk. John Williams, Bettwsycoed. Henry Williams, Pentir, Clerk. Benjamin Wyatt, Lime Grove, Bangor. William White, Glasynfryn. John Williams, Carnarvon, Clerk. Peter B Williams, Llanrug, Clerk.

The names of representatives of the Rhiwlas Estate are not shown in these lists, the reason being that, it is said, they had given land for the road foundations from Bronygadair Bach, Pentrefelin, to the boundaries of Coed y Cefn, free of charge.

POSTSCRIPT

In the year 1836 there was an enthusiastic movement in Caernarfonshire to get a railway between London and Porthdinllaen as the route to Ireland. An influential meeting was held at Carnarvon by the top gentry of the county and others. It appears that there was a motion to make Porthdinlleyn into a harbour as early as the reign of George I – £600 was spent at that time to build a pier.

Another meeting was held in Dublin, with many from this country in attendance. It was shown that the distance to Dublin from London would be less if the Porthdinllaen route was used; in addition Porthdinllaen was considered to be a safer harbour. The matter was not pursued further and when it was raised a second time later the railway between Chester and Holyhead had been established, as it is today. In 1866 a railway was built from Oswestry to Pwllheli, which passed through Tre'r Gest. This, The Cambrian Railway, was expected to terminate at Porthdinlleyn, but only reached as far as Pwllheli.

EXPLANATORY NOTES ON THE TWO SIR HOWELS

HYWEL Y PEDOLAU (Howel of the Horseshoes) was the son of Griffith ap Iorwerth ap Methuselem ap Hugh ap Cynddelw from Gwenllian, daughter of Ririd Flaidd. Howel's mother was nurse to Edward II; that is how Howel was created a Baron by the King as well as receiving other favours. He was buried at Carmarthen, there being a memorial to him at St Peter's Church with a picture of a horseshoe on it. He was born at Treiorwerth, Anglesey. In a poem by Dafydd Trefor, Vicar of Llanallgo in 1483, to 'the heroes of the world' the name of Hywel y Pedolau is mentioned.

The second Sir Howel was HYWEL U FWYALL (Howel of the Battle-axe), or Howel ap Rhys. Rhys's mother was Margaret (or Gwladus), daughter of Griffith ap Howel y Pedolau ap Griffith ap Iorwerth, etc. Iolo Goch called him Howel ap Einion ap Griffith ap Howel ap Meredydd Goch ap Collwyn ap Tango, but Sir John Wynn of Gwydir calls him Howel ap Rhys fychan ap

Howel fychan of Bronyfoel; who is correct, and does it matter? He died in the year 1372.

ADDITIONAL EPITAPHS AT YNYS CYNHAIARN

Thomas Williams, Cross Keys, who died October 24, 1844, aged 42. Also Ellen Griffiths, his wife, September 14th 1866, aged 61.

The children of Richard Williams of Beuno, Blacksmith, and Mary, his wife of Porthmadoc. Jane, who died January 12th 1840, aged 13 days. John, their son, who died June 24th 1867, aged 23 years from Tuberculosis. Also William, their son, aged 16 years, who was lost at sea with the rest of the crew with the sinking of the ship 'Ada' of Porthmadog on its voyage from Huelfa to Newcastle in the terrible storm of October 18th to 20th 1889. The Captain was Lewis Evans Davies, son of Rees and Mary Davies of 2 Cornhill, Porthmadog. One of the hands was the Captain's brother named Evan and the above William who was a brother in law of the captain. Edward, their son, who died February 6th 1879, aged 29 years. Also Mary Jane, who died May 26th 1884, aged 32 years.

Epitaph of Edward Williams, son of Richard and Mary Williams of 14 Cornhill, Portmadoc.

The death of one so virtuous fills the heart
With sadness and longing;
Long will he be mourned,
O young man of beauty and true piety.

Finis.

That is the end of *Gestiana*; the following are extras that may be of interest.

The task is o'er, the pen is laid aside.
The ghosts of memories long since gone are told again.
Now, in another tongue, the life of Gest re-awakens
And spans the void of a hundred years.
Undimmed by these passing years,
Echoes of the past reach out to charm.
And we, the inheritors now,
Salute those who have gone before. – CYFIETHYDD

A ROUGH TRANSLATION OF THE WORK OF GLASYNYS ON THE HARPIST, DAFYDD Y GARREG WEN

Copied from an unknown source.

Sometime during a pilgrimage to 'my dear old Eifionydd', I happened to meet a man by accident, if such a thing as meeting a man by accident is possible. What is clear, anyhow, is that he had not the vaguest idea who I was and there was nothing premeditated on my part about starting a conversation with him, but as things happen, we started to talk, and I do not regret doing so.

I shall not describe my colleague, but will turn at once in his company to the cemetery of Ynys Cynhaiarn, where there are many graves and trim memorial stones. Everything neat and tidy, and I do not believe it is possible to find as many good epitaph stanzas in any other cemetery in Wales.

Whilst walking to and fro amongst the graves, we came at last to a gravestone that was different from the rest; a stone with a harp carved on it. I commenced to read and found out straightaway that it was the grave of David Owen or David of the White Rock.

After reflecting a moment over the small section of his grave, I requested a few details of the harpist's life. As the wind was keen we both went to the porch and there we sat down to talk of various matters and amongst those some were given to those who slumber there, my friend telling me in a simple unceremonious way something like this about David Owen, David of the White Rock. His parents lived in rather a small cottage in the parish of Treflys; his mother was the daughter of a place called Isallt Fawr, her baptismal name being Gwen. The family of Isallt was quite learned in medical matters and it is said that they descend directly in line from the doctors of Myddfai, that is from Rhiwallon and his sons. The family of Dolfanog also sprang from the same source. Owen had the ability to compose a poem on the spur of the moment, and was very fond of singing to harp Accompaniment. I cannot remember for the life of me, who or what her husband's name was but it was at Garreg Wen that they lived.

They had many children and amongst then was Dafydd. It is not known when he started to play the harp, but one can easily assume that it was at an early age.

Dafydd stayed at home with his parents, but Rhys, his brother left home and after roaming around from place to place eventually turned up as a gardener in a gentleman's house in Scotland. Dafydd used to keep 'Merry evenings' in various places quite often. He became an able musician and his fame spread around the length and breadth of the country. Sometime when he was returning home one early summer morning after playing his harp at a mansion not far from his home, he sat down on a mossy stone and rested his head on the harp; no doubt he was tired after being out all night. A lark rose from its grassy home close by him, rising up to meet the sun and started to sing. As someone said about him, most probably Dafydd felt:

> In a cloud above the meadow sweet music filtered down,
> It rose straight on wings dampened by early dew
> The lark's magic voice, with its poetic song
> It showered down its gentle Hymnal voice.

Simultaneously, undoubtedly before Dafydd and in a flash off came the harp's coverlet and the maestro played 'The Rising of the Lark', one of the most melodious tunes that belong to Wales.

Another time when bored at home he started off with his harp on his back to find his brother, Rhys, and after a long search found him amongst the mountains of Scotland; he stayed there out of respect and delight for quite a while. After tiring there, and as he was getting ready to depart, the gentleman for whom his brother worked, asked him for a tune as a memento of his stay at the house. What Dafydd did was to give him the air that he had just composed for the Criccieth Fair before leaving home. This was 'The Pleasures of the Men of Criccieth'. This was renamed 'Rosslyn Castle in Scotland'.

After he arrived home it was plain to see that travelling did not agree with him; he had developed a bad cough, his eyes had sunk deep into his head and the fair countenance had paled, and signs were showing that death was playing a dirge on the 'strings of his life'.

He weakened and it was not long before he had to forego pulling the strings as his strength became too weak but, even so, when he had an hour or two free from pain, he would stagger to his old instrument and play a few of the tender airs that had drawn tears 'from the eyes of time'. He continued to weaken until at last he was unable to leave his bed.

One day, watched by his dear mother, he appeared very drowsy. She noticed a wry smile on his face, and his fingers appeared as if he was starting to play his harp. His features relaxed and his face appeared more like what it was before he had been taken ill, the hollows in his cheeks filling out. Gwen feared that he was dying, but the next minute his eyes opened and he said distinctly 'Oh!, Mother, I saw the most beautiful thing I have ever seen in my life', he took a deep breath, half turned his head and went ahead. 'Never before in my life have I heard such singing, the music, Oh! Mother!, give me my harp, I can, yes I can play it'. Then he fell into a comfortable coma, his mother watching him. Who knows whether she was able to see a light through the tears that streamed from both loving eyes?

As the rays of the sun on the morning dew, why did she not respond to the Divine Spirit also? Dafydd awoke a second time and pleaded with his eyes as well as his voice, 'Please, Mother can I have my harp once more?' Who could refuse such a request – not Gwen, his mother.

The harp was brought and tenderly and slowly she raised the harpist and let him sit on the side of the bed. She placed cushions and pillows around him to hold him up as if he was sitting in a chair; then Dafydd commenced playing, his mother holding his head. From the sweet strings he drew the melodious 'The White Rock'. After taking his fill of the old instrument she replaced him in his bed, he felt better and in less pain.

After resting a while he told his mother how he had learnt the tune. He had, so he said, been in another world. These were his words:

> I saw myself in a wonderful wooded country, each leaf was green, each twig was fresh, each branch was full of sap, the hedges were neat and the meadows full of scented clover. The river was clear and slowly meandered by, quiet and peaceful. I saw myself in a beautiful mansion. In front of the door was a flower garden; in a leafy bower in the centre of the garden I heard someone playing a harp, and the tune was the one I played to you, mother. In front of the bower two grey doves were listening. Slowly and humbly I moved to the spot and to my great surprise found there was no trace of a harp or anything else.
>
> I pondered over this but yet the music continued. But what it was, was it the sound of the breeze coming through the orchard to the bower through plaited osiers?
>
> Oh, Mother, how I was wishing you were there to hear the singing, but for the life of me I could see no other than the two doves, after this I woke up, and saw you, my dear Mother.

He went quiet and it was plain that he had worsened and that his 'earthly house' was rapidly disintegrating; that his tent was being struck. Death whistled its own elegy in his breast. He lingered on for a few more days and his mother related it all and she also told her friends that she also knew the air from memory, and that nothing pleased the harpist more than to hear his mother singing the new tune. Before long he slept; he went home to the quiet area of the golden harps.

'He was buried at Ynys here' said the reciter 'and this is his grave.' On the day of his funeral they sang the song 'The White Rock' all the way to the church, not pausing until they reached the graveside; but the oddest thing of all was that two doves came to the house at Garreg Wen when the coffin was brought to the door, and they both followed the cortege all the way. They entered the church, resting there quietly whilst the service was going on and when he was carried to the graveside they were still there close to the coffin. But when the clergyman intoned the words 'Dust to dust, earth to earth, ashes to ashes' they both flew away and were never seen again, and that is what I was given of the history of Dafydd y Garreg Wen.

There was also a poem but this was the same as the one in the article on Dafydd y Garreg Wen.

SOME EXTRACTS FROM 'THE HISTORY OF THE GWYDIR FAMILY'

Again from an unknown source

> Hoell ap Rees ap Hoell Vaughan's sister being Evan ap Robert's wief went a mile or therabouts with her husband and the companye takinge with them, and soe p'ted with them, and in her waye homwards shee met her brother a horseback, with a great companye of people armed ridinge after her husband as fast as they could, shee cried

out upon her brother and desires him for the love of god not to harme her husband that ment him noe harm, and withall steps to his horse meaning to have caught him by the bridle which he seeinge, turned the horse; she caught the horse by the tayle, and hanginge upon him soe longe, crying upon her brother, that in the end he drew out his short sword and aboute stroke at her arm w'ch she p'ceavinge, was fain to lett slip her hould, and running before him to a narrow passage wherefore he must passe thorow a brooke where there was a footbridge neere the forde she steps to the bridge and takes away the 'canllaw' or hand stave of the bridge and with the same lette flye at her brother and yf he had not avoided the blowe she had struck him off his horse.

An ould woman that dwelt there in Rees ap Meredith's time tould him tha shee had seene his grandfather Evan ap Robert at that house both in going and cominge from his voyage to Chirkeland, and that he was the tallest and goodliest man shee had ever seene, for sittinge at the fire among the spure, the hynder p'te of his head was to be seen over the spure, w'ch shee never saw to any other man. Also she said that in his return from Chirkeland she sawe Lowrie, vz Hoell, Rees ap Merediths wief his kinswoman, wash his eyes with white wine being bloodshotte by long wachings.

Griffith ap John ap Gorono challenged Hoell ap Rhys to the fielde which he refusinge, and assemblinge his coosens John ap Meredith sonnes and his friends to gather assaulted Hoell in his own house after the manner he had seene in the French Warrs consumed with fyre. His barns and outbuildings and afterwards assaulting the hall where Hoell ap Rhys and many other people kept beinge a very string, was shotte out of a cravies of the house, thorugh the sight of his bever into his head, and slaine outright beinge otherwise armed at all points.

Notwithstanding his death the assault on the house was continued with great vehemence, the doors fired with great burthens of straw besides the smoake of the outhouses and barnes nott farr distant anoyed greatly the defendants, soe that most of them laye under boords and benches upon the floore in the hall the better to avoid the smoake onelie the ould man Hoell ap Rhys verstoopt but stood valiantlie in the midst of the floore armed with a gleve in his hands and called out to them and bid arise like men, for shame, for he had known as great a smoake in that hall upon a Christmas even.

Bill of complaint by Morris ap Griffith to the Court of Star Chamber.

But the said William Morris in contempt of yor highness's lawes having no respect for the severall offices with which he is yyett invested nor regard for the owth admynistered to him when made Justice of the Peace presently commanded one Rowland Ellis, a person very lewd and of light behaviour and a common suborner of perjury and matteyner of other detestable and abobynable vices . . . . and sundry other lewd and desperate persons to the number of one hundred as yett unknown to your subject to sett upon the said sheriff with force and violence to rescue him.

.. . . . to the peril of the lives of the sheriff and his small number of servants and did take and convaye awye him the said William Morris from his custodye and arrest of the sherriff through the streets to the shirehall of the said towne where he satt upon the Bench there upon the day of the said arrest among other Justices of the Peace.